Institutional Economics and National Competitiveness

This book offers a strong contribution to the growing field of institutional economics, going beyond the question of why institutions matter and examines the ways in which different types of institutions are conducive to the enhancement of competitiveness and economic development. Adopting a variety of approaches, ranging from New Institutional Economics, Public Choice, Constitutional Political Economy and Austrian Economics, to more traditional economic approaches, contributors examine the important issues of interest to development economics.

This book asks whether democracy is a pre-condition for economic development, what the proper role of government is in the age of globalization and whether successful government led policies were the cause of South Korea's economic development. As well as these key questions, the book covers the issues of whether the government should rely on the market process to encourage economic development or must they interfere, and by what criteria one can judge a proposal for policies for economic prosperity. The book tries to make a contribution by introducing a variety of perspective, some argue in favour of industrial policies while others argue for a lesser role for the government and greater entrepreneurial freedom. Some question the wisdom of promoting democracy as a necessary condition for economic development while others argue that political liberalization is the basis of lasting competitive edge of an economy.

The book should be of great interest to students and researchers in need of a multi-perspective collection covering several approaches to the issues of institutional economics and national competition.

Young Back Choi is Professor of Economics at St. John's University, New York, USA, and a faculty associate of the Colloquium on Market Institutions and Economic Processes at New York University, USA.

Routledge frontiers of political economy

Institutional Economics and National Competitiveness

Edited by Young Back Choi

Routledge
Taylor & Francis Group

LONDON AND NEW YORK

First published 2012
by Routledge
4 Park Square, Milton Park, Abingdon, Oxon OX14 4RN
605 Third Avenue, New York, NY 10017

Routledge is an imprint of the Taylor & Francis Group, an informa business

British Library Cataloguing in Publication Data
A catalogue record for this book is available from the British Library

Library of Congress Cataloging in Publication Data
Institutional economics and national competitiveness/edited by Young Back Choi.
  p. cm.
Includes bibliographical references and index.
1. Institutional economics. 2. Competition. I. Choi, Young Back, 1949–
HB99.5.I563 2011
330.15′52–dc22

2011007111

ISBN: 978-0-415-75016-5 (pbk)
ISBN: 978-0-415-60026-2 (hbk)
ISBN: 978-0-203-80554-1 (ebk)

Typeset in Times
by Wearset Ltd, Boldon, Tyne and Wear
First issued in paperback in 2013

Contents

Contributors

Young Back Choi is Professor of Economics at St. John's University and a faculty associate of the Colloquium on Market Institutions and Economic Processes at New York University. He has a PhD in Economics from the University of Michigan. His wide-ranging interests are reflected in publications including 'Political Economy of Han Feitzu' (*History of Political Economy*, 1989), *Paradigms and Conventions* (University of Michigan Press, 1993), 'On the Rich Getting Richer' (*Kyklos*, 1999), and 'Path Dependence and the Korean Alphabet' (*Journal of Economic Behavior and Organization*, 2009). His primary areas of research interest are entrepreneurship, economic mobility, and economic development.

Roger D. Congleton joined the Department of Economics and the Center for Study of Public Choice at George Mason University in 1988, after being a Visiting Fellow at the Center in 1986. His most recent books focus on the political economy of institutions: *Perfecting Parliament: Liberalism, Constitutional Reform and the Rise of Western Democracy* (Cambridge University Press, 2011), *40 Years of Research on Rent Seeking* (two edited volumes, Springer, 2008, with A. Hillman and K. Konrad), *Democratic Constitutional Design and Public Policy* (MIT Press, 2006, with B. Swedenborg), and *Improving Democracy through Constitutional Reform* (Springer, 2003). In addition to his books, Prof. Congleton has published more than 100 papers in academic journals and volumes on such topics as the politics of constitutional reform, the importance of information in democratic decision-making, the emergence and significance of norms, and on policy-making within national governments and international organizations.

Randall G. Holcombe is DeVoe Moore Professor of Economics at Florida State University. He received his PhD in Economics from Virginia Tech. He is also Senior Fellow at the James Madison Institute, a Tallahassee-based think tank that specializes in issues facing state governments. He served on Florida Governor Jeb Bush's Council of Economic Advisors from 2000 to 2006, and is past president of the Public Choice Society and the Society for the Development of Austrian Economics. He is the author of 12 books and more than 100 articles published in academic and professional journals. His books include

The Economic Foundations of Government (1994), *Public Policy and the Quality of Life* (1995), *From Liberty to Democracy: The Transformation of American Government* (2002), and *Entrepreneurship and Economic Progress* (2007). His primary areas of research are public finance and the economic analysis of public policy issues.

Sung-Hee Jwa is President of Gyeonggi Research Institute. A graduate of Seoul National University, Dr. Jwa earned his PhD in Economics at University of California, Los Angeles in 1983. He then worked as an economist at the Federal Reserve Bank of Minneapolis for two years before joining the Korea Development Institute in 1985. From 1997 to 2006 he was President of the Korea Economic Research Institute. His publications include The New Wealth of Nations (2006), *A New Paradigm for Korea's Economic Development* (Palgrave, 2001), *The Evolution of Large Corporations in Korea* (Edward Elgar, 2002), and *Competition and Corporate Governance in Korea* (Edward Elgar, 2004). He is a member of the Presidential Council on National Competitiveness, and serves in a variety of public task-forces. His areas of specialty are development economics, new institutional economics, the Korean economy, monetary economics, and industrial organization.

Sung-Kyu Lee is an Associate Professor of Andong National University in Korea. Previously, he was an analyst of the Fiscal Policy Analysis Division at the National Assembly Budget Office in Korea. He also taught at Hankuk University of Foreign Studies, Seoul Women's University, Myungji University, and Sungshin Women's University. He has a PhD in Economics from the University of Southampton. His main research interests are on public finance, public choice, and international trade policy. He is the author of *International Trade and Strategic Trade Policy* (2007), *Political Economy of Tax Policy and International Taxation* (2008), *Essays on Voting, Policy and Campaigning* (2009), and *Political Economics of Trade Policy* (2010).

Md. Dulal Miah is Assistant Professor of Finance, American International University, Bangladesh. He has received his PhD on Development Economics from Ritsumeikan Asia Pacific University, Japan. He has several research publications mainly focusing on new institutional economics in peer reviewed journals. Dr. Miah's research interests include property rights, corporate governance, comparative financial system, and bank rents.

Sung Sup Rhee has been Professor of Economics at Soongsil University since 1986. He was the President of the Korea Institution and Economics Association (2004–8) and a Vice-President of the Korea Economic Association (2010–11). He was a Research Fellow at the Korea Development Institute (1982–6) and a visitor at Moscow Institute of Physics and Technology (1992) and George Mason University (2003–4). He received his PhD in Economics from State University of New York, Buffalo in 1982.

J. Barkley Rosser, Jr. is Professor of Economics and Kirby L. Cramer, Jr. Professor of Business Administration at James Madison University, where he has taught since 1977. He received his PhD in Economics from the University of Wisconsin – Madison in 1976. He has published about 150 books, articles, comments, book chapters, and book reviews. His books include *From Catastrophe to Chaos: A General Theory of Economic Discontinuities* (1991, 2nd edn., 2000), *Comparative Economics in a Transforming World Economy* (1996, 2nd edn., 2004), *Complexity in Economics* (2004), *The Changing Face of Economics* (2004), *Handbook of Complexity Research* (2009), and *European Economics at a Crossroads* (2010). He has served on numerous editorial boards, and served for nearly a decade as Editor of the *Journal of Economic Behavior and Organization.* In 2010 a *festschrift* was published by Springer for him entitled, *Nonlinear Dynamics in Economics, Finance, and the Social Sciences: Essays in Honour of John Barkley Rosser, Jr.*

Marina V. Rosser is Professor of Economics at James Madison University where she has been on the faculty since 1987, after she arrived from Russia. She received her PhD in Economics from Moscow State University in the former Soviet Union, and from 1980–1984 was a Senior Researcher at the Institute of World Economy and International Relations. She was removed from her position that year when she became engaged to J. Barkley Rosser, Jr., only being allowed to emigrate after much difficulty and diplomatic activity. She is the first person to have received a PhD in Economics in the former USSR to receive tenure in an American economics department. She is author of numerous papers on transition and comparative economics and is coauthor with J. Barkley Rosser, Jr. of the textbook, *Comparative Economics in a Transforming World Economy* (first edition, 1996, Irwin; second edition, 2004, MIT Press).

Yasushi Suzuki is Professor at the Graduate School of Management, Ritsumeikan Asia Pacific University, Oita, Japan. He has an undergraduate degree from Waseda University and a PhD from the University of London. His main work is on the institutional political economy of financial development, and he has published on the Japanese financial system as well as on financial fragility, credit risk monitoring, and bank rent effects in South and East Asia. His work has appeared in *Review of Political Economy*, *International Review of Comparative Public Policy*, *Asian-Pacific Economic Literature*, and *Journal of Policy Informatics.*

Viktor J. Vanberg is Professor Emeritus at the University of Freiburg, Germany, where he taught from 1995 to 2009, and Member of the Board of the Walter Eucken Institute, Freiburg, which he directed from 2001 to 2010. From 1985 to 1995 he taught as Professor of Economics at George Mason University, Virginia. He is author of *Rules and Choice in Economics* (1994) and of *The Constitution of Markets: Essays in Political Economy* (2001).

Joon-Mo Yang is Professor of Economics at Yonsei University, Wonju Campus. He received his PhD in Economics from the University of California,

Los Angeles, in 1994. He has written more than 43 academic articles in refer-reed journals, book chapters, and more than 15 consulting reports to the public sector including the government, the Bank of Korea, and government agencies. He was the Editor-in-Chief of the *Journal of Korean Economic Studies*, and the Editor of *Journal of Economic Theory* and *Econometrics* and other academic journals.

Jungho Yoo is a Visiting Professor at the Korea Development Institute School of Public Policy and Management. Recently, he was the C.W. Lim and Korea Foundation Chair of Korean Studies in the School of International Services, American University (Washington, DC). He was a researcher at the KDI, 1981–2004, where he served as the Vice-President. Earlier, he also served as the Senior Counselor to the Deputy Prime Minister in charge of Economic Affairs, Republic of Korea. His areas of research interest include international trade, economic development, and related policy issues. Before joining KDI, he was an Assistant Professor of Economics at Wheaton College in Norton, MA. He graduated from the College of Law, Seoul National University. He earned an MA in Public Policy and Administration and a PhD in Economics at the University of Wisconsin – Madison.

Yong Yoon is a Lecturer in the Faculty of Economics at Chulalongkorn University. Prior to moving to Thailand, he worked as a researcher for the Korea Economic Research Institute (1999–2006) while studying for his PhD at Seoul National University. Yong Yoon has also lived, studied, and worked in Eastern and Southern Africa. He regularly lectures in Korea and in Vietnam. His areas of interest are econometrics, development economics, and the Korean economy.

Yong J. Yoon is a Professor of Economics, Department of Economics and Center for Study of Public Choice at George Mason University. His major area of interest in economics is increasing returns and public economics/public choice. His current research includes partial anarchy: an economic theory of the state.

Foreword

James M. Buchanan

'Institutional economics': in its modern usage, this term has become the rubric for an inclusive set of related research programs, all which were initially stimulated, in a negative way, by the increasing formalization of the Economics of academia. For several decades, institutions were largely neglected by the economic 'theorists.' The emerging critical programs shared the common purpose of bringing inquiry closer to empirical reality.

This shift in interest was accompanied temporally by the increasing globalization of all markets during the half-century after World War II. Clearly, the impact of globalization on economic institutions as well as the adjustments of institutions to the expansion in the extent of markets, were subjects that demanded careful inquiry.

Because, however, there are dimensions to the rules and conventions of exchange that vary as among national economies, some delineation based on geography becomes necessary. In this sense, some of the chapters in this book are uniquely relevant to Korea, but they are properly set within the more inclusive research program that treats the competitiveness dimension as it relates the Korean economy to world markets. Experiences and problems that describe recent Korean history become lessons that offer spillover lessons for comparable efforts.

Why institutions matter

[Reprint of a letter from Oliver Williamson to the KIEA on the occasion of the Conference]

Oliver Williamson

Greetings and best wishes for a successful conference on 'Institutions and National Competitiveness' [August 18–19, 2009, Seoul, Korea]!

It is always gratifying to be associated with and to contribute to a successful program. Your conference on the New Institutional Economics speaks to the vitality of the NIE in South Korea, and is part of a growing world-wide movement – in other parts of Asia, in Europe, in North and South America, Africa, Australia, and other corners of the globe. The annual conference of the International Society for New Institutional Economics was held at Berkeley this June. My former student Scott Masten gave the Presidential Address and my Berkeley colleague Pablo Spiller organized the conference in his capacity as President-Elect. It attracted the largest attendance ever for an annual ISNIE conference and also speaks to the vitality of the movement.

Institutions matter for economists, if not more generally, if and as they are made susceptible to analysis using economic reasoning. The NIE owes its conceptual origins to deep insights and critiques of orthodoxy that were advanced in the 1930s. After a long gestation period, the NIE began to take on operational significance in the 1970s and new contributions to this project continue to this day. R.C.O. Matthews, in his Presidential Address to the Royal Economic Society in 1986, pronounced that economics. Events have borne him out. Twenty-three years later the NIE has substantial accomplishments under its belt and continues to develop in theoretical, empirical, and public policy respects.

The NIE program breaks down into two major parts: the 'rules of the game,' of both formal and informal kinds, much of it dealing with the public sector and the institutional environment (as worked up by research on Positive Political Economy); and the 'play of the game,' which deals with the governance of contractual relations and the economics of organization (much of it as worked up by Transaction Cost Economics). It has been my pleasure to participate in this project and to see it take hold in South Korea and elsewhere.

Most of Transaction Cost Economics can be thought to be complementary to yet differs from orthodoxy in the following respects: it works out of the lens of contract (exchange) rather than the lens of choice (the resource allocation paradigm); it is a more interdisciplinary undertaking in that it joins law, economics, and organization; the firm is described not as a production function (which is a technological construction) but as a governance structure (which is an organizational construction); the emphasis is on transaction cost economizing rather than production cost economizing; and it is a much more microanalytic undertaking, in that the action is in the details of transactions on the one hand and governance structures, on the other. Pertinent to this last is that the student of transaction cost economics needs to know a lot more about the details of the phenomena under investigation than is customary when examined in neoclassical (lens of choice) terms. That is demanding, but it is also rewarding and sometimes exhilarating to examine complex phenomena through the focused lens of contract in a 'modest, slow, molecular, definitive way.'

Congratulations. Your contributions are important to your country and to the Institutional Economics movement of which you are a part.

Sincerely yours,
Oliver Williamson

Preface

Young Back Choi

In August 2009 an international conference on Institutions and National Competitiveness was held in Seoul, Korea. The conference reflected a growing interest in the study of the nature of institutions and their role in economic development. Papers presented at the conference cover wide-ranging topics with diverse approaches. This volume collects a selection of papers presented at the conference. The following is the outline of the chapters of the volume.

Western nations have promoted democracy and political freedom in Less-Developed Countries as a necessary institution for economic prosperity. Randall Holcombe argues in Chapter 1 that what truly produces prosperity is not democracy, which is just as prone to rent-seeking and predation as autocracy, but rather economic freedom, which gives a free reign to the entrepreneur.

In Chapter 2, Viktor Vanberg argues that increasing globalization demands a clear distinction of two roles of the state – as the joint enterprise of providing public services for its citizens only and as a territorial enterprise of defining and enforcing the rules of the market within its territory, binding to citizens and non-citizens alike. That is, governments are increasingly forced to distinguish between citizens and jurisdiction-users as they have different implications for taxation and regulations.

Mercantilist policies are implied by the rent-extraction model of the state. Successful liberal economic reforms reduce opportunities for rent extraction and promote an enduring basis of economic development. But how can a rent-extracting state adopt liberal economic reforms? Roger Congleton argues in Chapter 3 that strategies of export-led growth are often politically possible even in a rent-extracting state. Historically, liberalization of export sectors of the economy tends to be the first step in a series of liberal reforms in the West.

There have been all sorts of proposals for economic prosperity, including various industrial promotion schemes, free trade combined with social safety net, encouraging investment of various sorts, counter-cyclical policies, reducing inequality, job creation, investing in education and/or R&D, and so on. How are we to evaluate the proposals? In Chapter 4, Young Back Choi argues that the entrepreneur is the agent of wealth creation and therefore any policy proposal for economic prosperity should be judged by whether or not it allows freedom to the entrepreneur. By this criterion, he judges many extant proposals wanting.

He further argues that as regulations and taxes by and large reflect people's beliefs about the role of the entrepreneur in wealth creation, the advocates of liberal economic reform must not ignore beliefs that are mistaken and hostile to entrepreneurship.

Yong J. Yoon argues in Chapter 5 that, increasingly, economic progress depends on scientific discoveries, which differ from the pre-scientific technical know-how. Science as an institution of organized inquiry and persuasion among specialists allows the process of sustained inquiry and the benefit of cumulative learning.

In Chapter 6, Joon-Mo Yang surveys the evolution of the linkage between universities and industries that is becoming increasingly important as the Korean economy has moved to higher level of technologies and the need for innovation has intensified. Even as leading firms in Korea invest substantially in R&D, they have become more and more reliant on various support from universities, beyond supplying well trained human resources and consultancy of professors, including incubation of innovative ventures. The burgeoning innovative ecosystem in Korea, according to Yang, has been shaped by government policies by providing a legal framework for ventures, introducing an evaluation system of professors for their research productivity, and aligning incentives of researchers with the success of ventures.

In Chapter 7, Sung Sup Rhee argues that industrial policy, widely denounced by free-market economists as misguided, can be justified within the framework of the New Institutional Economics, in which the government plays a crucial role in shaping institutional changes. He argues that the South Korean policies of promoting the heavy and chemical industries (HCIs) in the 1970s were successful and provides detailed description of the steps the government took to make it possible.

Jungho Yoo argues, in Chapter 8, against the commonly held view that rapid industrialization of Korea was made possible by the government's interventionist policies. For Yoo, the real reason for rapid economic development is not so much switching from import substitution to export promotion, but eliminating over-valuation of the currency and removing obstacles to participation in the international division of labor. In his view, government export-promotion in the 1960s amounted to neutralizing severe distortions introduced through various protectionist measures. When the Korean government actively promoted the HCIs in the 1970s, government policy miserably failed, resulting in mal-investment and a severe recession. Yoo does not deny that the Korean economy is heavily regulated by government.

In Chapter 9, Barkley and Marina Rosser examine the two Koreas from the perspective of the economics of civilization, their synthesis of two distinct approaches in the New Institutional Economics and the new traditional economy. When a traditional society goes through a modernization process, it draws on the existing institutions, especially traditional belief system and religions, which offer diverse possibilities. They argue that South Korea has been able to draw from its Confucian tradition such elements as the emphasis on education and social harmony to enhance its competitive edge. North Korea, however, has managed to combine socialism with Confucian elements of authoritarianism and *juche*, a distorted notion of self-reliance.

Under progressive taxation, inflation causes bracket creep and increases the tax burden. Sung-Kyu Lee calls the increasing tax burden, both from people being pushed into higher tax brackets and from more people being subject to taxes by crossing the threshold, fiscal drag. In Chapter 10 he advocates indexation of the tax schedule for inflation to offset fiscal drag.

In Chapter 11, Md. Dulal Miah and Yasushi Suzuki argue that reduction of transaction costs is not sufficient reason for property rights. Given that uncertainty cannot be eliminated even if one had perfect information, for example, uncertainty arising from strategic interactions, perfect delineation of property rights is not possible. They argue that there is logic to vaguely defined property rights in the Chinese Township and Village Enterprises (TVEs), in slacks as a means of dealing with ineliminable uncertainty.

In the last chapter, Sung-Hee Jwa and Yong Yoon survey the development literature and try to debunk what they regard as myths – that any country can develop, that democracy is necessary for development, that balanced growth is necessary for development, that markets will take care of development, that development policies should avoid ideological commitment, that one must choose between the market and the government, and so on. They see development as an uneven process involving the generation of new orders. They argue that the essential feature of institutions that are conducive for development is discrimination, between those who are productive and innovative from those who are not, and rewarding for the former. They argue that policies and institutions that emphasize equality retard the development process and that government can amplify rewards for the successful to accelerate the process of economic development.

In closing, I would like to express my appreciation to Dr. Sung-Hee Jwa, President of Gyeonggi Research Institute and the current President of the Korea Institution and Economics Society (KIEA) and Prof. Sung Sup Rhee, former President of the KIEA, for their unstinting efforts to make the 2009 Conference a success and the present volume possible. I also would like to thank Prof. James Buchanan for gracing the volume with a word of wisdom in the foreword and Prof. Oliver Williamson for allowing the reprint of his letter to the Korea Institution and Economics Society on the occasion of the Conference on which the volume is based.

Acknowledgment

I am very pleased to see the publication of this volume, which is the outcome of the very first annual international conference of its kind in Korea under the general theme 'Institutions and National Competitiveness,' held in Seoul in August 2009.

My sincere appreciation goes to all participants at the conference as well as all KIEA International Conference Committee members and supporting staff that helped at the Conference. I would like to thank all the chapter contributors to this volume and especially my old friend, and the editor of this volume, Prof. Y.B. Choi, without whom this volume would have been impossible. The generous support of various organizations, including the Presidential Council on National Competitiveness and Gyeonggi Research Institute as well as other supporting institutions, is also acknowledged. It is my privilege to work with such a distinguished set of people.

As President of the Korea Institution and Economics Association, I promise to ensure our institution's role as a pioneer in research aimed at better understanding the relationship between institutions and national development. Your continued support in the years ahead in our research and gathering of new knowledge is greatly appreciated.

Dr. Sung-Hee Jwa
President
Korea Institution and Economics Association
September 2010

1 Democracy and prosperity

Randall G. Holcombe

1 Introduction

Much of the post-World-War-II twentieth century was dominated by the Cold War division between the Eastern bloc, led by the Soviet Union, a political dictatorship with a centrally planned economy, and the Western bloc, including Western Europe and the United States, with democratic governments and market economies. After the collapse of the Berlin Wall in 1989, followed by the breakup of the Soviet Union in 1991, Fukuyama (1992) declared that the triumph of capitalist economies and democratic governments was 'the end of history.' Indeed, the triumph of the West in the Cold War was a direct result of the citizens of the Eastern bloc looking across the Berlin Wall and deciding that they would prefer to live their lives as those in the West were living theirs, rather than being impoverished in centrally planned economies and dominated by political dictatorships.

Political and intellectual leaders in democratic nations were quick to push the virtues of democratic government on those who once lived behind the Iron Curtain, and citizens of those newly freed countries were ready to accept democratic government as the vehicle through which they could transition toward the lifestyle of the West. Two decades after the collapse of the Berlin Wall, that transition has not gone smoothly for many of those countries. Despite the adoption of democratic political institutions, economic progress has been slow. Meanwhile, two of the world's fastest-growing economies in the first decade of the twenty-first century have been India and China. India has been a democracy since its independence from Britain, but a socialist democracy until the 1990s, when with the adoption of more market-friendly institutions came increased economic growth. China has never been democratic, but like India, saw increasing prosperity as its economic system moved away from central planning and toward the market allocation of resources.

In Hayek's (1944) classic argument that a centrally planned economy is the road to serfdom, he placed heavy emphasis on the institutions of economic freedom and discounted the importance of democratic government. Hayek argued that market institutions led to prosperity, and that enduring democracy was not possible without a free-market economic system. Like Schumpeter

(1950), Hayek was concerned that under a democratic government people could vote their economic freedoms away, and lose their political freedoms in the process. Similarly, Friedman (1962) argued that political freedom was possible only within the framework of a market economy. Despite the intellectual arguments of Hayek, Schumpeter, Friedman, and others, democratic political leaders have consistently pushed the virtues of democratic government to transitioning economies, neglecting the significance of market institutions to the prosperity of the West.

The evidence linking democracy with prosperity is tenuous at best. Barro (1996) finds little relationship between political freedom and economic growth, once economic institutions are taken into account. Similarly, Gwartney *et al.* (1999) find that when economic freedom is taken into account, political freedom makes no contribution to prosperity. De Haan and Sierman (1998) and Sturm and de Haan (2005) present some evidence that political freedom increases economic growth, but Acemoglu *et al.* (2008) argue that once other factors are taken into account, democracy and political freedom do not affect prosperity.

This chapter critically examines the nature of democratic political institutions to demonstrate that there is no reason why there should be any link between democracy and prosperity. The crucial characteristics of government that foster prosperity are constitutional constraints on the size and scope of government. Without such constraints, democracies have the potential to be as predatory as dictatorships, and predatory governments undermine the market institutions that generate prosperity.

2 Government and coercion

The only reason governments exist is to coerce their citizens into doing things they would not freely choose to do if uncoerced. Government forces people to conform to its regulations because without being forced they would not conform. Government forces people to pay taxes because without the coercion they would choose not to pay. Government forces people to obey its laws because without coercion they would act otherwise. If people would do what the government demands without being coerced, there would be no reason to have a government, because people would freely choose those actions anyway. Force underlies everything government does.

As Yeager (1985, 2001) insightfully notes, the threat of force is at the foundation of all government action, no matter how much one agrees with one's government. For example, many governments mandate that people fasten their seatbelts when riding in an automobile. Fastening one's seatbelt seems like a prudent action, and many people would fasten their seatbelts regardless of a law mandating that they do so. But there are such laws and even those who would voluntarily choose to fasten their seatbelts are threatened with penalties should they choose not to. Similarly, many people may support government spending programs sufficiently that they would voluntarily contribute their taxes to fund them, but government threatens even those who would voluntarily comply.

Regardless of how much people agree with their governments, government runs by force, and compliance with its policies is not voluntary.

A centuries-old line of reasoning argues that citizens somehow agree with each other to abide by the government's mandates, but the obvious flaw in this line of reasoning is that, in fact, there are people who do not agree. Rousseau was perhaps the strongest advocate of this argument that citizens are party to a social contract to follow the mandates of government. Rousseau (1762, IV: ch. 1, no. 2) says

> The citizen gives his consent to all the laws, including those which are passed in spite of his opposition, and even those which punish him when he dares break any of them.... When in the popular assembly a law is proposed, what the people is asked is not exactly whether it approves or rejects the proposal, but whether it is in conformity with the general will, which is their will. When therefore the opinion that is contrary to my own prevails, this proves neither more nor less than that I was mistaken, and that what I thought to be the general will was not so.[1]

Thus, citizens are bound by a social contract and all have the same general will. Democratic decision-making is a method of finding the general will, with which all agree.

Hobbes (1651) argued that without government, life in anarchy would be nasty, brutish, and short, so obedience to the sovereign's rules is necessary for a civilized society. The social contract binds all members of a society, and everyone must agree to its provisions because order cannot exist if people can pick and choose which rules they want to follow. This old idea remains current as contemporary contractarians argue that people agree to a social contract. Rawls (1971) argues that if people would agree from behind a veil of ignorance, they are in agreement; Buchanan (1975) argues that if people would agree if a social contract were renegotiated from Hobbesian anarchy, they are in agreement. Thus, the argument goes, people agree to be coerced, because they benefit from belonging to a society where everyone is forced to go along with the government's rules.[2]

Modern public expenditure theory makes similar arguments. Because people have the incentive to be free riders, government forces people to pay taxes to produce public goods, improving everyone's welfare in the process. The argument has even been extended by Hochman and Rodgers (1969) to redistribution programs. They argue that people are better off if government forces them to pay taxes so that their incomes can be transferred to others, even if they do not want to pay those taxes! The transparent flaw in the argument, when applied to the real world, is that if there is even one stingy miser who would really rather keep his money than have it taxed away to be given to someone else, forced redistribution is not a Pareto improvement. Even if it is, however, the argument remains that the government accomplishes its ends through force. There would be no reason to force people to fund income-transfer programs if they would voluntarily transfer the money themselves. Similarly, there would be no reason to force people to pay taxes to fund public goods if people would voluntarily pay for those goods.

Coercion lies at the foundation of all government action, and without this foundation there would be no reason for government to exist. Theories that purport to show that governments act through consent rather than coercion are fictions. As Schumpeter (1950: 198) observed: 'The theory which construes taxes on the analogy of club dues or of the purchase of the services of, say, a doctor only proves how far removed this part of the social sciences is from scientific habits of mind.' Government is based on coercion, not agreement, and exists only to force people to do things they would not freely choose to do in the absence of the force of government.

3 Democracy and autocracy

Viewed narrowly, the difference between representative democracy and autocracy is the way in which the government's leaders are chosen. In a democracy citizens choose their government's leaders, whereas in autocracy the government is run by a self-appointed leader. This fundamental difference can produce other differences as a result of how the political leadership in the two types of systems must act to retain power. Those who control the government need the support of others to maintain their power. In both democracies and autocracies, those who control the government must keep potential challengers from taking their power away from them, but because of the differences in design, different strategies are likely to be used to wrest control from an autocrat versus democratically elected leaders.

In either system, those with political power do not willingly give it up, although in both systems they may choose to step down if they see that their replacement is inevitable. The difference is that democracies have an institutionalized process for challenging those with government power in the form of elections, whereas autocrats remain in power unless they are forced out through a process not specified by formal institutions.

Autocrats can be replaced through revolution, where groups from outside the government unseat the autocrat and form a new government, or through coups, where someone within the existing governmental power structure ousts the autocrat and establishes a new government. For obvious reasons, military leaders are likely suspects to initiate coups, because they control a substantial amount of physical force which could be used to seize political power.[3] Thus, the autocrat who wants to maintain power must maintain a military service strong enough to deter revolutionaries from attempting a violent overthrow of the government, and loyal enough not to attempt such an overthrow themselves. Similarly, others who hold powerful positions in government are potential rivals whose loyalty the autocrat needs to cultivate.

An autocrat will be surrounded by a nucleus of people who aid the autocrat in maintaining political power, and the autocrat cultivates their loyalty by making it more rewarding for them to remain a part of the existing power structure rather than trying to unseat the autocrat to try to become part of a replacement power structure. This is done by taxing citizens to provide benefits to those who help the autocrat maintain power. The autocrat's hold on power will be more secure if the citizens themselves are content with this situation, and citizen support can be cultivated by policies that increase economic productivity. Thus, the autocrat may have an incentive to keep taxes low, to minimize regulatory barriers to productivity, and to maintain secure property rights. In a bi-causal relationship, the longer the autocrat's time horizon, as Levi (1988) notes, the greater the incentive for the autocrat to support an institutional structure that generates long-run growth, because the autocrat expects to be in power in the long run to tax that future productivity. In the other direction, the more productive the institutional structure, the greater the popular support, which can help increase the autocrat's tenure.

In this sense, autocrats might view themselves as effectively the owners of a country and therefore residual claimants, in that the more productive the economy, the more there will be to tax for the benefit of the ruling class. For a secure autocrat – say, a king who people believe serves at the will of God – the autocrat has every incentive to act as a benevolent despot who does what is best for the well-being of the country's citizens. Autocrats with shorter time horizons – those who fear being overthrown – have incentives to be more predatory, confiscating as much of a country's wealth as they can before someone else overthrows them. The predatory autocrat will enjoy a greater short-term gain, but at the expense of long-run gains that are uncertain in any event.

Herein lies the threat to the benevolent despot. By limiting his take now for the sake of the long-run productivity of his country, he is giving up short-run benefits in exchange for long-run benefits that potential competitors might try to seize by force. The autocrat can receive those long-run benefits only by remaining in power for the long run. Thus, the autocrat must compensate those who support him sufficiently so that they would not view it as beneficial to join a movement to replace him. Those who support the power of the autocrat are in a position to demand such compensation, which will produce autocracies that are less economically productive than potentially they could be, because as Bueno de Mesquita *et al.* (2003) and Niskanen (2003) note, the autocrat must plunder the citizens, to some degree anyway, to support his base of power.[4]

Those who maintain political power in democratic government also must maintain support, but elections provide an institutionalized opportunity for challengers to attempt to take control of the apparatus of power. Rather than investing in weapons and threatening physical force to oust the current leadership, opponents invest in political campaigns to elect themselves into positions of power. This institutionalized channel for replacing the existing power structure reduces the threat of violent overthrow by opening up an alternative channel whereby power can be seized. Democratic leaders, like autocratic ones, need support to maintain their power, but in a democracy that support must be more broadly based. At the simplest level, the support of a majority of voters is required to gain and maintain power, and the classic analysis of Downs (1957) explains the basic strategy by which candidates appeal to the median voter to win elections.

The analysis becomes more complex when it recognizes that interest groups can strengthen the political power of some voters relative to others, but the essential element remains that retaining political power requires the support of a majority of the electorate. Thus, whereas autocrats must cultivate the support of a relatively narrow power group to maintain their power, those who hold the reigns of democratic governments must cultivate the support of a majority. This implies spreading out the benefits more widely. In theory this suggests that democratic governments produce more public goods than autocratic governments, but in practice the bulk of what democratic governments produce is redistribution, not public goods, as Holcombe (2008) notes. It appears that even in democracies, political support is more effectively generated through transfers than through public goods production.

The differences between the sources of political support in autocracies and democracies result in differences in their behaviors. For example, as Niskanen (2003) notes, autocracies, with their limited base of support, can increase the take of the ruling coalition by conquering additional territory, which gives them additional subjects to tax. This will not necessarily be true for democracies, which must maintain the support of a majority of the voters. If a democratic country takes over a poorer territory, the median income of the aggregated territory falls, which will result in a reduction in the potential for redistribution to the median voter. Thus, autocracies tend to be more aggressive in acquiring new territory, which unambiguously increases the potential income of the ruling coalition, than democracies, which could find their ruling coalition's income fall if they acquire territories poorer than their current territory.

Despite the differences between autocracies and democracies, they share in common the need for those with political power to maintain the support of their power base in order to maintain their power. They do so by using the force of government to transfer income and wealth from taxpayers in general to those whose support they need to remain in power. In democracies, voters are the ultimate support group that must remain satisfied with the incumbents, but this does not alter the fact that government uses coercion to provide benefits to its supporters. If coercion is approved by a majority, that does not make the coercion less coercive.

4 Maintaining majority support

Consistently maintaining the support of a majority in a democracy is a difficult undertaking, and as a result, in many nations the reins of political power – both for individuals and for parties – frequently change hands. This may be because, as Downs (1957) suggests, all candidates are competing for the support of the median voter, so the median voter is nearly indifferent between the alternative choices. It may be, however, that candidates target different groups for support, as Peltzman (1984) suggests, and McKelvey (1976) demonstrates that in a multi-dimensional issue space, regardless of the platform adopted by the incumbent, a challenger's platform could always dominate it and gain the support of a majority. Enacting policies that will continue to maintain the support of a majority is a non-trivial task, because there always is a way for a challenger to craft a platform that a majority of the voters will prefer to the status quo. A simple example can illustrate why.

Assume that three people will vote on how they will divide up a dollar among them. One strategy could be Riker's (1962) minimum winning coalition, where the division would be (1/2, 1/2, 0), a division that would be supported by two of the three voters. Voter 3 could offer the alternative of (2/3, 0, 1/3), which would be supported by the first and third voters, and which would break up the minimum winning coalition. This could prompt voter 2 to offer (0, 1/3, 2/3), which would gain a majority, and prompt voter 1 to offer (1/3, 2/3, 0). Voter 3 could then re-offer his original proposal, setting up a cyclical majority that introduced Arrow's (1951) analysis of collective decision-making. The general point is that when democratic decision-making is used to engage in redistribution, there is always an alternative that can gain majority support to replace any given alternative. The reason, illustrated in the simple example above, is that those in the current minority can always propose taking something from some recipients in the current majority to bribe some members of the current majority to switch coalitions and form a new majority.

This suggests that democratic governments should be inherently unstable, yet as Tullock (1982) observes, democratic outcomes tend to be very stable. Incumbents tend to get re-elected, and programs and expenditures tend to have even more staying power than individuals. The reason, following along the lines of the previous section, is that those with political power use that power to maintain their support so they can continue in office. Incumbents want to use their political power to provide benefits to their constituents, as described by Weingast *et al.* (1981) and Holcombe (1985), and engage in logrolling so that all incumbents are successful, buying political support to enhance their chances of re-election. Weingast *et al.* refer to this as a system of universalism and reciprocity. Universalism because all incumbents participate, and reciprocity because they support each other's projects, enabling all of them to offer constituent benefits to gain electoral support.

In the context of the cyclical majority described above, all representatives recognize that they do better to break the cycle with a (1/3, 1/3, 1/3) division – universalism – and support each other's efforts to buy voters with government-provided benefits. If they could get even more money for the redistributive game, an outcome of (1/3, 1/3, 1/3) could be even more politically successful. This will mean higher taxes, but constituents tend to credit their representatives for the benefits they get from government, but are less ready to blame them for the taxes they pay to finance those benefits. Their assessment is, in fact, correct, in that the benefits to specific constituents would not have been forthcoming had their representatives not worked for them, but most of their taxes would remain, to pay for the benefits that go to others.[5] The political process allows democratic governments to bribe constituents for their support, using the constituents' own money to pay the bribes!

In a democracy, incumbents hold political power, and want to retain that power. They use the power they have to buy the support of their constituents. Unlike purchases in the market, they use the force of taxation to pay for their programs, and while some taxpayers may not like the outcome, they have no choice. Incumbents must allocate the proceeds such that a majority believe they are better off allowing the incumbents to retain power than to replace them with challengers. The system does not change if the challengers win, however. The old challengers become the new incumbents, and have the same incentive to use the power of government to purchase the support of the majority.

5 Democracy provides the appearance of legitimacy

One challenge that faces any government is maintaining the appearance of legitimacy in the eyes of the government's citizens. The appearance of legitimacy enhances the ability of those in charge to enforce compliance, as Edelman (1964) argues. To the extent that citizens view those in government as a band of thieves, taking money from taxpayers in order to buy political support, their legitimacy will be eroded, meaning that taxpayers will work harder to avoid having the government appropriate their resources, and constituents will be less likely to repay any transfers with political support. The earlier quotation from Rousseau (1762) illustrates the social contractarian argument that the actions of a democratic form of government represent the public will, and if citizens hold Rousseau's ideology they have no basis for objecting to anything a democratic government does, even if they, personally, find themselves in disagreement. Democracies are not alone in devising institutions that increase the appearance of legitimacy. Historically, dictatorships and hereditary monarchies have presented their leaders as being chosen by the gods, or at least having the approval of the church; more weakly, hereditary monachy might be defended as a popularly approved selection process, or even one required for an orderly society, as Hobbes (1651) suggested.

Indeed, the contrast between Hobbes and Locke (1690) is striking, because Hobbes argues the social contract requires that citizens obey the rules of the sovereign, whereas Locke, a few decades later, argues that if the sovereign acts against the public interest, citizens have a right to overthrow and replace the sovereign. As Locke's arguments gained acceptance, the legitimacy of all but the most benevolent dictators would come into question, and one possible reason for the displacement of autocrats by democrats among world governments in the last few centuries is that autocrats lost their appearance of legitimacy due to arguments just like Locke's – and Rousseau's – destabilizing autocratic government and paving the way for its replacement by democratic government. Democracies, after all, are institutionalized to reflect the popular will.

The apparent legitimacy of democratic decision-making, in contrast to autocracy, enhances the ability of democratic governments to use the force of government to engage in transfers to politically powerful groups. Autocratic governments certainly undertake such transfers to those with political connections, but those transfers are recognized as the result of political favoritism, and increases in transfers reduce the government's appearance of legitimacy, placing some constraints on the ability of autocracies to engage in transfer activities. Yes, political insiders in autocracies can receive handsome rewards for their insider status, but as Niskanen (2003) notes, insiders are a relatively small group in autocracies. In contrast, there are fewer constraints on transfers in democracies because of the apparent legitimacy of outcomes generated by a democratic process, so aggregate transfers can be much larger.

6 Rent seeking in democracy

Autocracies, with a limited and (almost) fixed ruling group, institutionally constrain rent seeking, and with it, the welfare losses from rent seeking. The autocrat wants to pay off those in the ruling group to maintain their support, limiting the need for rent-seeking waste, while those outside the group have little hope of obtaining rents, except perhaps from finding a way to join the autocrat's coalition, or by revolution. Those in the autocrat's favored group recognize their favored positions, and pushing too hard for more – that is, rent seeking – could backfire, and the rent seekers could be replaced by the autocrat. Rent seekers in democracies are exercising their constitutional rights. They may not be successful, but the only penalty for unsuccessful rent seeking in a democracy is the resources used up in the rent seeking.

Autocracies are what North *et al.* (2009) refer to as limited access orders, where personal relationships are important, which limits the ability of outsiders to join the ruling coalition, and with it, the rent-seeking losses associated with trying. Revolution, as Kurrild-Klitgaard (1997) notes, is potentially costly, but unlikely because of an extreme free-rider problem. Not only do discontented citizens have an incentive to free-ride on other discontented citizens who might overthrow the government, unsuccessful revolutionaries will pay a substantial cost at the hands of the incumbent government. Thus, even if there is a sufficient mass of citizens to successfully overthrow the incumbent government, they are unlikely to make an attempt because of the free-rider problem and the substantial cost in the event of failure. The point is, autocratic governments have institutions in place that limit the amount of rent-seeking losses they will incur.

In democracies the potential for rent-seeking losses is nearly unlimited. The political process provides a mechanism within which citizens can participate to try to generate private gains for themselves at public expense, and the democratic nature of the process gives it the appearance of legitimacy. When rent seekers succeed in obtaining a rent in a democracy, the very process by which they succeed legitimizes their success. Following along the lines of Rawls (1971) and Buchanan (1975), an outcome is legitimate if the process that produces it is legitimate. Democratic governments establish legitimate institutions through which collective decisions are made, so when rent seekers work through those processes and receive government-granted rents, the rents they receive appear legitimate.

In an autocracy one can fault the plunderers, who are political insiders, for taking from the general public for their own benefit. In a democracy, the plunderers – the rent seekers – work through legitimate political channels and receive their plunder through government approval. One might fault those in government for approving the rents, but one cannot fault the rent seekers, because seeking private benefits at public expense is a legitimate practice in democratic government, whereas it is a questionable practice in autocracy. Democratic institutions encourage interest groups to enter the political process and engage in rent seeking. Participation in the political process is not only accepted but is viewed as a patriotic activity on the part of citizens. Political apathy – the refusal to participate – is viewed as unpatriotic. Lobbying government is not only a generally accepted practice in democracies, but is even painted as virtuous because people are involving themselves in political discourse and lobbying allows their voices to be heard.

The concept of rent seeking, introduced by Tullock (1967), was named by Krueger (1974), who described the rent-seeking waste she observed in India, which had been democratic since its independence from Britain in 1947. McChesney (1987, 1997) discusses the way that politicians can extract rents, with associated rent-seeking losses, from groups simply by threatening to pass legislation that would harm them. The concept of rent seeking and the associated rent-seeking losses was developed with reference to democratic decision-making because that is where the potential for these losses is most significant. Observers at least as far back as Tocqueville (1835) have noted the potential inefficiencies that arise when people in democracies discover that they can vote themselves benefits at the expense of others.

Olson (1982) saw the potential for rent-seeking losses to grow over time in democracies as political coalitions become more firmly entrenched. With limited government, productive activity is more rewarding than predatory activity, but as government grows and interest groups become more firmly entrenched in public policy, forced transfers increase and predatory activity becomes relatively more attractive when compared to productive activity. Over time, the rent-seeking losses in a democracy increase, sapping productivity and eroding prosperity. This is the essential tension between democracy and prosperity.

7 The ideologies of capitalism and democracy

The Cold War of the second half of the twentieth century pitted capitalist democracies like the United States and countries in Western Europe against the socialist dictatorships like the Soviet Union and China. This taxonomy tended to separate economic and political systems, much as Fukuyama (1992) did when identifying the triumph of democratic governments and capitalist economies. In this two-dimensional vision, countries sat between the extremes of democracy and dictatorship in the political dimension and between capitalism and socialism in the economic dimension. It is easy to envision countries independently locating in various positions in either dimension.

The United States would be an example of a capitalist democracy and the Soviet Union an example of a socialist dictatorship. But other combinations are possible. Sweden and India could be cited as examples of socialist democracies, and fascism such as that of Hitler's Germany has often been depicted as a capitalist dictatorship.[6] Thus, any combination of political and economic systems would be possible in this two-dimensional framework, and the framework itself was reinforced by the Cold War tension between democracies and dictatorships, and between capitalist nations and socialist nations.

This framework has the liability that it does not take into account the scope of government. Another way to envision political and economic order is to view a continuum with liberty and limited government at the extreme of one axis and coercion and big government at the other extreme. In the extreme libertarian society people make their own choices about their lives and how they allocate their incomes; at the coercive extreme government tells them what they must do. In the extreme libertarian society, as Holcombe (2002) notes, there is little room for either democracy or autocracy, because those are two systems for controlling the power of government and in the extreme libertarian society there is almost no government control. Seen in this way, democracy and autocracy fall at the government end of the liberty–government continuum, and are two ways of determining who does the coercing. Under autocracy it is the autocrat; under democracy it is the majority.

In the libertarian extreme, there is little room for either democracy or autocracy, because people make their own decisions. With a constitutionally limited government of minimal size, whether the government is democratic or autocratic makes little difference to people's lives. The bigger factor is the constitutional limits on the power of government. As the society moves from liberty to coercion, the type of government makes more difference, as the previous sections have described. During the Cold War era the prosperity of Western nations was not due to the type of government they had – that they were democracies rather than dictatorships. It was due to their economic systems – that they were capitalist rather than socialist.

The Cold War ideology obscured the differences between capitalism and socialism, on the one hand, and democracy and dictatorship on the other, because on one side were capitalist democracies and on the other were socialist dictatorships. As a result, the beneficial effects of capitalism tended to be ascribed excessively to those countries' democratic politics. Capitalist economies allocate resources based on individuals' choices, not on government direction, so with reference to government, the key factor in this Cold War division was not that capitalist nations were democratically governed but that the scope of their governments was constitutionally limited. It was limited government, not democratic government, that led to the prosperity of capitalist democracies.

8 Institutions and prosperity

Over the last few decades a considerable literature has developed that has identified those institutions that lead to prosperity. Mokyr (1990) and Landes (1998) both offer compelling arguments that prosperity is the result of the adoption of capitalist economies with market institutions, limited government, and the protection of property rights. Throughout history, and throughout the world, countries that have done so have prospered; those that have not have languished in poverty. Perhaps the most compelling natural experiment was the division of Korea into two countries with different economic institutions following World War II. Both countries started with the same people, the same culture, the same language, and the same level of economic development. South Korea, with market institutions, has grown to be among the more prosperous countries in the world, while North Korea, with its centrally planned economy, is among the world's poorest countries. A similar experiment was done with the division of Germany into East and West Germany, with similar results.

India and China, two of the world's fastest-growing economies since the 1990s, offer interesting case studies. For both countries, their economic growth accelerated when they allowed market institutions to substitute for government planning, but an interesting contrast between the countries is that India has been a democracy since its independence from Britain, whereas China has never had democratic government. It appears that the adoption of market economies is the common element that has allowed both economies to grow, despite their very different political environments. Economic institutions appear to make the difference, independent of political institutions.

Gwartney and Lawson (2004) have created an Economic Freedom Index to quantify those economic institutions that define a market economy, and Berggren (2003) reviews a substantial literature that has used Gwartney and Lawson's index to demonstrate empirically the connection between economic freedom and prosperity. The key features of a market economy, following Gwartney and Lawson, are protection of property rights, rule of law, low taxes and government spending, minimal regulatory restraints on economic activity, freedom of trade, and a stable monetary system. As Gwartney *et al.* (1999) note, when measures of economic freedom and political freedom are considered together, differences in economic freedom explain differences in levels of income and changes in economic freedom explain differences in economic growth. Once economic institutions are accounted for, differences in political institutions have little impact on prosperity.

9 Constitutions and democracy

Looking at Gwartney and Lawson's list of institutions that lead to prosperity, they are all market institutions, but in contemporary societies all are overseen by some form of government. The legal structure, protection of property rights, freedom of trade, the monetary system, and, most obviously, taxes, government spending, and regulation are determined by political institutions. Thus, while economic institutions are the key to prosperity, political institutions are the key to maintaining those economic institutions. Prosperity requires that political institutions be designed to preserve economic freedom. To use Hayek's (1960) phrase, a constitution of liberty is required for prosperity.

In constitutional democracies, there has been a tendency – especially in the past few decades – to overemphasize the importance of democracy and underemphasize the importance of constitutional constraints on the power of government. After the collapse of the Berlin Wall in 1989, followed by the demise of the Soviet Union in 1991, the leaders of Western nations were emphatic about the importance of establishing democratic governments in those nations in transition. Market institutions – the key to prosperity – received relatively little emphasis.

The instrumental feature of constitutional democracy is constitutional constraints on government so that government protects the rights of individuals and is constrained from limiting their freedom. Political freedoms, such as the right to free speech, are important in their own right, but economic freedoms are essential to the production of a prosperous society. In constitutional democracy, constitutional constraints are the key feature of the political design. Democracy is only a means to that end.

Government powerful enough to protect the rights of its citizens is also powerful enough to violate the rights of its citizens. Constitutional constraints on government are designed to prevent government from violating citizens' rights, but how is the power of government to be controlled? Democracy is one way, and perhaps the best way. But, as Polanyi (1944: 234) remarked, 'Socialism is, essentially, the tendency inherent in an industrial civilization to transcend the self-regulating market by consciously subordinating it to a democratic society.' In a constitutional democracy it is the constitution, not the democracy, that enables prosperity.

Democracy is a means to an end. It is a method whereby citizens have the ability to determine who will hold the reins of government power. In a democracy, if citizens are dissatisfied with their political leaders, citizens can vote those leaders out of office. In an autocracy, political leaders remain until they are forced out. Elections provide not only a non-violent method of forcing leaders out of office, but also a periodic referendum on whether they should stay. This is the advantage democracy offers over autocracy. But, to emphasize, democracy is a means to an end – a means to maintain constitutional government – and not an end in itself.

10 Uncontrained democracy

Unconstrained democracy suffers from the obvious problem that a majority can vote themselves benefits at the expense of a minority. This provides such a clear argument against designing public policy to follow the will of the majority that it needs little support. It is worth noting, however, that the democratic decision-making process will lend more legitimacy to predatory majorities than to a predatory autocrat. Citizens recognize that the predatory autocrat's plunder is an abuse of power, and will be ready to forcibly remove such autocrats from office at the first sign of the autocrat's weakness on the grip of power. Ferdinand Marcos, the Shah of Iran, and a host of Eastern European dictators after the fall of the Berlin Wall provide evidence.

The majority in a democracy can be just as predatory as an autocrat, but unlike with the autocrat, the predatory majority is only a symptom and the real problem lies mostly with the political system within which that majority operates. Those leaders of the predatory majority can be voted out of office, but the political institutions within which they operated remain, and are filled with a new set of democratic leaders who are ready to use their offices for plunder. The fault lies not with the individuals but with the system. As noted earlier, political leaders in a democracy must win the support of a majority to remain in office, and as long as the institutions allow it, this support can most effectively be bought by using the coercive force of government to tax and regulate some for the benefit of others. Applying the logic of competitive politics depicted by Downs (1957), if the incumbent leaders do not use all the power at their disposal to provide benefits for a majority, challengers can make a majority a better offer and unseat the incumbents.

Democracy requires constitutional constraints to keep it from turning into a system in which a majority plunders and oppresses a minority. Alexis de Tocqueville (1835) described this as a 'tyranny of the majority,' which he saw as an inherent tendency in democratic government. Nobody explicitly advocates unconstrained democracy, which would give a majority the power to use government for whatever ends they saw fit. However, public policy arguments are frequently implicitly supported with this argument. Policies are advocated because of their popular support, independent of any constitutional foundation. These are the types of policies that erode the constitutional foundations of government and create the conflict between democracy and prosperity.

11 Constitutional design

In the most abstract framework, constitutional democracy consists of a set of constitutional rules that define the scope and powers of government. The US Constitution is drawn up according to this framework, because it enumerates the powers government has and explicitly states that its powers are limited only to those the Constitution enumerates. Thus, the constitution specifies the government's activities, and the role of democracy in this constitutional democracy is limited to determining who will exercise the government's power to carry on those enumerated powers. Buchanan and Tullock (1963) make a clear distinction between the design of constitutional rules and the post-constitutional decisions that are made within those rules. The constitutional rules determine the government's enumerated powers.

The constitutional rules required for prosperity have already been noted. Getting those rules in place to begin with is not a trivial task. In hypothetical settings, Rawls (1971) argues that optimal constitutional rules are those that would be agreed to from behind a veil of ignorance; Buchanan (1975) argues that optimal constitutional rules are those that would be agreed to in a renegotiation of the rules from a setting of anarchy. One feature of the Rawls–Buchanan framework is that in their hypothetical settings, everyone agrees to the rules. Another feature is that in both instances, the settings within which agreement takes place leaves citizens with substantial uncertainty as to their roles in society under the resulting constitutional rules. If people do not know what roles they will occupy under constitutional rules they are considering, they will naturally want those constitutional rules to be impartial, and conducive to prosperity.

In reality constitutions are not designed by impartial observers; rather, those who hold power in pre-constitutional society will have the ability to design the constitutional rules. Even the US Constitution was designed to further the interests of its authors, Beard (1913) argues. The American Founders tended to be entrepreneurs and businesspeople, which is why the Constitution was slanted to favor productive activity over predation. In other settings, those who design the rules are more predatory, and the constitutional rules are designed from the start to favor some people over others. Designing a constitution that supports an institutional structure of prosperity is a difficult task. Even if that task is accomplished, maintaining such a constitution is a challenge that democracy tends to undermine.

12 Democracy erodes liberty

In an ideal setting of constitutional design, the structure of constitutional rules remains separate from the post-constitutional decisions made under those rules. In the real world, the division between constitutional and post-constitutional decision-making is not so clear-cut, and post-constitutional decisions effectively change the constitution. Olson (1982) describes a process in which a political structure, derived *de novo*, sets a structure of impartial rules within which people can interact. As the nation matures, interest groups form and gain strength, and with their growing strength comes an increasing ability to influence government policy to favor those interest groups at the expense of the general public. This produces the rent-seeking losses described by Tullock (1967) and Krueger (1974). Government grows as interest groups gain political power, which in turn encourages others to lobby government for benefits.

Baumol (1990) paints this contrast between institutional structures nicely. When institutions protect property rights, treat everyone the same under the law, and prevent government from favoring some groups over others, entrepreneurial individuals will prosper by engaging in productive activities that add to the prosperity of everyone. When institutions allow some people to use the political system to effect transfers from others to themselves, entrepreneurial individuals will engage in rent-seeking activities to try to use the force of government to enrich themselves. Successful entrepreneurship in the first case is directed toward productive activity; in the second case it is directed toward predatory activity.

Herein lies the long-term problem with democracy. Those with political power must be re-elected to maintain that power. To be re-elected they must win the support of a majority, which means proposing a platform that a majority sees as preferable to competing platforms. Thus, both incumbents and challengers propose using the political structure for the benefit of the majority. Some votes can be won by using the force of government to design transfers from some citizens to those potential supporters. With constitutionally constrained government, the ability to effect such transfers is limited, but because there is not a clear dividing line between constitutional and post-constitutional decisions, constitutional constraints erode over time as politicians push the limits to expand the power of government. Those expanding limits give those in power the ability to increase the support they give to the majority that elects them.

This is especially clear when looking at the US case, because the US Constitution is so clearly a document that enumerates the powers of the federal government and nominally prevents the government from expanding beyond those enumerated powers. In a literal reading of the US Constitution one would be hard-pressed to find any constitutional authority for the government to run a compulsory retirement system, yet somehow the Supreme Court ruled the Social Security program constitutional in 1937. Similarly, one would be hard-pressed to find any constitutional authority for the federal government to run a healthcare program, yet when Medicare and Medicaid were established in 1966 those constitutional limits had been eroded so far that the programs were not even challenged.

The issue is not whether Social Security and Medicare are desirable programs. If they are, the Constitution has provisions for amendment to allow them. The point is that the Constitution did not require amending, even though there is no authority for those programs in the Constitution's enumerated powers, because the constitutional constraints on the scope of government have been eroded to such a degree that there are no effective constitutional limits remaining. The principle of constitutional constraints to protect the liberty of its citizens has been eroded and replaced by the 'principle' of democracy, which in effect says that if most people favor a certain policy the government should do it. But democracy is not, in fact, a principle. Unconstrained, it is a political system that allows a majority to use the force of government for their benefit, at the expense of a minority. When this happens, predation, using the power of government to extract resources from some for the benefit of others, becomes a more effective method of generating income than production, and democracy erodes prosperity.

13   The legitimization of coercion

While Rousseau (1762) saw democracy as a way of revealing the public will, an analysis of the actual institutions of democracy shows that democratic decision-making opens the door to rent seeking and provides an avenue for some to use the political process – that is, the force of government – to transfer resources from others to themselves. While all government action is coercive at its foundation, one pernicious aspect of democratic government is that it legitimizes the use of the force of government to benefit some at the expense of others. In autocratic government, it is apparent that the autocrat controls the coercive powers of the state, and the autocrat that abuses those powers runs the risk of being overthrown and replaced. In a democracy, government actions are justified as being an expression of the popular will.

As Edelman (1964) notes, democracy has symbolic value that legitimizes the policies of democratic government. Every citizen is given the opportunity to participate, through voting, contacting elected representatives, joining interest groups, and participating in lobbying. The selection of representatives is the result of a process in which every citizen can participate, legitimizing their selection as, indeed, representative of all citizens. Therefore, the decisions those representatives make are legitimized as the result of their democratic selection process. After that, citizens can make their voices heard in varying ways, so unlike autocracy, where the autocrat determines policy, in a democracy public policy can be traced directly back to the citizenry. Some individuals may not agree with some government policies, but because one set of policies must be implemented for everyone, policies implemented by democratic governments express – albeit indirectly – the will of the majority and are thus appear more legitimate than policies imposed by the will of an autocrat.

Are the policies of democratic governments really more legitimate? The social contract theory of the state, running through Rousseau, Rawls, and Buchanan, makes democratic decision-making appear to be the result of agreement, but policies of democracies are just as coercive as those of autocracies. Consider, for example, firms that lobby government to use the force of government to protect them from competitors, perhaps through tariffs to protect them from foreign competition, perhaps through regulation to exclude competitors from the market, perhaps through government contracts to buy their output, or perhaps through outright subsidies. Rent-seeking activities that lead to this type of benefits to some who have political power at the expense of the general public can hardly be called the will of the majority. As Olson (1965) notes, concentrated interests have an advantage in the political process because they can more effectively organize themselves, and the concentrated benefits they receive make political action worthwhile, whereas when the costs are spread among a large group their incentive to oppose those special interest benefits is diluted, and in any event it will be difficult for large interests to organize.

The result is that concentrated special interests are able to use the institutions of representative democracy to create policies that forcibly transfer benefits from diluted interests to themselves. This rent seeking is nothing the majority agreed upon, nor is it anything the majority would favor. Democratic political institutions have the appearance of legitimacy, but it is no more legitimate for politically connected interest groups to plunder the general public than it is for a robber to take someone's property. As Downs (1957) notes, most people are rationally ignorant of most of what government does. This rent-seeking activity is simply a matter of some people using the force of government to effect transfers from others to themselves. However, when the government is demo-cratic there is the appearance of legitimacy simply because of the democratic form of government. If an autocrat did the same thing, it would be more clearly seen for what it is: those with political power using the force of government for their own private benefit. When the same thing happens in a democracy, the symbolism associated with democracy legitimizes what amounts to taking the property of some for the benefit of others.

Democracy does not enable prosperity, it legitimizes plunder – more benignly referred to as rent seeking in the academic literature – which erodes prosperity. Democratic election of a nation's political leaders has much to recommend it, but the common notion of democracy at the beginning of the twenty-first century goes well beyond that, to the notion that if a policy is supported by a majority, the government should enact it. This broader twenty-first-century notion of democracy stands at odds with the prosperity that has been produced by the market economy.

14 Democracy in a historical context

Unconstrained democracy allows a majority to use the force of government to transfer resources from productive members of society to themselves, undermin-ing the incentive structure that is required for prosperity. This thesis might appear alarmist considering the widespread and growing prosperity that the world has seen for as long as anyone alive today can remember. However, one does not have to look too much further back in history to find a time when this was not the case. The economic progress the world sees today began with the Industrial Revolution around 1750, so is only a few hundred years old. It is a short time in human history indeed, begun only when the institutions allowing for economic progress solidified in eighteenth-century Britain and then spread around the world. Meanwhile, the modern concept of democracy that threatens to undermine the institutions of prosperity is only about a century old and is still evolving.

Prior to the twentieth century, democracy was not viewed as an end in itself, but rather as a means to an end. Democracy was viewed not as a method of implementing the will of the majority, but rather as a method of selecting a gov-ernment's political leaders, and those leaders were viewed – and viewed them-selves – as subject to constitutional constraints on their use of governmental power. As Higgs (1987) describes, in the nineteenth century people viewed the role of government as the protection of individual rights. In the late nineteenth century this ideology changed so that people came to view an expanded role of government, where government was not only responsible for protecting their rights but for also looking out for people's economic well-being.[7]

This ideological change transformed democracy from a method of selecting a nation's political leaders into a method for determining the role of government in the economy. That evolution of the concept of democracy, begun in the Pro-gressive era around the beginning of the twentieth century continued through the

New Deal and years of the Great Depression as the government became increasingly involved not only in direct transfers to support some people at the expense of others but also in regulating the market activities of individuals. By the end of the twentieth century democracy meant the determination of public policy according to the will of the majority. By some measures modern democracy might be viewed as having a history that dates back centuries, but democracy in the modern sense of the role of government being to implement the will of the majority really only dates back a few decades.

Higgs (1987) notes that government has ratcheted up its power during periods of crisis, like wars and depression. Indeed, in the twentieth century this is apparent as effects of two world wars and the Great Depression of the 1930s. Modern democracy finally emerged full-strength, Holcombe (2002) argues, in Lyndon Johnson's Great Society, where a major expansion of the scope and power of government occurred not as a result of a crisis, but rather because a majority supported it. In the United States, Medicare and Medicaid were created in 1965 not because healthcare was deteriorating – in fact, healthcare was improving – but because of the optimism of the majority behind Johnson's Great Society. Government programs were expanded to create a War on Poverty in the 1960s not because poverty was increasing – in fact, it was rapidly decreasing – but because a majority supported it. During this same period the welfare state greatly expanded in Europe, again because of its popular appeal, not because welfare was deteriorating. Constitutionally constrained government gave way to democratic government, which meant government directed by the will of the majority.

One might view this chapter's critique of twenty-first-century democracy as alarmist, thinking, 'Things have always worked this way.' That may appear true to people who are only remembering what they have experienced in their lifetimes, but one does not have to go back too far in history to see that, in fact, the contemporary concept of democracy is relatively new. Modern institutions of democracy, in which people view the plunder of some for the benefit of others through democratic government as a legitimate exercise of government power, is a post-World War II phenomenon.

15 Conclusion

At the beginning of the twenty-first century, democracy is held in such high regard that any criticism of it might even be taken as a stance against a basic human right. Yet public policy designed by democracy is antithetical to prosperity and ultimately harmful to human rights. Prosperity requires liberal economic institutions, and democracy should be seen as a means to an end, not an end in itself. Government is at its foundation a coercive institution, and covering it with a veneer of democracy does not change the fundamentally coercive nature of government.

Markets work through voluntary agreement. In market transactions people obtain things only from people who agree to an exchange. Government works through force. It obtains its revenues through compulsory taxation and requires obedience to its regulations. The common notion that democratic government legitimizes this coercion is dangerous, because it conveys to the majority the appearance of a legitimate right to confer benefits to themselves at the expense of those who are taxed and regulated.

What would appear as plunder if done by an autocrat, or simple theft if done by a fellow citizen, appears as the will of the majority in a democracy. If a poor and hungry person approaches a citizen on the street, pulls out a knife, and says, 'Give me your money, and I will force you and harm you if you don't comply,' that would be viewed as robbery. If a democratic government says, 'Pay your taxes to fund food stamps and other transfers to a subset of citizens, and we will harm you and extract those resources from you by force if you don't comply,' that, in a democracy, is viewed as a part of the social contract. Rothbard (1982: 163, emphasis in original) says, 'It would be an instructive exercise for the skeptical reader to try to frame a definition of taxation which does not *also* include theft.'

Democracy and prosperity are at their foundations incompatible. Prosperity requires the protection of property rights, equal protection under the law, and transfers of resources only through the voluntary consent of those who own them. Democracy means imposition of the will of the majority, which allows the majority to violate property rights, favor some over others under the law, and to forcibly transfer resources from some to others.

The democratic legitimization of government coercion does not remove government's coercive element, and when one looks at democratic institutions in detail, rather than at a distance with a romantic notion of democracy, one sees that democratic political institutions allow those with political power to use the force of government to benefit themselves by imposing costs on others. Democratic government has the potential to be more pernicious precisely because it appears to be more legitimate.

Prosperity is produced by market institutions, and market institutions require the protection of property rights, rule of law, and low tax and regulatory barriers to exchange. Those conditions require a certain set of economic institutions, and a constitutionally limited government can help implement and maintain those institutions. In this framework, democracy can be used as a means to the end of prosperity, but if democracy is viewed as an end in itself, constitutional constraints will be eroded and democratic politics will find itself at odds with the economic institutions that create prosperity. There is an inherent tension between market institutions and democratic government, a tension that can be controlled though constitutional constraints on the scope of government. Without such constraints, democracy will undermine prosperity.

Notes

1 This is a translation from the original French, but it is still worth noting that in the translation 'people' is treated in the singular twice: first when Rousseau says 'when the people is asked' and then again saying 'whether it approves.' Thus, Rousseau treats the people not as a group of individuals, but as a single entity with a single general will.

2 Rawls (1971) and Buchanan (1975) do not argue that all government rules are a part of the social contract, and develop a conceptual framework for identifying those that are. Their frameworks fall somewhat short in this regard, however, because (despite the attempt of Rawls to do so) it is unclear which specific provisions the social contract contains.

3 Recognizing this potential, governments design institutions to make military coups less likely. For example, in the United States military personnel are routinely shifted to new assignments every few years in which they will be relocated so they have a different peer group. This prevents the formation of long-standing personal relationships among military leaders, reducing the possibility that a small group of close friends in control of the military can engineer coups. The network of military leaders would have to be much larger to engineer a successful coup, because a group of people working together today will not have long-standing relationships with each other, but will have longer relationships with their former military colleagues who now have different assignments in different places. In such an institutional setting, it is unlikely that a small group of military leaders could design and effect a coup without information spreading outside the group, to others who may be in a position to stop it. Military people tend to move frequently, and be reassigned, as a method of protecting against a military take-over of the government.

4 Deacon (2009) provides evidence that democracies produce higher levels of public goods than dictatorships, perhaps indicating preferences of dictators for plunder over production.

5 This is not unlike the way people view the healthcare they receive when paid for by insurance. They get benefits from their own healthcare providers, paid for by the premiums assessed on everybody, so even though people want lower health insurance premiums, they still ask their own providers for the highest-quality – and most expensive – care.

6 Hayek (1944) argued that this depiction is incorrect. In fact, fascist governments exercised considerable control over their economies, making them more centrally planned than market-based. Nonetheless, fascism has commonly been depicted as capitalist and dictatorial.

7 Higgs (1987) discusses this change in ideology with reference to American politics, but the same general thesis applies to European politics as well, although the transition came ahead of the American transition by a decade or two.

Bibliography

Acemoglu, D., Johnson, S., Robinson, J.A. and Yared, P. (2008) 'Income and Democracy,' *American Economic Review* 98: 808–42.

Arrow, K.J. (1951) *Social Choice and Individual Values*, New Haven, CT: Yale University Press.

Barro, R.J. (1996) 'Democracy and Growth,' *Journal of Economic Growth* 1: 1–27.

Baumol, W.J. (1990) 'Entrepreneurship: Productive, Unproductive, and Destructive,' *Journal of Political Economy* 98: 893–921.

Beard, C.A. (1913) *An Economic Interpretation of the Constitution of the United States*, New York: Macmillan.

Berggren, N. (2003) 'The Benefits of Economic Freedom: A Survey,' *Independent Review* 8: 193–211.

Buchanan, J.M. (1975) *The Limits of Liberty: Between Anarchy and Leviathan*, Chicago: University of Chicago Press.

Buchanan, J.M. and Tullock, G. (1963) *The Calculus of Consent*, Ann Arbor: University of Michigan Press.

Bueno de Mesquita, B., Smith, A., Siverson, R.M., and Morrow, J.D. (2003) *The Logic of Political Survival*, Cambridge, MA: MIT Press.

Deacon, R.T. (2009) 'Public Good Provision under Dictatorship and Democracy,' *Public Choice* 139: 241–62.

De Haan, J. and Sierman, C.L.J. (1998) 'Further Evidence on the Relationship between Economic Freedom and Economic Growth,' *Public Choice* 95: 363–80.

Downs, A. (1957) *An Economic Theory of Democracy*, New York: Harper & Row.

Edelman, M. (1964) *The Symbolic Uses of Politics*, Urbana: University of Illinois Press.

Friedman, M. (1962) *Capitalism and Freedom*, Chicago: University of Chicago Press.

Fukuyama, F. (1992) *The End of History and the Last Man*, New York: Free Press.

Gwartney, J. and Lawson, R. (2004) *Economic Freedom of the World, 2004 Report*, Vancouver, BC: Fraser Institute.

Gwartney, J., Lawson, R., and Holcombe, R. (1999) 'Economic Freedom and the Environment for Economic Growth,' *Journal of Institutional and Theoretical Economics* 155: 643–63.

Hayek, F.A. (1944) *The Road to Serfdom*, Chicago: University of Chicago Press.

Hayek, F.A. (1960) *The Constitution of Liberty*, Chicago: University of Chicago Press.

Higgs, R. (1987) *Crisis and Leviathan: Critical Episodes in the Growth of American Government*, New York: Oxford University Press.

Hobbes, T. (1950 [1651]) *Leviathan*, New York: E.P. Dutton.

Hochman, H.M. and Rodgers, J.D. (1969) 'Pareto Optimal Redistribution,' *American Economic Review* 59: 542–57.

Holcombe, R.G. (1985) *An Economic Analysis of Democracy*, Carbondale: Southern Illinois University Press.

Holcombe, R.G. (2002) 'Liberty and Democracy as Economic Systems,' *The Independent Review* 6: 407–25.

Holcombe, R.G. (2008) 'Why Does Government Produce National Defense?' *Public Choice* 137: 11–19.

Krueger, A.O. (1974) 'The Political Economy of the Rent-Seeking Society,' *American Economic Review* 64: 291–303.

Kurrild-Klitgaard, P. (1997) *Rational Choice, Collective Action, and the Paradox of Rebellion*, Copenhagen: Institute of Political Science, University of Copenhagen.

Landes, D.S. (1998) *The Wealth and Poverty of Nations: Why Some Are So Rich, and Some So Poor*, New York: W.W. Norton.

Levi, M. (1988) *Of Rule and Revenue*, Berkeley: University of California Press.

Locke, John (1970) *Two Treatises of Government*. Cambridge: Cambridge University Press, [orig. 1690].

McChesney, F.S. (1987) 'Rent Extraction and Rent Creation in the Economic Theory of Regulation,' *Journal of Legal Studies* 16: 101–18.

McChesney, F.S. (1997) *Money for Nothing: Politicians, Rent Extraction, and Political Extortion*, Cambridge, MA: Harvard University Press.

McKelvey, R.D. (1976) 'Intransitivities in Multi Dimensional Voting Models and Some Implications for Agenda Control,' *Journal of Economic Theory* 12: 472–82.

Mokyr, J. (1990) *The Lever of Riches*, Oxford: Oxford University Press.

Niskanen, W.A. (2003) *Autocratic, Democratic, and Optimal Government*, Cheltenham: Edward Elgar.

North, D.C., Wallis, J.J., and Weingast, B.R. (2009) *Violence and Social Orders: A Conceptual Framework for Interpreting Recorded Human History*, Cambridge: Cambridge University Press.

Olson, M., Jr. (1965) *The Logic of Collective Action*, New York: Shocken Books.

Olson, M., Jr. (1982) *The Rise and Decline of Nations*, New Haven, CT: Yale University Press.

Peltzman, S. (1984) 'Constituent Interest and Congressional Voting,' *Journal of Law & Economics* 27: 181–210.

Polanyi, K. (1944) *The Great Transformation*, New York: Farrar & Rinehart.

Rawls, J. (1971) *A Theory of Justice*, Cambridge, MA: Belknap Press.

Riker, W.H. (1962) *The Theory of Political Coalitions*, New Haven, CT: Yale University Press.

Rothbard, M.N. (1982) *The Ethics of Liberty*, Atlantic Highlands, NJ: Humanities Press.

Rousseau, J.J. (1762) *The Social Contract, Or Principles of Political Right*, trans. G.D.H. Cole. Online: www.constitution.org/jjr/socon.htm.

Schumpeter, J.A. (1950) *Capitalism, Socialism and Democracy*, 3rd edn., New York: Harper & Row.

Sturm, J.-E. and de Haan, J. (2005) 'Determinants of Long-term Growth: New Results Applying Robust Estimation and Extreme Bounds Analysis,' *Empirical Economics* 30: 597–617.

Tocqueville, A. de (1963 [1835]) *Democracy in America*, New York: Alfred A. Knopf.

Tullock, G. (1967) 'The Welfare Costs of Tariffs, Monopolies, and Theft,' *Western Economic Journal* 5: 224–32.

Tullock, G. (1982) 'Why So Much Stability?' *Public Choice* 37: 189–202.

Weingast, B., Shepsle, K.A., and Johnsen, C. (1981) 'The Political Economy of Benefits and Costs: A Neoclassical Approach to Distributive Politics,' *Journal of Political Economy* 89: 642–64.

Yeager, L.B. (1985) 'Rights, Contract, and Utility in Policy Espousal,' *Cato Journal* 5: 259–94.

Yeager, L.B. (2001) *Ethics as a Social Science*, Cheltenham: Edward Elgar.

2 Competition among governments

The state's two roles in a globalized world

Viktor J. Vanberg

1 Introduction

The development called 'globalization' reflects most visibly the evolutionary dynamics of an economic and social world that is subject to permanent change, driven by creative human action. The world-wide integration of markets that this term describes is but the significantly accelerated modern phase in a process that has unfolded throughout the entire history of humankind, namely the expansion of markets. Since humans discovered that gains can be had from trade, their advantage-seeking ambition led them to explore ever new trading opportunities beyond their already established exchange networks and thereby, as an unintended byproduct, to widen the extent of the market.

That the expansion of markets – by allowing for specialization and its effects on the productivity of human labor – is the main wellspring of the 'wealth of nations' has been the message behind Adam Smith's famous dictum 'the division of labour is limited by the extent of the market' and it has been a principal message of economics ever since.[1] Its wealth-creating effect, the advantages it produces for consumers, is the unambiguously beneficial side of globalization. The more burdensome flipside of the coin is the intensified competition that comes with it, the constant pressure to adapt to changes that originate in some, be it the most remote, corners of the global economic network.

The competition aspect of globalization, the adaptive pressure it exerts, is the subject of this chapter. Specifically, I want to explore the issue of what the need to adapt to the forces of globalization means for the role of the state as the agency that, within the territorial limits of its jurisdiction, defines and enforces the 'economic constitution,' i.e., the legal framework within which economic activities take place. The main conjecture that I will seek to support in this chapter is that adapting to the conditions they face in a globalized world requires governments to distinguish more clearly than has traditionally been the case between two distinct roles or functions of the state. This is, on the one hand, the state's role as a *joint enterprise of its citizens*, i.e., as the organization that defines and enforces the rights and duties *among its members*, the citizens. And this is, on the other hand, its role as a *territorial enterprise*, i.e., as the agency that defines and enforces the legal terms to which everybody – citizens and non-citizens alike – is subject who resides or carries out activities within its territorial boundaries.

2 Globalization, competition among governments, and democratic rule

The accelerated extension and integration of markets we are witnessing in our times may well be – and is often – described as 'second globalization' in recognition of the fact that the late nineteenth century witnessed comparable developments in the world economy, developments that were driven by a similar combination of technological and political-institutional factors as today's globalization. These were, and are today, on the one side advances in transport and communications technology that significantly reduce transportation and communication costs, and, on the other side, political-institutional changes that remove or lower artificial barriers to trade and capital mobility.[2] It is the reduction in transaction costs made possible by these technological and institutional changes that allows goods and services, information and technology, productive resources, and financial as well as human capital to move more easily across national boundaries, creating new choice opportunities for people in their various capacities as consumers, producers, investors, etc.

In a world that provides persons with increased opportunities to choose where to buy, where to produce, where to invest, and where to live, national governments are naturally increasingly in competition with other governments, both directly and indirectly.[3] Governments compete *indirectly* with each other to the extent that the legal and other terms to which they submit economic activities within their respective territories have an impact – via their effects on the costs of production – on the competitiveness of domestic producers in international markets for goods and services. And governments compete *directly* with each other to the extent that the legal-institutional framework and other attributes of their jurisdictions that they can control provide a more or less attractive environment for mobile persons and economic resources, compared to other jurisdictions.

It is a common theme in the literature on globalization that competition in both its forms imposes constraints on what governments can do in the sense that they cannot with impunity, i.e., without negative consequences for their tax base, ignore the ways in which their policy choices affect the competitiveness of domestic producers and the attractiveness of their respective jurisdictions for internationally mobile persons and economic resources. Thus, studies on globalization generally agree that the competitive constraints globalization imposes on governments limit their power to act. These studies usually do not limit themselves, though, to just diagnosing this fact but include, whether explicitly or implicitly, normative views on how it is to be judged in light of the proper tasks that governments are supposed to perform. On this issue there is less agreement.[4] In this context the argument that globalization forces democratic governments to cater to the interests of mobile resources, in particular mobile capital, supposedly at their citizens' expense, plays a prominent role.[5]

Beyond analyzing the factual claim that globalization requires governments to distinguish more strictly between the two noted functions – its role as joint enterprise of its citizens on the one side and its role as territorial enterprise on the other – this chapter will, therefore, also be concerned with the *normative* issue of how this separation affects governments' capacity to perform their proper tasks. With regard to this normative issue I shall presume that we are dealing with *democratic* governments and that the relevant question therefore is how the proper performance of democratic governments is to be measured. If democracy, as is often done, is simply identified with majority rule, globalization may indeed be an impediment to democratic government, since in a globalized world there will surely be occasions where majority wishes are obstructed by the constraints of competition. In line with John Rawls' (1971: 84) characterization of democratic society 'as a cooperative venture for mutual advantage,' I shall adopt here a different standard for judging the proper performance of democratic government, namely its capacity to create *mutual advantages* for its citizens or, in other words, to serve their *common interests* (Vanberg 2000).

Majority rule is a decision-making tool that a democratic polity adopts for pragmatic reasons, but it is not always a reliable instrument for making governments best serve their citizens' common interests. Quite obviously, there are instances in which majority decisions produce outcomes that, instead of creating mutual advantages for all citizens, benefit only some groups at the expense of others, and their cumulative results may sometimes even be in nobody's interest. This is the reason why additional constraints on majority rule, such as the constraints imposed by competition among jurisdictions, may well serve to bring governments more in line with their proper task of working to the common benefit of their citizens.

To sum up, as 'cooperative ventures for mutual advantage' or, in brief, as 'citizens' cooperatives,' democratic polities, like ordinary cooperative enterprises, are supposed to be operated in the common interest of their members, i.e., the citizens. The appropriate measuring rod for the performance of democratic governments is, accordingly, how well they serve to advance citizens' common interests and refrain from taking measures that serve the interests of particular interest groups at the expense of other citizens, or even their own interests at the expense of the citizenry at large. This normative standard will be used in the following sections when assessing the constraints that governments face in a globalized world.

3 The state as citizens' joint enterprise and as territorial enterprise

As noted above, the purpose of the present chapter is to focus on a particular aspect of the constraints that the competitive dynamics of globalization impose on governments, namely the growing necessity to distinguish more strictly between two functions of the state. States have always performed these two functions, but the need to keep them separate from each other was of less urgency as long as the mobility of persons and economic resources remained below a critical threshold. The process of globalization has moved societies beyond this threshold.

As already stated, on the one hand the democratic state is the *joint enterprise* of its citizens, i.e., the organization that its member-citizens form to undertake projects of common interest, projects that they can better realize as a politically organized community than in private organizational forms. On the other hand, the state is the *territorial enterprise* that, within its geographically defined jurisdiction, legislates and enforces rules and regulations to which everybody is subject who resides or operates within the jurisdiction, whether they are citizens or not. Corresponding to these two roles of the state, persons can be affected by governmental measures in two capacities, namely as *citizens* and as – what, in want of a better name, I propose to call – *jurisdiction-users*. As citizens, persons are *members of the polity*. They are the constituents in whose common interest governmental authority is to be exercised and to whom political agents are responsible. In this capacity they are subject to rights and duties that the state as a citizens' cooperative defines for its members. By contrast, as jurisdiction-users persons are subject to governmental authority in their *private capacities*, as private law subjects. As jurisdiction-users they can take advantage of the generally accessible public amenities a polity offers within its territory, subject to the rules that the state as territorial enterprise defines for all – natural as well as legal – persons who engage in economic or other activities within its domain.

While as citizens persons are *members* of the state as a cooperative enterprise, their relation as jurisdiction-users to the state as territorial enterprise is comparable to that between a commercial business and its *customers*. This is equally true for citizens as jurisdiction-users in relation to their own government, as it is for non-citizens who enter the territory of a state as jurisdictions-users. In their private capacities, in their decisions where to work, where to take residence, where to invest, etc., citizens can, no less than non-citizens, compare the advantages and disadvantages that their home-jurisdiction offers to the conditions they might enjoy in other jurisdictions, and decide in favor of the most attractive alternative.

Just as we can, according to the two roles of the state, distinguish between citizens and jurisdiction-users, the totality of rules and regulations that a state legislates and enforces can be sub-divided into two categories. These are, on the one hand, rules that concern the conditions of membership in the citizens' cooperative, i.e., the rights and duties that come with being a member of the state as joint enterprise of its citizens. And these are, on the other hand, rules that apply to jurisdiction-users, to non-citizens as well as to citizens in their private capacities. In other words, as *citizens' joint enterprise* the state manages the internal affairs of the citizens' cooperative, i.e., the relations between citizens *in their capacity as members of the polity*. As *territorial enterprise* it provides the legal-institutional framework for the private law society, i.e., the framework of rules within which citizens *in their private capacities* can interact with each other as well as with non-citizens who enter the state's territory as jurisdiction-users.

These rules include the system of private law or civil law that governs the relations among individuals as private law subjects and the public regulations that the state imposes on private activities within its territory. From this perspective, the set of rules referred to as public law can be distinguished into two parts, rules that concern the internal relations among the citizen-members of the polity and rules that concern all private law subjects, citizens as well as non-citizens, who undertake activities within the state's jurisdictional boundaries.

The economic order that we call *market* is nothing but the system of economic relations that emerges within a private law society. As Franz Böhm, co-founder of the Freiburg School of Law and Economics (Vanberg 1998) aptly put it, the market economy is the twin sister of the private law society (Böhm 1966). A market economy emerges naturally where a private law society exists, and it can only come into being to the extent that a private realm exists in which individuals can freely act as private law persons, separate from their status as members of the polity.

It is worth noting that there is only one case in which the state's two functions cannot be separated, namely the limiting case of a perfectly totalitarian society in which persons are nothing but members of the citizens' cooperative. In such a totalitarian society no separation between the state as a collective enterprise and private law society is possible. All rights are collectively owned and exercised through the state's collective decision procedures. Individuals have rights only in their capacity as members of the cooperative organization, not as private persons. In such a society there is no room for a market economy whatsoever. As we move away from the totalitarian extreme there will be a division between rights collectively exercised by the political community and rights that individuals hold and exercise in their private capacity. In other words, there will be a division between state and private law society, the former functioning as the organization that provides citizens with public services (including the service of legislating and enforcing the rules of the private law society), and the latter functioning as a spontaneous order formed by individuals who interact and cooperate with each other as private law subjects within the 'rules of the game' defined by the private law system and the state's regulations for private activities. In different polities the dividing line between state and private law society may be drawn quite differently, giving more or less scope to individual liberty and to the emergence of markets. Of relevance in the present context is the fact that where it exists individuals are affected by government in two distinguishable capacities, as citizen-members of the polity and as private law subjects.

Why with increasing mobility of persons and economic resources states are increasingly required to separate their two functions from each other can best be seen if one imagines the world of states arranged along a continuum at the one end of which is a world in which states, for geographical or other reasons, exist in perfect isolation from each other, without any mobility between them, and at the other end of which is a world in which people can entirely freely and easily move between states in the sense that they are free in their choice of citizenship and are unimpeded in moving as jurisdiction-users from one state to another.

In a world of perfectly isolated states governments are pure monopolists. Birth and death are the only events by which the population of their 'subjects' can change. Even for the perfectly isolated state we can conceptually distinguish between the role of the state as citizens' joint enterprise and its role as territorial enterprise that provides the legal framework for the private law society. Yet, materially the distinction between the two roles is of little consequence. The population of members of the citizens' cooperative and the population of jurisdiction-users are identical. Since they are confined to the state's territory without exit option, individuals are faced in both their capacities, as member-citizens of the polity and as jurisdiction-users, with the same monopolist. Whatever the state does in one of its two roles, those who live within its borders are inescapably affected thereby. In the absence of any exit option, individuals subject to the state's authority can only use their 'voice' (Hirschman 1970), an option that, by itself, is of limited and, with growing population size, decreasing effectiveness.

At the opposite end of the spectrum, in a world of uninhibited mobility between states, the difference between the two roles of government becomes most visible. In this world individuals can freely decide, in both matters, to which polity they wish to belong as citizen-members and how they wish to allocate their activities as private law subjects across alternative jurisdictions. In regard to both kinds of choices they can weigh the respective costs and benefits of being a member in one polity rather than another and of opting, as jurisdiction-users, for one jurisdiction rather than another. By contrast to the world of isolated states, in this world the population of citizens and the population of jurisdiction-users are no longer identical in any given territory. Member-citizens of one state will, in smaller or larger numbers, engage in various activities or even reside in the territory of other states while keeping up their citizenship, and citizens of other polities will, as jurisdiction-users, live, work, and invest in the state's territory.

The real world of states has never corresponded to either of the two polar cases. States have never existed in perfect isolation from each other, nor is today's world one of perfectly uninhibited mobility. But over time the world has surely moved significantly away from one end to the other end of the spectrum. Globalization has markedly accelerated this development creating new constraints on the powers of government that will be the particular focus of the remainder of this chapter. More specifically, the focus will be on the implications of globalization for the state's power to tax and to regulate.

4 Taxation in a globalized world and the benefit principle

In the theory of public finance, two different principles of taxation have been in long-standing conflict, namely the ability-to-pay principle and the benefit or interest principle (Musgrave and Peacock 1967: ix ff.; Buchanan and Flowers 1987: 50ff.).[6] Traditionally the first principle has been dominant in the theoretical debate and even more so in the practice of taxation.

The *ability-to-pay principle* corresponds to the *non-affectation principle* that is widely practiced in budgetary policy. According to this principle the revenue-generating side of the public household is systematically separated from the expenditure side, that is, no direct connection is supposed to exist between how taxes are collected and the purposes for which they will be used. In other words, public decisions on how to raise the funds for public activities are kept separate from the decisions on how the budget is to be spent. And typically the ability-to-pay principle is then considered the natural principle to be applied on the revenue-generating side.[7] Persons are supposed to be charged taxes according to their 'capacity' – however specified – entirely independent of the benefits they receive from the state's activities. Notwithstanding its widespread application, the ability-to-pay principle has not only been challenged on theoretical and normative grounds, in a world of mobile people and resources its sustainability is seriously challenged by the choices people can make.

One of the most influential critics of the ability-to-pay principle, Knut Wicksell (1967 [1896]), has argued that the principle of taxation according to benefit or interest is not only more consistent with the subjectivist-individualist thrust of theoretical economics, but is also more consistent with the normative foundations of a democratic society (Musgrave and Peacock 1967: xiv).[8] In a spirit similar to Rawls' notion of a democratic society as a 'cooperative venture for mutual advantage,' Wicksell insisted that in a society of free and equal individuals public expenditures can be considered legitimate only if they are 'intended for an activity useful to the whole of society and so recognized by all' (Wicksell 1967: 89). From this he concluded: 'It would seem to be a blatant injustice if someone should be forced to contribute towards the costs of some activity which does not further his interests or may even be diametrically opposed to them' (ibid.).

The task of ensuring that the benefit principle is actually honored in budgetary practice has, according to Wicksell, to be solved in a democratic society by adopting a suitable decision-making procedure, one that best protects the interests of everyone. In his view this asks for a decision rule that essentially aims at consent.[9] The unanimity (or approximate-unanimity) rule that Wicksell suggested adopting for every single budgetary decision[10] has obvious limitations as a practical instrument for implementing the benefit principle. Following up on Wicksell's notion that legitimacy in budgetary matters – and, more generally, in social matters – derives from voluntary consent among the persons involved, James M. Buchanan has developed the research paradigm of contractarian constitutional economics that shifts the unanimity requirement from the level of sub-constitutional ordinary, day-to-day policy choices up to the constitutional level where the rules for making ordinary policy choices are chosen (Buchanan 1990).

Of interest in the present context is the fact that the Wicksellian project can count on the assistance of a substitute force that he did not consider, namely the opportunity for people to vote with their feet and to exit with their economic resources from jurisdictions that do not respect their interests. In a world of isolated monopoly-states the ability-to-pay principle may be easy to implement, because people have no way of escaping whatever taxes are imposed on them. Just as a monopoly enterprise may be able to differentiate the prices for its products according to its customers' wealth, a monopoly-state may tax its citizens according to their ability to pay, independent of the benefits that its services provides to them. And in the absence of any exit option their co-determination rights in democratic procedures can only provide limited protection from being exploited. The situation is obviously different, however, in a competitive world. Just as a business that has to compete with others would soon lose its better-off customers if it were to try to charge them differentially higher prices, in a mobile world a state would soon see its wealthier taxpayers move away if it were to try to tax them according to their ability to pay, entirely independently of the benefits that they may reap from remaining in the jurisdiction. And this applies equally to their citizens' choice to keep up or give up their citizenship as it applies to their jurisdiction-users' choice of where to take their business, even though, as will be discussed below, there are significant differences between the two groups that need to be considered in this context.

An early author to recognize the significance of increasing mobility for the practice of taxation is the German public finance economist Georg Schanz.[11] In an article 'On the Issue of the Liability to Pay Taxes' published in 1892 he observed that the increasing mobility of persons and economic activities, primarily across local communities but more and more also across national boundaries, had to be taken into account in the ways taxes are levied, because, as he argued, the different ways in which persons are affected by public activities need to be reflected in the taxes they pay. Pointing in particular to the difference between the member-citizens of a polity and others who enter the respective jurisdiction for various economic purposes, he noted:

> As long as taxes are a general payment for expenditures of the community it will not be compatible with the nature of taxes if the community does not tax a number of people who benefit from its expenditures while taxing others who do not benefit.
>
> (Schanz 1892: 8)[12]

Anticipating the objection that he was reviving the 'old, strongly contested benefit principle,' he argued:

> To this objection I can only reply that a tax which does not include some kind of a benefit relation does not exist. Of such a tax one could speak only if one were to suppose … an absolutely coercive membership in a community, which does not exist; one can exit from every community, also from the national polity, one can weigh whether the services of the community, the amenities and happiness it provides, compensate for the sacrifices it demands.
>
> (ibid.: 9f.)[13]

The forces that Schanz described have significantly intensified in the process of globalization with the consequence that governments are increasingly under pressure, on factual grounds, to move their taxation practices in the direction of the benefit principle that Wicksell argued for on grounds of justice. While in a closed society persons who feel unduly burdened by the taxes they are forced to pay can only raise their voice, in a globalized world they can with relative ease exit from inhospitable jurisdictions and relocate their activities to places where they feel more fairly treated. In such a world governments will find it more difficult to sustain the ability-to-pay principle, in particular with regard to jurisdiction-users.

The ability of persons to exit from one jurisdiction and to move to another clearly differs between citizens and jurisdiction-users. This reflects the interrelated facts that, on the one hand, to shift one's allegiance as citizen between states is generally much more difficult than to move as jurisdiction-user between polities and, on the other hand, that the cost–benefit calculus that underlies a person's choice of citizenship (to the extent that such choice option exists) is characteristically different from the cost–benefit calculus that guides her choices as jurisdiction-user. Not only are the political barriers to changing one's citizenship typically much higher than the barriers jurisdiction-users face in moving between polities, it lies in the nature of things that shifting one's membership between polities is a more complex undertaking than relocating one's activities as jurisdiction-user. The packages of services and benefits that come with being a member of a polity are significantly more extensive and multifaceted than the bundle of location-specific services and benefits that jurisdiction-users are typically interested in. As a trans-generational cooperative enterprise, the state allows its members to enter into joint commitments the costs and benefits of which can be appropriately assessed, if at all, only in a long-term perspective. In particular, solidarity- or mutual-insurance arrangements by which citizens can provide each other and their offspring with a measure of protection against the misfortunes of life that they could not obtain from private-law arrangements are the most obvious of these benefits. It is, in fact, because of the more complex and long-term nature of the benefits that political communities can provide for their members that persons can change their citizenship not nearly with the same ease with which they can move as jurisdiction-users between polities. Most importantly, in choosing one's citizenship, where such choice is feasible, one must choose between the inclusive bundle of costs and benefits from being a member of polity A instead of B, bundles that on either side may well include components that one would rather do without.

By contrast, in their capacity as jurisdiction-users persons are much more flexible in their choices. There is no need for them to concentrate all their potential activities in one jurisdiction. Instead, they can separate the various dimensions of their inclusive interests from each other and choose separately for each of them the jurisdiction that offers, with regard to the respective activity, the most attractive conditions. They can choose different jurisdictions for different kinds of investments or financial engagements, others for their own professional activities, and still others for other purposes including their place of residence.

To be sure, even though as jurisdiction-users persons can choose with greater ease among alternative polities than they can choose their citizenship, there remain significant differences depending on the different capacities in which they may be engaged in a jurisdiction. Where immovable resources, such as land and real estate, or sunk investments are concerned, jurisdiction-users are, for obvious reasons, less mobile than with their flexible investments or their financial capital. And in relocating their residence or long-term employment from one jurisdiction to another they obviously face more serious obstacles than in choosing where to take a temporary job or where to spend their vacation. Various issues raised by these differences have been discussed extensively in the literature on inter-jurisdictional competition (Vanberg 2000, 2008).

Of particular interest in the present context is the question of how the differences in mobility between citizens and jurisdiction-users, as well as between the latter, affect the power of governments to tax their citizens and their jurisdictions-users.[14]

5 Taxing citizens and taxing jurisdiction-users

In a world in which the benefit principle were generally practiced, taxes would fall into two principal categories, corresponding to the two roles of the state: namely, on the one hand, taxes that citizens would have to pay in their capacity as members of the polity and, on the other hand, taxes that would be collected from jurisdiction-users. In their capacity as citizens, persons would be charged taxes as payment for the right to benefit from the services that the state provides for its members, comparable to the *membership fees* persons pay to the private clubs or associations to which they belong as payment for the opportunity to take advantage of the rights that come with being a member. By contrast, in their capacity as jurisdiction-users they would be charged taxes as payments for the right to carry out in a state's sovereign territory the kind of activities they are interested in, comparable to the *access-* or *user-fees* that a private territorial enterprise (such as a recreation park or a developer of a private community) charges its customers for the right to take advantage of the facilities it offers.

The traditionally and still widely practiced systems of taxation in the real world of states are scarcely organized in ways that reflect the systematic separation between taxes as citizens' *membership-fees* and as jurisdiction-users' *access-* or *user-fees*. Yet, the same forces of globalization that require governments to move in the direction of taxation according to benefit will require them to distinguish more strictly between the two kinds of taxes than has been the case in the past. It is the need to adopt principles of taxation that can be sustained in a world of mobile persons and resources that will leave governments no choice other than making these adjustments or see their tax-base erode.

The possibility of jurisdiction-users to divide the various activities they engage in between different jurisdictions and to respond with exit to adverse treatment in any one jurisdiction makes it impossible for governments to impose on them tax burdens that exceed the price they are willing to pay for the benefits the jurisdiction offers them, compared to the cost–benefit packages that other jurisdictions offer. The ease with which jurisdiction-users can escape unwanted tax burdens, the more so the easier they can move with their respective activities from one jurisdiction to another, is often diagnosed in the globalization literature as the source of two major problems. It is argued, first, that the need to compete for mobile taxpayers, in particular for investors of mobile capital, forces governments into a 'race to the bottom' in the sense that they underbid each other with ever lower tax rates with the consequence that the tax burden will be increasingly shifted to less mobile taxpayers, specifically the citizens. And it is argued, second, that the competition for taxable mobile jurisdiction-users inhibits governments in their capacity to carry out public projects that serve their citizens' interests, such as, in particular, redistributive policies.

As far as the first charge is concerned, the fear that competition among governments leads to a race to the bottom seems to be based on the tacit assumption that jurisdiction-users consider in their choice among jurisdictions only the tax price they are required to pay without regard to other jurisdictional attributes. This is, however, an assumption no more realistic than the assumption that customers of any ordinary business make their choice where to buy exclusively in light of what the price tags say without regard to the quality of the products that are at stake or the quality of the services they can expect. Prudent jurisdiction-users, such as investors of mobile capital, will surely compare the tax prices they have to pay with the advantages that jurisdictions have to offer with regard to the kinds of uses they might be interested in, such as a functioning infrastructure, protection of the law, reliable courts, an effective public administration, an educated work-force, etc. Among alternative jurisdictions that are open to them they will choose the one that offers the most attractive cost–benefit package for their purposes, not simply the one with the lowest tax rate. The fear that competition among governments leads to a ruinous race to the bottom is as implausible as the fear of ruinous competition in ordinary business life. What competition does in both realms is to require enterprises – be it states as territorial enterprises or producers of ordinary goods and services – to offer their customers attractive price–quality combinations.

Discussing the second charge provides an opportunity to add a specifying comment to the conjecture that the forces of globalization require governments to adjust their taxation systems in the direction of the benefit principle. With regard to taxes as citizens' membership-fees this conjecture needs to be clarified. Because of the specific nature of the benefit packages that polities extend to their citizen-members, in particular because of the solidarity or insurance arrangements that their members enter into, citizens have prudential reasons for taking persons' ability to pay into account when determining their tax obligations. The uncertainty about their own longer-term fate in life – and even more so the uncertainty about the fate of their offspring – is the reason for citizens' common interest in a mutual commitment to assist each other in case of need. The very logic of such a mutual insurance arrangement requires that the funds from which assistance to needy members of the polity is given must be fed by those who are able to make the necessary contributions. In an uncertain world it can therefore be assumed to be in the mutual interest of the members of a citizens' cooperative to agree on a taxation system that takes the ability to pay into account.

Beyond the sheer technicality of financing a solidarity fund there are more general reasons why citizens may have a mutual interest in adopting a taxation system among themselves that takes the ability to pay into account, reasons that have to do with the extent of the services that the state as citizens' joint enterprise can provide to its members. The package of services that governments could finance would inevitably be rather slim if what the poorest members of the polity are able to contribute would define the upper limit of the taxes that citizens might be charged. Given the uncertainty about their own and their offspring's long-term income-earning capacity, citizens have good reasons to accept a taxation system that charges them in line with their ability to pay, if they wish to ensure that a generally desired level of public services can be financed.

Note that, to argue, as I have done above, that there are prudential reasons for citizens to adopt, for the internal operation of their citizens' cooperative, a taxation system that takes their ability to pay into account does not mean to reintroduce the ability-to-pay principle through the backdoor. The rationale for organizing the taxation system in such a manner is not axiomatically derived from a presupposed ability-to-pay principle but is, instead, located in the very interests of the citizens themselves. In other words, it is the benefit principle that provides the rationale for considering citizens' ability to pay in determining their tax-obligation[15] – and it will also limit the extent to which unequal tax burdens can be sustained. To the extent that citizens can gain membership status in other polities, they will compare the inclusive cost–benefit package that their home country offers them with what they could realize elsewhere, and this will set limits to the tax burden they willingly accept.

Returning to the issue of what the mobility of jurisdiction-users means for the capability of governments to engage in redistributive policies, it should be noted first that redistribution is clearly part of the solidarity or insurance arrangements that citizens may organize among themselves for their mutual benefit. The charge that the ease with which mobile factors can move between polities unduly limits the power of governments to impose on them redistributive taxes (Sinn 1994: 101) implicitly presumes that jurisdiction-users ought to pay their share in financing citizens' solidarity projects.[16] It is, however, difficult to see how such demand could be justified. Jurisdiction-users are customers of the state as a territorial enterprise; they are not members of the state as citizens' joint enterprise and, accordingly, not among the beneficiaries of the solidarity arrangements that this enterprise provides for its members. There are neither legitimate normative grounds on which jurisdiction-users could be required to contribute to citizens' solidarity projects, nor factual grounds on which one could expect them to willingly make such contributions, except to the extent that, besides the direct benefits to citizens, there are indirect effects, such as a reduced likelihood of social unrest or criminal offenses, that would make the jurisdiction a more attractive place for prospective users.

What is true for redistributive policies in the service of citizens' mutual insurance arrangements applies to all public projects that create benefits for the members of the polity without contributing to a more hospitable environment for jurisdiction-users. Any attempts to shift the burden of such projects to jurisdiction-users will be difficult to sustain in a mobile world in which persons as private law subjects can compare the cost–benefit packages of different polities and choose the one that offers conditions most attractive for the kind of activities they are interested in. This does not mean at all that the state in its capacity as citizens' joint enterprise is prevented from carrying out projects that serve common interests of its members. It only means that the costs of such projects must be covered by contributions from its citizens-members, i.e., by taxes as membership-fees, and cannot be shifted to mobile jurisdiction-users, except, again, to the extent that such projects add indirectly, in one way or another, to the attractiveness of the state as territorial enterprise. Generally, as customers of the state, jurisdiction-users can be charged taxes as access- or user-fees only to the extent that – compared to available alternatives – a state offers an attractive environment for their respective activities.

The principle that citizens' projects ought to be financed by taxes as membership-fees has surely not been the guiding rule of traditional taxation practices. Instead, taxes have been – and continue to be – quite commonly collected from jurisdiction-users to (co-)finance such projects. In a less mobile world governments may have felt little pressure to change this practice, yet in an increasingly mobile world the pressure intensifies. The principal reason why governments are typically reluctant to adjust their taxation systems accordingly is that it is all too tempting for (re-)election-seeking politicians to promise voters benefits without having to present them with a corresponding tax bill. And shifting the financial burden on to jurisdiction-users may work as a successful short-term strategy to give voters the illusion of a cost-free gift. Yet, while it may possibly bring success at the next election, this strategy will not improve the longer-term economic prospects of the citizenry. Since it is bound to make the jurisdiction a less attractive place for wealth-producing jurisdiction-users, it reduces, in the longer run, the income-earning opportunities of citizens themselves and, thereby, their own ability to finance the kinds of projects, including solidarity projects, that they may wish to fund for their mutual advantage.

The difficulties in sustaining a taxation system that seeks to burden jurisdiction-users with the costs of citizens' projects are most visible in the case of business taxes. Business enterprises are legal entities and as such cannot be members of a citizens' cooperative that, by its very nature, can only be composed of natural persons. Businesses are pure jurisdiction-users and their calculus of advantage in choosing a jurisdiction for their activities is exclusively based on a comparison between the costs they have to incur and the benefits they can expect.[17] It does not include benefits that the state as citizens' joint enterprise provides exclusively to its members. Any attempt to impose on them tax-burdens that are not compensated by jurisdictional advantages, such as the costs of pure citizens' projects, runs the risk of provoking their exit from or deterring their entry into the jurisdiction. In a globalized world with an increasingly mobile corporate tax base, governments are under intense competitive pressure to recognize this fact. And, it is indeed in the realm of corporate taxes that the most far-reaching adjustments in national taxation systems have occurred in recent decades (Edwards and Mitchell 2008).

6 Regulation in a globalized world

Just as the increased mobility of persons and resources imposes competitive constraints on governments that limit their power to tax it imposes similar constraints on their power to regulate. As in the case of taxation, in the field of regulation competition among governments creates the need for a stricter separation of the two roles of the state in the sense that governments are required to distinguish more clearly between, on the one hand, regulations that they legislate in their capacity as citizens' joint enterprise, i.e., regulations that concern the internal relations among the members of the citizens' cooperative, and, on the other hand, regulations that they legislate in their capacity as territorial enterprise, i.e., regulations that define the terms under which private law subjects – citizens and non-citizens alike – are allowed to operate as jurisdiction-users within the state's territory.

As citizens' joint enterprise the state can use regulation as an instrument to advance its members' common interests if by jointly submitting to the respective regulatory constraints citizens can realize among themselves mutual benefits that they would otherwise forgo (Vanberg 2005: 29ff.). As territorial enterprises states face the challenge of defining the terms under which private law subjects are allowed to operate within their sovereign territories in ways that are, in comparison to the terms in other polities, sufficiently attractive for jurisdiction-users they want to draw to their domain. In the traditional discussion on issues of regulation the distinction emphasized here can scarcely be found in explicit terms, and it may in fact be often difficult in practice to classify particular regulatory provisions unambiguously in one or the other of the two categories because they simultaneously affect common concerns of citizens as well as the interests of jurisdiction-users. Nevertheless, it is a distinction that governments cannot disregard with impunity in a globalized world.

The relevance of conceptually separating the two regulatory roles of government is, in fact, not so much a matter of unambiguously classifying each and every act of regulation. It is, instead, in the first instance a matter of clarity about the purposes that a regulatory provision is meant to achieve, namely whether its principal aim is to serve interests that citizens share in their capacity as members of the polity or whether it aims at improving the institutional framework within which the private law society and the market economy function. Only to the extent that clarity about the intended purpose exists is a meaningful assessment possible of the balance between intended positive and potential unintended negative effects in such cases, where a regulatory provision that aims at serving citizens' interests has negative side-effects for the polity's attractiveness for jurisdiction-users or vice versa.

Note that distinguishing between the two regulatory roles of the state is not meant at all to suggest that as a territorial enterprise the state derives legitimacy for its actions from a different source than it does in its capacity as citizens' joint enterprise. In both its capacities the democratic state is supposed to act as agent of its citizen-members, as custodian of their common interests. The difference between the two roles concerns the means and ways by which democratic government carries out its mandate as agent of its citizens, namely, on the one side, by regulating the internal affairs of its members and, on the other side, by providing, as territorial enterprise, a regulatory environment within which citizens in their capacity as private law subjects can best realize mutual gains from interacting and cooperating with each other as well as with other jurisdiction-users. That is to say, the ultimate normative standard against which a democratic government's actions as territorial enterprise are to be judged is not the attractiveness for jurisdiction-users per se but citizens' common interests in how the private law society should function. The two criteria are connected, though, by the fact that the attractiveness of the polity for jurisdiction-users is an essential determinant of citizens' income-earning prospects and, thereby, of their prospects of realizing mutual benefits as private law subjects as well as of their ability to finance mutually beneficial citizens' projects.

There will be instances where regulatory provisions that may serve common interests of the citizen-members of the polity have negative side-effects on their jurisdiction's attractiveness for private users, and in such cases a trade-off exists that citizens must account for in deciding whether or not to adopt such provisions. Of particular interest in the present context, though, are those cases in which governments seek to use regulatory constraints on jurisdiction-users as an instrument to serve citizens' interests without imposing the full burden of such concerns on them, i.e., cases where, instead of taking care of such interests directly by regulating the internal affairs of the citizenry, governments seek to enlist jurisdiction-users to carry (part of) the burden. The temptation to employ such strategy is surely present among (re-)election-seeking politicians because it allows them to promise voters benefits that seem to come at no costs, and one does not need to search long in order to find examples in standard regulatory practice that illustrate this very strategy. A preferred area for it to be employed is, in particular, the labor market.

Labor market regulations, like regulations in other areas, can be intended to rectify deficiencies in this market and to improve its overall working properties. Alternatively they can be intended to serve concerns that citizens share as members of the polity such as, in particular, their interests in being insured against risks of life and market adversities that threaten their income-earning prospects. Whether regulations such as minimum wage legislation, regulation concerning dismissal protection, mandatory social benefits, etc., are indeed suitable instruments for improving the overall working properties of labor markets, in the sense that they improve the employment and income prospects of the population at large, is, according to standard economic insights, rather questionable, but this is an issue that can be left aside here. Of interest here is the issue of whether such regulations can be suitable instruments of serving interests of the citizen-members of the polity. My principal conjecture is that attempts to impose, by means of regulation, the burden of citizens' projects on jurisdiction-users cannot be sustained in a mobile world.

As in the case of taxation, jurisdiction-users can be expected to accept regulatory burdens that are offset by advantages that a jurisdiction offers them for the kind of activities they are interested in. Yet, attempts to impose on jurisdiction-users the burden of projects, including the solidarity or insurance provisions that labor market regulations are often intended to provide, the benefits of which are exclusively concentrated on the citizen-members of the polity, risks provoking their exit and deterring their entry. Again, as in the case of taxation, their competition for mobile resources does not prevent governments from providing their citizens with benefits, such as insurance arrangements, the costs of which they are willing to carry and to share among themselves. It merely limits their opportunities to require jurisdiction-users to shoulder the regulatory (or tax) burden of citizens' projects beyond the extent to which indirect benefits may accrue to them as well. In other words, competition among governments limits the possibilities for (re-)election-seeking politicians to promise voters benefits under the pretence that somebody else will cover the costs.

7 Conclusion: competition among governments and the welfare state

It is a common theme in the literature that globalization and the intensified competition among governments that comes with it pose a particular threat to the welfare state as it has developed, especially since World War II, in many Western countries. The basic rationale of the welfare state is to find a balance between, on the one side, taking advantage of the productive dynamics of a market economy and, on the other hand, providing a safety-net that insures citizens against major misfortunes of life and fundamental uncertainties that are inherent in a dynamic market process. Both concerns are likely shared by citizens and the question is whether indeed, and if so why, the forces of globalization should impede governments in their ability to respond to them. The argument outlined in this chapter can throw some light on this issue.

As has been argued above, the competitive constraints that governments are facing in a globalized world cannot prevent them from serving common interests of their citizenry, at least not as long as citizens are willing to bear the costs of the services the state as their joint enterprise provides for them by paying the necessary taxes as membership fees or by accepting the required regulatory burden. However, competition does impose constraints on the ability of governments to shift the regulatory or tax burden of such provisions on to jurisdiction-users to whom they provide no benefit. Most Western welfare states have surely grown beyond the level that can be sustained under these constraints, and they have been able to do so because they have spared their present citizenry the burden of fully covering the costs of their favors by shifting them in part to jurisdiction-users and future generations of tax-payers. These strategies of concealing the true costs of welfare provisions from citizens are less and less sustainable in a world of mobile persons and resources.

Stated differently, the reason why competition among governments poses a threat to the welfare state is not that citizens were no longer able to use the state as their joint enterprise for carrying out projects of mutual advantage. The reason is, instead, the failure to adequately separate the role of the state as citizens' cooperative from its role as territorial enterprise, combined with the failure to recognize that it is in its first role and not in the second that the state must carry out its welfare policies. The forces of globalization increasingly require governments to rectify this failure, to face their citizens with the necessity of carrying the regulatory and tax burden of whatever welfare services they wish to provide for themselves, and to realize that the regulatory and tax burden they can impose on jurisdiction-users is limited by the advantages that the state has to offer as territorial enterprise.

Notes

1 Smith (1981: 31). This statement is to be read in conjunction with the very first sentence in *The Wealth of Nations*: 'The greatest improvement in the productive powers of labour, and the greater part of the skill, dexterity, and judgement with which it is anywhere directed, or applied, seem to have been the effects of the division of labour' (Smith 1981: 13).

2 The 'second globalization' has, of course, also been most significantly affected by singular historical events such as the collapse of the Soviet Empire and its secondary effects as well as the reform policies in China.

3 More generally speaking, such competition among governments exists, of course, not only at the level of nation-states but likewise at the sub-national level between local communities or between states within a federal union, and it exists at the supranational level in the sense that entities such as the European Union are also exposed to a competitive environment (Vanberg and Kerber 1994).

4 While, for example, authors like G. Brennan and J.M. Buchanan (1988: 212ff.) emphasize that such competitive constraints have the beneficial effect of limiting the power of governments to serve special interests, H.-W. Sinn (1997: 248) concludes:

> Since governments have stepped in where markets have failed, it can hardly be expected that a reintroduction of a market through the backdoor of systems competition will work. It is likely to bring about the same kind of market failure that justified government intervention in the first place.

5 For references and a more detailed discussion see Vanberg (2000, 2008).

6 Wicksell (1967: 74): 'As is well known, there are essentially two opposing basic principles ... They are the principle of ... "taxation according to benefit" and "taxation according to ability-to-pay" or to the capacity of each.'

7 Actually the non-affectation principle allows for two interpretations, only one of which is in conflict with the benefit principle. The case of the German tax system may serve as an illustration. In its legal foundation, the so-called 'Abgabenordnung,' taxes are defined (in §3.1) as follows: 'Taxes are monetary payments that are not made in return for a specific service.' If this definition is meant to imply that there is a difference between taxes and fees that are charged for specific services, such as issuing a driver's license or a passport, it is not at all in conflict with the benefit principle. Such conflict exists, however, if it is meant to imply that no connection exists between tax obligation and benefits received from public services. The issue of whether or not

public services can be generally financed by specific fees (which they surely cannot) is entirely different from the issue of whether taxes should be levied according to the ability-to-pay or according to the benefit principle. Only the latter is at stake in the present context.

8 Wicksell (1967: 88) describes the democratic ideal as 'equality before the law, greatest possible liberty, and the economic well-being and peaceful cooperation of all people.'

9 Wicksell (1967: 106): 'There seems to be a clear case for the requirement of full unanimity of all parties as the only possible guarantee against prejudicing these interests.' Wicksell did explicitly not identify democracy with simple majority rule. As he put it: 'It is not the purpose of the [democratic] movement ... to have ... shaken off the yoke of ... obscurantist oligarchies only to replace it by the scarcely less oppressive tyranny of accidental parliamentary majorities' (1967: 88).

10 Musgrave and Peacock (1967: xv) comment on Wicksell's approach:

> While there are issues on which public policy must be determined by simple majority, Wicksell argues that most matters of budget policy are not of this type. Specific public services should be voted upon in conjunction with specific cost distributions; and their adoption should be subject to the principle of voluntary consent and unanimity.

11 Already Adam Smith (1981: 848f.) commented on this matter when he noted:

> The proprietor of land is necessarily a citizen of the particular country in which his estate lies. The proprietor of stock is properly a citizen of the world, and is not necessarily attached to any particular country. He would be apt to abandon a country in which he was exposed to a vexatious inquisition, in order to be assessed to a burdensome tax, and would remove his stock to some other country where he could, either carry on his business, or enjoy his fortune more at his ease.

12 My translation.

13 My translation.

14 An issue that deserves special attention but will not be separately discussed here concerns the relevance of the difference between the capacity of individuals as citizen-members of a polity on the one side and their capacity as residents, i.e., as jurisdiction-users, on the other for the power of government to tax and to regulate. This issue has received little attention because permanent residents have typically been, and still are, citizens of the country in which they reside. In an increasingly mobile world there is, however, a growing and non-trivial number of persons who reside for longer periods or even permanently as 'alien residents' in a foreign country. Since permanent residents tend to share to a large extent in the services that governments provide for their citizen-residents, distinguishing the state's relation to its resident-citizens from its relation to its alien residents and its citizens living abroad raises a number of questions that are important but will, for reasons of space, not be discussed here.

15 A statement in Adam Smith's *Wealth of Nations*, the first part of which is often cited as supporting the ability-to-pay principle, can, on closer inspection, well be read as an argument that derives the justification of taxation according to ability from the benefit principle:

> The subjects of every state ought to contribute ... in proportion to their respective abilities; that is in proportion to the revenue which they respectively enjoy under the protection of the state. The expense of government is like the expense of management to the joint tenants of a great estate who are all obliged to contribute in proportion to their respective interest in the estate.
>
> (Smith 1981: 825)

Musgrave and Peacock (1967: ix) comment on Smith's statement: 'Thus Smith ingeniously cuts across the ability-to-pay and the benefit theories of taxation.' It is, as they add, in the post-Smith era that 'a distinct cleavage between the two approaches emerges.'

16 Sinn (1997: 262): 'Suppose the country's borders are opened and both capital and labor can freely migrate across them. This liberty ... will affect insurance through redistributive taxation since the government loses its power to enforce the payment of taxes.'

17 Business firms are, of course, owned and operated by natural persons who act in both capacities, as citizen-members of a polity and as jurisdiction-users. Business enterprises themselves as legal persons can, however, only be jurisdiction-users.

Bibliography

Böhm, Franz, 'Privatrechtsgesellschaft und Marktwirtschaft,' *ORDO – Jahrbuch für die Ordnung von Wirtschaft und Gesellschaft* 15, 1966, 75–151.

Brennan, Geoffrey and James M. Buchanan, *Besteuerung und Staatsgewalt. Analytische Grundlagen einer Finanzverfassung*, Hamburg: S+W Steuer- und Wirtschaftsverlag, 1988.

Buchanan, James M., 'The Domain of Constitutional Economics,' *Constitutional Political Economy* 1, 1990, 1–18.

Buchanan, James M. and Marilyn R. Flowers, *The Public Finances: An Introductory Textbook*, Homewood, IL: Irwin, 1987.

Edwards, Chris and Daniel J. Mitchell, *Global Tax Revolution: The Rise of Tax Competition and the Battle to Defend It*, Washington, DC: Cato Institute, 2008.

Hirschman, Albert O., *Exit, Voice and Loyalty: Responses to Decline in Firms, Organizations, and States*, Cambridge, MA: Harvard University Press, 1970.

Musgrave, Richard A. and Alan T. Peacock, 'Introduction,' in R.A. Musgrave and A.T. Peacock (eds.), *Classics in the Theory of Public Finance*, London: Macmillan, 1967, ix–xix.

Rawls, John, *A Theory of Justice*, Cambridge, MA: Harvard University Press, 1971.

Schanz, Georg, 'Zur Frage der Steuerpflicht,' *Finanzarchiv* 9, 2, 1892, 1–74.

Sinn, Hans-Werner, 'How Much Europe? Subsidiarity, Centralization and Fiscal Competition,' *Scottish Journal of Political Economy* 41, 1994, 85–107.

Sinn, Hans-Werner, 'The Selection Principle and Market Failure in Systems Competiton,' *Journal of Public Economics* 66, 1997, 247–74.

Smith, Adam, *An Inquiry into the Nature and Causes of the Wealth of Nations*, Indianapolis, IN: Liberty Classics, 1981 [1776].

Vanberg, Viktor J., 'Freiburg School of Law and Economics,' in Peter Newman (ed.), *The New Palgrave Dictionary of Economics and the Law*, Vol. 2, London: Macmillan, 1998, 172–9.

Vanberg, Viktor J., 'Globalization, Democracy and Citizens' Sovereignty: Can Competition among Governments Enhance Democracy?' *Constitutional Political Economy* 11, 2000, 87–112.

Vanberg, Viktor J., 'Market and State: The Perspective of Constitutional Political Economy,' *Journal of Institutional Economics* 1, 2005, 23–49.

Vanberg, Viktor J., 'Can Competition between Governments Enhance Democracy?' in Andreas Bergh and Rolf Höijer (eds.), *Institutional Competition*, Cheltenham, UK, and Northampton, MA: Edward Elgar, 2008, 113–28.

Vanberg, Viktor J. and Wolfgang Kerber, 'Institutional Competition among Jurisdictions: An Evolutionary Approach,' *Constitutional Political Economy* 5, 1994, 193–219.

Wicksell, Knut, 'A New Principle of Just Taxation,' in R.A. Musgrave and A.T. Peacock (eds.), *Classics in the Theory of Public Finance*, London: Macmillan, 1967 [1896], 72–118.

3 Rent extraction, liberalism, and economic development

Roger D. Congleton

1 Introduction: liberalization and economic development

This chapter provides a rent-seeking and rent-extraction based explanation for the association between liberalization and economic development, and for the durability of the economic advantages associated with liberalization. The analysis is based on the rent-seeking, rent-extraction, and constitutional political economy literatures, which together provide a public choice explanation for the slow rate of adoption of liberal economic and political institutions throughout the world.

Simply put, the persons that have sufficient authority to adopt major and minor institutional reforms often benefit from unproductive forms of political and economic competition. The interest of rent recipients, together with institutional conservatism, makes liberal reforms difficult to adopt and less likely to be copied than other organizational and economic innovations. In contrast, liberal polities tend to adopt policies that promote productive forms of competition. As a consequence, liberal reforms, once adopted, can be a nearly permanent source of competitive advantage that affects long-run trade flows, patterns of international investment, and economic development.

A possible exception to this rule occurs in the area of exports, where rent-extraction rates may be adjusted to encourage growth. Reductions in the rate of rent extraction in the export sector may increase, rather than reduce, total rent extraction in the short and medium run, as demonstrated below. In the long run, the economic growth encouraged by export-led growth strategies may indirectly support liberalization of other sectors of the economy and of the political system.

2 Rent seeking, the rules of the game, and competitive waste

Most methods of obtaining wealth and status are competitive to some extent, because of the scarcity of wealth, status, and authority. Scarcity induces persons from all walks of life to invest their scarce time and attention in activities that protect and/or increase their holdings of scarce economic and social resources (Congleton 1980, 1989).

Individual decisions to invest in such contests can be modeled in a number of ways. Suppose, for example, that there are m contests and that the expected payoffs from contest j have the form:

$$R_{ij} = s_j \left(f_j(x_{ij}),\ g_j(x_{oj}) \right) P_j - c_i(x_{ij}) \tag{3.1}$$

where x_{ij} is the investment by the i-th rent seeker in contest j and x_{oj} is the investment of all rent seekers other than i. P_j is the prize or profit at stake, f_j and g_j are influence production functions. The individual's cost of participating in rent-seeking activities, C_i, varies with the resources committed to the game and the opportunity cost of i's resources in non-rent-seeking activities, such as farming and leisure. Function s_j is a sharing rule or probability function for contest j. i's anticipated share of the prize is determined by his or her effort and that of all other persons in the game, $S_j = s_j(F_{ij},\ G_{oij})$.

For the purposes of this chapter, I assume that the various contests resemble extended forms of the Tullock contest in which relative effort, rather than absolute effort, generates one's share of the 'prize' (wealth or status) or probability of winning. In that case, the typical rent seeker, i, will invest in rent-seeking contest j so that the expected (risk-adjusted) marginal rate of return is the same in all contests.

$$PjSj_{fj}Fj_{xij} = Ci_{xij} \tag{3.2}$$

for every i in all j games.

In rent-seeking societies a very large fraction of personal resources are invested in such contests. Whether the results are a disaster in which all these resources are wasted – as assumed in much of the rent-seeking literature – or increase total wealth – as assumed in much of the economics literature – depends on the nature of the contests (Congleton 1980).

When the contests are such that *relative influence*, rather than absolute influence, determines the shares of a pre-existing prize or the probability of winning the entire prize, considerable waste results unless the contest produces benefits for non-participants. Because relative rather than absolute effort determines expected payoffs, all players could simultaneously halve their efforts to influence the outcome without affecting their shares of the 'prize' or probability of winning. This would free resources for activities that directly or indirectly increased the stock of knowledge, comfort, or health. Excessive investments in rent-seeking contests are nonetheless individually sensible whenever the expected net benefit of participation is at least as great as that associated with other activities.

Law and culture largely determine the extent to which resources are wasted in the contests in which people invest, because law and culture largely determine the nature of the competition that take place in a society's contests, through effects on the rates of return from different activities. If the most likely routes to personal wealth and status require political contacts and favors, prudent persons will spend time seeking such contacts and favors. If the most likely routes to personal wealth and status are produced through military prowess, people will invest in the discipline and destructive skills required to be good soldiers. In liberal societies, the most likely routes to personal wealth and status involve pleasing consumers and/or voters by creating attractive products or policies, and so 'upward bound' persons invest in product and policy refinement and innovation – activities that benefit many persons who are less engaged in contests for status and wealth.

Insofar as legal and social factors can be considered the formal and informal 'rules of the game,' the rules can be said to determine the intensity and manner of competition in society's contests. Such rules determine magnitude of the prizes, the sharing rule, and the influence functions, which jointly determine s_j, F, and F_{xij} in the model above and thereby the relative rates of return in a society's contests for status, wealth, and satisfaction.

3 Rent extraction: creating rent-seeking and status-seeking contests

Most of the rent-seeking literature assumes that the number and nature of a society's contests are determined exogenously. This is a reasonable place to start in most cases, because so many rent-seeking and status-seeking contests emerge spontaneously, or are grounded in quasi-constitutional rules such as the civil law and a nation's constitution. Many contests, however, are products of design. Within firms and academic institutions, for example, contests for raises and promotion are designed to increase productivity of 'team members' and to solve team-production problems. Well-designed contests can simultaneously increase the efforts of team members, the production of useful outputs, and the profits of firm owners.

Similar contests may also be devised by government officials with similar gains (profits, revenues, deference) in mind. For example, government can create special privileges, barriers to entry, exclusive rights to buy or sell, etc., that are available to only a subset of the persons who wish to obtain them. It may also determine who is eligible to compete for those prizes and the procedures through which such privileges can be obtained by interested persons and organizations. In this manner, government officials may create a complex series of nested contests.

Figure 3.1 illustrates the simple microeconomics of a contest to obtain a government-created monopoly in a market in which it is difficult to discriminate among buyers. It bears noting that monopoly 'profits' are not always monetary, but may also include 'social rents' in the form of status, deference, and political authority.

Tullock (1967) pointed out that the prospect of gaining monopoly profit (area T) can induce a good deal of political activity to obtain such market privileges. He also pointed out that resources used to obtain such privileges can often be regarded as additional sources of deadweight loss, because the resources used to seek monopoly privileges from government reduce social net benefits and have

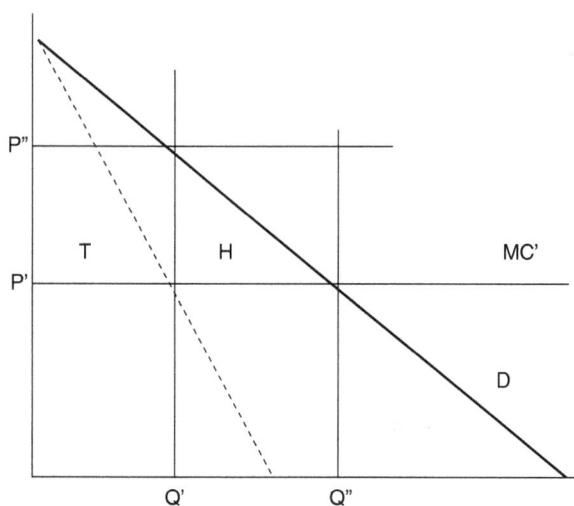

Figure 3.1 Monopoly profits and rent-seeking effort.

an opportunity cost. They could have been used to increase social net benefits by producing other products that could be sold at mutual advantage.

The resources invested in many personal wealth- and status-increasing contests tend to be value-decreasing, rather than value-increasing for society at large. In macroeconomic terms, they reduce national income and wealth, rather than increase it.

The use of such rent-extracting contests and of government monopolies as sources of government revenue is historically important in most societies. For example, during the Hang Dynasty, a state monopoly on salt was a major revenue source for the imperial government (Chen 1911: 542). State monopolies were also important sources of revenue in the Ottoman Empire (Mansfield 2004: 66). Revenues from state monopolies and sales of office were also important sources of revenue in medieval and late medieval Europe, as in France and England. Efforts to establish private monopolies were, in turn, often discouraged through punishments of various kinds.[1]

Efforts to obtain state monopoly privileges like the one illustrated can produce government revenues (and other forms of support) with a value of up to area T. Welfare economics implies that government 'sales' of monopoly privileges reduce social net benefits by triangle H. The cost of generating revenues from rent-seeking contests is at least area *H* and can be as much as *H + T*, an amount exceeding the revenues, as implied by the analyses of Tullock (1967), Hillman and Katz (1984), and Nitzan (1991).

The extent of the deadweight losses from such contests depends on how much the efforts of rent seekers benefit government officials (e.g., the rents extracted by government officials) and the extent to which the contests produce benefits for other non-contestants. These are affected by the procedures through which rents are obtained and rules that affect participation in the contests (Congleton 1980; Aidt and Hillman 2008).

3.1 Rent-extracting authority

It bears noting that the efforts of rent seekers normally produce benefits for government officials, as well as governmental revenues. A common strategy for those who hope to benefit from entry barriers and other protectionist policies is to lobby government officials who control parameters of existing contests or who have the authority to create new rent-seeking contests that restrict eligibility to persons and firms similar to themselves. Once criteria for contest participation are established, similar strategies are employed to persuade officials that they qualify for participation in the contests and/or to change the eligibility rules.

The authority of government officials as 'gate builders' and 'gate keepers' allows government office-holders to benefit from the deference, gifts, and bribes paid by those wanting 'new gates' to be constructed, old gates to be removed, or simply to be allowed through the 'gate' into pre-existing games of interest. Because government officials benefit from most government-sponsored rent-seeking and status-seeking contests, they have good personal reasons to create such contests and to maintain (and seek) authority to create contests in which they can determine winners and losers.

The creation of rent-seeking contests in order to 'profit' from the rent-seeking activities elicited is called rent extraction (McChesney 1997). Rent-extracting contests are more or less efficient according to the value of the services extracted by government officials relative to their value to the participants in the rent-seeking contests, and to the extent the contests produce positive or negative externalities. The greater the extraction, the lower is the deadweight loss of the contest, other things being equal. The greater the positive externalities or lesser the negative ones, the more efficient the contest is, other things being equal.

3.2 Intra-governmental rent seeking and anti-corruption laws

The ability of government officials (policy-makers) to create competitive contests for 'outsiders' indirectly creates higher levels of contests among insiders. Government officials will compete for positions of authority where rents are extracted and for additional authority to create new rent-extracting contests. That is to say, the rents associated with positions of authority induce competition among insiders. Such intra-governmental contests may be designed to increase governmental efficiency or may evolve haphazardly in a manner that tends to undermine it. Hillman and Katz (1987) provide an early analysis of intra-governmental rent-seeking contests in which government rents are entirely dissipated by competition among insiders, as office-holders compete for larger shares of a shrinking pie.

The Hillman and Katz analysis implies that there is a conflict between the interests of lower and upper officials with respect to rent extraction. The more rent extraction that takes place at low levels of governance, the less remains for top officials to 'harvest.' As a consequence, upper-level rent-extracting officials have incentives to adopt rules and regulations that restrict the types of rent extraction permitted by lower-level officials. Such rules *define* corruption and are supported by significant penalties, including the death penalty.

The rules against 'corrupt forms of rent extraction,' however, do not always apply to the senior officials who draft 'anti-corruption' laws, who can often continue selling favors for cash and political support. Rent extraction thus remains of interest in societies that have well enforced anti-corruption laws both as sources of state revenue and senior official wealth. Well designed and enforced anti-corruption laws tend to reduce the deadweight losses from intra-governmental rent seeking, although not necessarily the magnitude of investments in rent-seeking contests by outsiders.

3.3 Rent extraction by well run governments

In rent-extracting governments with tough, well enforced anti-corruption laws, senior officials are, in effect, residual claimants on 'their' country's economic production analogous to Olson's (1993) model of stationary bandits. This has predictable effects on the extent to which senior officials will extract rents from various sectors of their national economy. Senior officials will take account of the deadweight losses of rent-seeking contests and their overall effect on the economy (at least for their term of office), because these affect their net receipts from rent-seeking contests. In such polities, rent-extracting contests may resemble an auction analogous to those modeled by Helpman and Grossman (1994). The effect of rational rent extraction, nonetheless, is to reduce national income and wealth below levels that might otherwise be achieved (Congleton and Lee 2009).

In countries in which corruption runs throughout the bureaucracy, rent-seeking activities inside government reduce the revenues generated at the same time that rent-seeking activities outside of government reduce average income to near-poverty levels (Hillman and Katz 1984, 1987; De Soto 2003). As rent-extraction 'taxes' increase, a nation tends to become poorer, because fewer open-market transactions take place, more relatively inefficient black-market transactions take place, and because productive resources are wasted in unproductive rent-seeking activities (De Soto 2003; Schneider and Enste 2002; Tullock 1967).

Governments that carefully craft their rent-extraction systems tend to have higher average income than less well run rent-extraction regimes, because the 'rent extractors' take better account of losses from excessive rent extraction and harvest more rents from their contests in the long run (North *et al.* 2009; Mesquita *et al.* 2003; Hillman and Katz 1987; Tullock 1967).

The distribution of income in both sorts of rent-extraction states tends to be skewed, because of the implied net income differences among rent extractors, rent recipients, rent seekers, and rent payers.[2] Rent-extracting governments tend to reduce the rent-paying and rent-seeking parts of society to near subsistence levels of income, while the rent-extracting sector becomes relatively wealthy, particularly in well run rent-extraction states.

4   Escape from rent-extracting regimes through liberal reforms

Before the nineteenth century, during most times, and in most places, governments were rent-extracting regimes, although the efficiency of rent extraction varied among governments. Domestic and international barriers to trade were allocated on the basis of family, political support, and cash payments. Privileged persons and organizations had exclusive rights to sell, produce, import, and export particular goods and services. Occupations and positions in government were reserved for privileged members of privileged families, often living in privileged locations. Such state-sanctioned privileges created 'elites,' whose interests were well advanced in most medieval societies. These include relatively prosperous ones such as France, Spain, Turkey, Japan, Korea, and China. Such societies have been called rent-seeking societies (Ekelund and Tollison 1982), and their governments 'natural' states (North *et al.* 2009), although the term 'rent-extracting' states is more descriptive of their governments and policies.

European medieval society gradually disappeared in Europe during the eighteenth and nineteenth century as political and economic reforms were adopted that favored more open and productive forms of economic and political competition. The general direction of reform came to be referred to as 'liberal,' their philosophical and intellectual foundations as liberalism, and the persons advocating the reforms as liberals (Congleton 2011).

Liberals developed arguments that favored productive forms of competition that had previously been suppressed.[3] That is to say, liberal reforms did not reduce social conflict, per se, but rather increased prosperity by shifting resources from economic and political contests that reduce average wealth to ones that increased average wealth.[4]

4.1   Examples of economic reforms that reduce rent extraction

Reforms that reduce governmental discretion and/or 'gate-keeping' authority tend to reduce total investment in rent seeking, other things being equal. For example, a major consequence of the enclosure movements of the eighteenth and nineteenth centuries was making land easier to sell, which allowed voluntary exchange to more easily shift resources from lower- to higher-valued uses. More land could be transferred without the government's (the king's or parliament's) explicit support. Recording property titles also reduced the extent to which resources were consumed through private and public disputes over the control of particular pieces of land, by reducing the ability of neighbors and governments to shift property boundaries without compensating owners.

Opening up domestic markets to greater price and quality competition also reduced opportunities for rent extraction. The optimal rate of rent extraction is lower when firms face more or less competitive markets, because competition tends to increase the price elasticity of both demand and supply curves. The 'open-door' policies advocated by economic liberals reduced barriers to imports as well as exports, which tended to make both domestic and international markets more competitive and reduced opportunities for rent extraction by firms and governments.

4.2 Liberal economic reforms rewrote the economic constitution

The gains from liberal reforms did not emerge simply because private contracts and private property were better enforced, as modern Coasians might argue. Contracts and property rights (privileges) were well enforced in earlier periods as well. Instead, liberal reforms redefined economic and political property rights in a manner that promoted productive forms of competition and reduced unproductive forms. Some pre-existing property rights were reduced and some opportunities for exchange were also reduced.

Liberal reforms allowed some assets to be traded more easily (land) and made others (people and government positions) less tradable. The enclosure movements of the eighteenth and nineteenth centuries made property a more tradable asset. On the other hand, the abolitionist movement made people less so. Slavery was eliminated, rather than slave markets made to function more efficiently. Many long-standing monopoly privileges for towns, firms, and families were reduced. Political reforms reduced the inheritability and private sale of government offices, which reduced the capital value of the rents associated with many government offices, and also often created new merit-based contests for those offices. Cartel agreements and many other 'contracts' between private persons and public officials (purchasing votes and governmental positions) were outlawed or not enforced.

Overall, monopolies became more difficult to own and government positions became more difficult to sell. Markets for slaves and long-term indentured contracts were eliminated. Liberal economic reforms changed the domain of contract, property, and public policy in a manner that encouraged value-increasing activities (trade, production, and innovation) and discouraged value-reducing activities (obtaining special privileges from governments). The elimination of slavery and extension of land-ownership rights allowed labor and capital to move more easily from less productive to more productive activities. Reductions in the sale of government offices tended to make governments more responsive to the average (typical) member of society.

4.3 Political liberalism limits rent extraction by the senior office-holders

Within hereditary or elite governments, efforts to reduce rent extraction tend to reduce, rather than increase, one's prospects for retaining high office, because other senior officials lose both economically and deferentially from efforts to limit rent extraction. In the absence of elections, high officials need only please each other.

Within elected governments, high officials also have to please voters. Most voters are consumers and few consumers benefit from rent extraction. They, consequently, tend to favor low rates of rent extraction, other things being equal. Electoral competition thus induces candidates to oppose 'corruption' and privilege (even if it reduces the income of elites). Corrupt and incompetent senior officials are often removed from office through elections, whereas this is much less common and more difficult in heredity-based systems of government.

As the opportunities for market opportunities expand and the ability of governments to distribute rents diminish, rent seekers realize smaller marginal benefits from rent-seeking activities and shift their attention to market contests. Together the economic and political reforms reduced the extent to which government revenue could be generated through rent extraction, and induced policy-makers to replace rent extraction with new or expanded formal tax systems.[5]

5 Evidence in support of the liberalization hypothesis

The above overview and synthesis of several strands of the public choice literature provides an explanation for the economic success of the West in the nineteenth century and for its continued success throughout most of the twentieth century. By changing the rules of the economic and political game, liberal reforms shifted resources from unproductive to productive competitive contests and reduced the number of rent-seeking contests. As a consequence, the countries that 'liberalized' became the most wealthy and powerful countries on Earth, using technologies and methods of political and economic organization that had never been seen before.

In places where liberals and liberal arguments were less successful, fewer liberal reforms were adopted. Rent-extracting states 'modernized' by adopting the railroads, telegraphs, air travel, and the Internet. However, their policy-makers could not adopt the West's system-wide political and legal innovations that encouraged productive forms of competition without undermining their ability to extract rents. Consequently, 'modernization' in illiberal states only modestly increased income levels and economic growth rates.

Table 3.1 provides evidence that supports the hypothesis that liberalization tends to increase national income by reducing rent-seeking losses (e.g., the misallocation of national resources). It lists 25 countries with the highest per capita gross domestic product, calculated using World Bank data. The list includes 22 countries that adopted more or less liberal economic and political institutions during the late nineteenth and early twentieth centuries. Of the three others – Singapore, Cyprus, and Equatorial Guinea – two may also be said to have adopted liberal legal institutions during that period: Singapore was established as a British trading post in 1819, and so has had British legal institutions for nearly two centuries. Cyprus was administered by Great Britain from 1878 until 1960, and its Greek half is presently a member of the European Union. All

Table 3.1 The world's highest income countries and indices of their political and economic liberalism

Rank	Per capita GDP	Civil liberties index	Economic freedom rank	Corruption RANK
1	Luxembourg	1	15	11
2	Norway	1	28	14
3	Singapore	4	2	4
4	United States	1	6	18
5	Ireland	1	4	16
6	Switzerland	1	9	5
7	Austria	1	23	12
8	Netherlands	1	12	7
9	Iceland	1	14	7
10	Sweden	1	26	1
11	Denmark	1	8	1
12	Canada	1	7	9
13	Australia	1	3	9
14	Belgium	1	20	18
15	Finland	1	17	5
16	United Kingdom	1	10	16
17	Japan	2	19	18
18	France	1	64	23
19	Germany	1	25	14
20	Greece	2	81	57
21	Spain	1	29	28
22	Equatorial Guinea	7	142	171
23	Italy	2	76	55
24	Cyprus (Greek)	1	24	31
25	Slovenia	1	68	26
Average		1.48	29.28	23.04

Notes
The GDP per capita rankings (using purchasing power parity international dollars) come from the
World Development Indicators database (2008) assembled by the World Bank. Civil liberty data
from the *Freedom House* 2009 website (downloaded June 2009), economic freedom rankings from
the Heritage Foundation's *2009 Index of Economic Freedom* (downloaded July 2009), and corruption rankings from the *2008 Corruption Perceptions Index* (downloaded from Transparency International's website July 2009).

but five of the listed countries have very liberal economic policies by Heritage
Foundation's measures. All but three have very low levels of corruption (locally
illegal forms of rent seeking). The outlier in the table – Equatorial Guinea – has
very large oil sales relative to its population and is the only country on this high-
income list without liberal economic and political institutions.

Other lists of high per-capita GNP nations include more oil countries than the
one used above, but are otherwise broadly similar. Oil-rich nations tend to have
lower scores on economic and political liberalism. These countries are not of
interest for the purposes of this chapter, because high per-capita geological
endowments are largely matters of geological luck, rather than public policy or
institutions that can be improved.[6]

Table 3.2 lists the 25 poorest countries and associated indices of political and economic liberalism and corruption using the same data sets as in Table 3.1. Note that all but four of these countries exhibit very illiberal political environments (CLI>3). All but four also exhibit very illiberal economic environments (EFR>100). All but three have very high levels of corruption (CR>100).

Together, Tables 3.1 and 3.2 clearly support the liberalization hypothesis. The tables suggest that democracy tends to reduce, although it does not eliminate, corruption and rent seeking as a fraction of GDP. Policies that reduce corruption and promote open competitive markets and politics, rather than closed monopolistic markets, tend to promote economic development. The distributions of polit-

Table 3.2 The world's lowest-income countries and indices of their political and economic liberalism

Country	Bottom per capita GDP rank	Civil liberties index	Economic freedom rank	Corruption rank
Republic of Congo	1	5	166	158
Burundi	2	5	153	158
Liberia	3	4	157	138
Guinea-Bissau	4	4	165	158
Eritrea	5	6	175	126
Niger	6	4	128	115
Sierra Leone	7	3	158	158
CAR	8	5	156	151
Malawi	9	4	129	115
East Timor	10	3	149	145
Ethiopia	11	5	135	126
Mozambique	12	3	113	126
Togo	13	5	154	121
Rwanda	14	5	124	102
Madagascar	15	3	73	85
Uganda	16	4	63	126
Nepal	17	4	133	121
Mali	18	3	114	96
Burkina Faso	19	3	85	80
Guinea	20	5	144	173
Comoros	21	4	172	134
Tanzania	22	3	93	102
Gambia	23	4	112	158
Bangladesh	24	4	160	147
Haiti	25	5	147	177
Average		4.12	134.32	131.84

Notes
The GDP per capita rankings (purchasing power parity international dollars) are computed from *World Development Indicators* database (2008) assembled by the World Bank. The civil liberties data come from the *Freedom House* 2009 website (downloaded June 2009), economic freedom rankings from the Heritage Fund's *2009 Index of Economic Freedom* (downloaded July 2009), and corruption rankings from the *2008 Corruption Perceptions Index* (downloaded from Transparency International's website July 2009).

ical and economic liberalism and corruption in Tables 3.1 and 3.2 overlap only for oil-rich Equatorial Guinea, which exhibits a degree of illiberality similar to those of countries in Table 3.2.

6 Export-led growth: improved rent extraction or economic liberalizm?

Incentives to adopt and maintain liberal reforms vary somewhat with the type of government, because political institutions indirectly affect the interests of senior government officials. Government officials in rent-extraction states have incentives to encourage monopolization and rent-seeking activities, rather than economic and political liberalization. In such cases, a broad program of economic liberalization may require changes in political institutions that realign governmental interests, as may be associated with political liberalization.

An exception to this general rule occurs in the export sector in countries that use more or less uniform rates of rent extraction.

6.1 'Neutral' rent extraction and reductions in international trade

The optimal tax literature, perhaps surprisingly, has implications about how a rent-extracting government tends to extract rents. In a setting in which economies are relatively simple, rent-extraction systems tend to resemble Ramsay tax systems, with greater 'protection' provided to markets with the least elastic supply and demand functions (Congleton and Lee 2009). As economies become more complex, devising entry barriers with market elasticities in mind becomes increasingly difficult. As a consequence, one can imagine that 'neutral' rent-extracting systems tend to be adopted. More or less uniform systems of rent extraction have far lower informational requirements than Ramsay extraction systems and so may have lower deadweight costs because fewer mistakes are made. They are also easier to administer.

Nonetheless, under a 'neutral' rent-extraction regime, the rate of rent extraction in some sectors of the economy will be above their revenue-maximizing levels. One such sector is likely to be the export sector.

Rent extraction tends to have relatively larger effects on international trade flows than on domestic markets, because international markets include more supply choices than domestic markets. Insofar as rates of rent extraction vary among countries, consumers and producers will tend to favor the products of countries with lower rates of rent extraction, because products from those nations tend to have lower (total) production costs and prices. This provides another explanation for trade flows among industrial nations that complements the Krugman (1983) model.

In the absence of international trade, a uniform rate of rent extraction has many of the same economically desirable effects as a neutral tax. It produces revenues for government officials without distorting patterns of trade. Unfortunately, as Figure 3.2 indicates, relatively high rent-extraction rates (such as t")

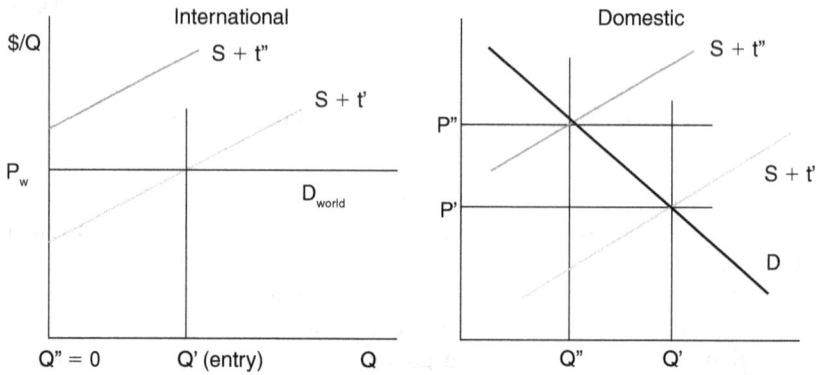

Figure 3.2 Competitive limits on rent extraction.

may maximize total rent extraction, but may eliminate foreign trade by domestic firms, because the full burden of such quasi-taxes in competitive markets falls entirely on the shoulders of domestic producers, rather than being (partly) shifted to consumers.[7]

For the purposes of the illustration, rent extraction is treated as an excise or profits tax on firms in the market of interest, which is a reasonable first approximation for rent-seeking games in which government officials squeeze a more or less uniform level of bribery, deference, and political support from all domestic firms and industries. The burden of quasi-tax t is shared with consumers in the home market, but this is less possible in the more competitive international markets. Indeed, in the case illustrated, high rates of rent extraction from national firms and industries with significant international competition prevent domestic firms from participating in world markets.

As a consequence, the 'usual' domestic rate of rent extraction may prevent even relatively efficient domestic firms from selling their products in competitive international markets. It is simply not profitable to do so given their country's rent-extraction quasi-taxes.

In this manner, a rent-extracting government's relatively high rates of rent extraction may accidently cause 'their' firms to fail in international markets. Exceptions to that rule may occur for domestic firms that sell unique natural resources (easily mined oil, gold, diamonds) and countries in which the revenues generated through rent extraction are used to reduce production costs in some way (education and infrastructure). In many other cases, however, high rates of rent extraction may price domestic firms out of international markets.

The same logic applies regardless of whether domestic firms are price-takers or oligopolists in the relevant markets, as long as foreign consumers have a broader range of alternative suppliers than domestic consumers.

Figure 3.2 also illustrates how relatively high rates of rent extraction can reduce national income. Relatively high rates of rent extraction reduce the number of domestic and international transactions, which reduces national output and income. These reductions are partly offset by greater spending by governments and government officials and by the emergence of black markets, but not completely so. In cases in which rent extraction is illegal, many bribes and kickbacks flow to foreign banks, rather than to public services or domestic producers of luxury goods. Black markets tend to rely on relatively less than efficient capital–labor ratios in order to avoid detection.

6.2 Export-led growth as improved rent extraction

Rent extraction tends to reduce the size of both domestic and export sectors, but the logic of Figure 3.2 implies that this effect is larger in export sectors than in domestic sectors of the economy. In such cases, 'liberalization' of the export sector may create additional revenues from rent extraction, rather than reduce them. This, however, tends not to be true of import barriers, which reduce competition within domestic markets and increase opportunities for rent extraction. As a consequence, the export sector may be the only sector that can be profitably 'liberalized' by rent-extraction states with relatively high rates of rent extraction.

As a consequence, a rent-extracting regime that recognizes the difference between domestic and foreign markets may be able to increase its total revenue from rent extraction by reducing the rate of extraction in the export sector.

Consistent with this hypothesis, Kang (2002: 161–3) shows that revenues from quasi-taxes in Korea increased as its export-led strategy was implemented. Kang (2002: 102–3) argues that informal 'quasi-taxes' emerged in Korea through which 'voluntary' donations of 10–20 percent were made to political parties and other well connected organizations in exchange for government-allocated loans. These quasi-taxes were legal contributions, so tax records are available for them. Kang (2002: table 4.1) reports that approximately 150 billion won were devoted to such purposes in the 1970s. He also provides some anecdotal evidence, noting, for example, that 'Hyundai founder Chung Ju-yong admitted [that] "I personally handed to the ruler about 1 billion won yearly during the 3rd republic, about 5 billion won yearly during the 5th republic, and 10 billion won yearly in the 6th republic"' (2002: 163).

Corruption in Japan and Korea have been increasing in the postwar period according to the Heritage Foundation's Economic Freedom subindex on freedom from corruption during the relatively short period of that index. Evidence of increased corruption (e.g., rent extraction) during the period of export-led growth in China is provided in Pei (2007) and Ngo and Wu (2009).

The success of export-led growth strategies of the 'Asian Tigers' together with increases in corruption suggest that the export sector had previously been overtaxed relative to what would maximize rent extraction from exports. That other markets were not simultaneously liberalized suggests that the aim was more effective rent extraction, rather than liberalization per se.

6.3 Secondary liberalizing effects generated by export-led growth strategies

Figure 3.2 suggests that rent extraction from international sectors is potentially greatest when domestic firms are relatively more efficient than the average firm in the relevant world market, because this increases potential profits for domestic firms. This efficiency effect aligns the incentives of government officials with efficiency in export markets, because the more efficient a country's exporters are, the more rents can be extracted from them. Rewarding efficiency in export markets may require changes in the procedures through which, for example, capital is allocated by the central government.

For example, preferential access to domestic capital (domestic or foreign) may be based on international market share and/or market share growth, rather than well connected firms run by relatives of state officials. By shifting capital to efficient parts of a nation's export sector and reducing quasi-taxes, rent extraction from that sector can be increased relative to more restrictive practices.

Adopting such relatively liberal practices in export sectors indirectly tends to induce modernization and increase the efficiency of related domestic markets. For example, successful exporters will tend to use their more efficient organizational methods and production techniques to produce products for domestic markets. This may increase an exporter's domestic market power (from which rents may be extracted) or may induce their domestic competitors to adopt more efficient production methods. The former increases opportunities for (net) rent extraction, insofar as the result is greater domestic monopolization of domestic production and sales, rather increased domestic competition. This provides another reason for policy-makers to support liberalization of the export sector. However, rather than monopolization, such policies may spur domestic competition. Domestic rivals may copy the methods of the exporter in a manner that increases domestic competition and reduces opportunities for rent extraction by reducing profits in the affected markets.

Similarly, government investments in infrastructure that improve the efficiency of the export sector also tend to reduce transport costs for domestic industries, which increases specialization and competition. The latter tends to reduce domestic opportunities for rent extraction in the long run. Government investments in human capital necessary for a competitive export sector may also affect the efficiency and competitiveness of domestic industry. State support for higher education, however, also indirectly tends to support the dissemination of liberal ideas, as is evident in Korean, Chinese, and Turkish history.

Whether rent-extraction rates in the domestic sector increase or decrease as a consequence of export liberalization depends in part on the extent to which exporting firms become important sources of government finance and support, which tends to constrain the government's domestic policy options. Modest support for exports in the form or reduced rates of rent extraction (reduced or less corrupt regulation), are less likely to produce major declines in domestic rent-extraction opportunities, than broader support. Nonetheless, over the course of a few decades of indirect liberalization, diminished revenues from rent extraction may induce governments to rely more extensively on other revenue sources such as income taxes. The experience of the Asian Tigers suggests that export liberalization can gradually induce political and economic liberalization by reducing opportunities for domestic rent extraction and increasing support for other liberal reforms.

7 Conclusion: institutions, rent extraction, and competitive advantage

This chapter has demonstrated that the political economy of rent seeking and rent extraction sheds light on a broad range of long-term economic and political phenomena that have been neglected by those literatures. Analysis of the incentives of senior government officials in rent-extracting governments helps to explain why liberal institutions affect economic growth rates and why they have not been universally adopted, although they have broadly increased economic income and the quality of life in essentially every society in which they have been adopted.

The poorest places on Earth have barely escaped from the Hobbesian jungle and suffer from the worst problems of rent-seeking contests. Per-capita income levels, corruption, and other forms of conflict in these countries are consistent with the predictions of the rent-seeking and anarchy literatures. Their unconstrained contests over scarce resources evidently consume most of their national resources (Tullock 1967; Congleton 1980). The wealthiest men and women in such rent-extracting societies are often 'warlords' and their top officials, rather than successful economic entrepreneurs. The political and legal institutions of relatively efficient rent-extracting states tend to protect the security and wealth of those already in positions of authority, but they often do so in a manner that limits opportunities for economic development (Krueger 1974; Murphy *et al.* 1991; Congleton and Lee 2009).

In contrast, liberal political and economic systems tend to have fewer state-produced privileges, with the consequence that more resources are invested in productive contests and fewer in unproductive contests. Liberal economic policies facilitate price and quality competition in markets and the development of national and international trading networks by reducing entry barriers, transactions costs, and increasing incentives for capital accumulation and economic innovation. Flows of trade tend to be between liberal market-based societies, because firms that operate in societies with greater rates of rent extraction have higher production costs, other things being equal. Liberal legal and political systems facilitate relatively productive forms of competition in courts and among political parties.

Tables 3.1 and 3.2 suggest that economic and political liberties and corruption tend to be inversely related. The most economically and politically liberal countries exhibit the least corruption and have the greatest average income. This is not to say that rent seeking and high income are entirely incompatible, as

Equatorial Guinea demonstrates. However, significant rent-seeking losses and high income are incompatible in countries in which income is based on production, rather than natural resources.[8]

Liberal system-wide reforms are politically more difficult to copy than railroads, telephones, and the Internet, because they reduce opportunities for rent extraction. Senior government officials tend to benefit from rent extraction, and cannot liberalize their economic and political policies without reducing their incomes, power, and status. As a consequence, liberal economic and political reforms can be a long-term source of comparative advantage in trade, innovation, and public policy, as is evident in modern international datasets and indices of institutional quality.

Export-led growth strategies may be exceptions to that rule, and may provide a possible route to other liberal reforms, as the recent experiences of Taiwan and South Korea suggest. It bears noting, however, that these countries required substantial liberalization of their economic and political systems before they 'took off.' Export-led growth was not enough to sustain long-term growth by itself.

Notes

1 The idea that monopolists earn higher rates of return than firms with many competitors is an ancient one; examples in Europe go back at least to classical Greece and, in Asia, back at least to the time of Confucius. For example, Aristotle mentions the case of the philosopher Thales, who monopolized the olive-press market for a season to prove that philosophers could be wealthy if they wished to (Aristotle 330 BC).

2 Evidence of the effect of corruption on the distribution of income is provided by Gupta *et al.* (2002) and Rosser *et al.* (2000).

3 Among well-known liberal theorists prior to 1800 are Locke, Rousseau, Smith, and Madison. Nineteenth- and twentieth-century liberals include Mill, Wicksell, Von Eucken, Hayek, Friedman, and Buchanan. Among nineteenth-century Asian intellectuals, Fukuzawa, Liang, Sô, and Minobe are often noted. See Congleton (2011) for a more complete discussion of liberalism's role in the European transitions of the nineteenth century.

4 These rough classifications of states parallel those developed in North *et al.* (2009), but in this chapter, states are classified by the extent to which those institutions promote welfare-enhancing or welfare-reducing forms of competition, rather than their political institutions. Political institutions tend to be correlated with the extent of welfare-reducing competition, because the 'political rules of the game' frame many of the most important contests that take place in a given society as developed in this chapter and elsewhere.

5 Of course, the ability to create rents does not entirely disappear with political and economic liberalization. However, many of the 'new games' encouraged by economic and political liberalization tend to increase innovation and economic efficiency in the long run at the same time that they create rents and new opportunities for rent seeking and rent extraction. For example, subsidies for transport grids (roads, canals, and railroads) and communication networks (telegraphs and telephones) provided the new entrepreneurs with rent-seeking opportunities (and substantial rents for winners). The subsidies (right of ways, access to government bond markets, and direct payments) allowed new technologies with economies of scale to be employed for production and distribution, which increased both specialization and competition within domestic and international markets.

6 The country rankings are taken from http://en.wikipedia.org/wiki/List_of_countries_by_GDP_(PPP)_per_capita.m.
7 In monopolistic or monopolistically competitive markets, the burden of such transaction fees tends to be shared by foreign investors and/or consumers, although again the number of transactions tends to fall, and again there are cases in which they fall to zero.
8 Most of the countries in Table 3.2 score even lower on Freedom House's political liberty index.

Bibliography

Aidt, T.S. and A.L. Hillman (2008) 'Enduring Rents,' *European Journal of Political Economy* 24: 545–53.
Baik, K.H. and S. Lee (2001) 'Strategic Groups and Rent Dissipation,' *Economic Inquiry* 39: 672–84.
Buchanan, J.M. and Y.J. Yoon (eds.) (1994) *The Return to Increasing Returns*. Ann Arbor: University of Michigan Press.
Chen, H.C. (1911) *The Economic Principles of Confucius and His School*. New York: Columbia University Press.
Congleton, R.D. (1980) 'Competitive Process, Competitive Waste, and Institutions,' in J.M. Buchanan, R.D. Tollison, and G. Tullock (eds.), *Toward a Theory of the Rent-Seeking Society*. College Park: Texas A&M Press, pp. 183–94.
Congleton, R.D. (1989) 'Efficient Status Seeking: Externalities and the Evolution of Status Games,' *Journal of Economic Behavior and Organization* 11: 175–90.
Congleton, R.D. (2003). 'Economic and Cultural Prerequisites for Democracy,' in A. Breton, G. Galeotti, P. Salmon, and R. Wintrobe (eds.), *Rational Foundations of Democratic Politics*. New York: Cambridge University Press, pp. 44–67.
Congleton, R.D. (2011) *Perfecting Parliament: Liberalism, Constitutional Reform, and the Rise of Western Democracy*. Cambridge: Cambridge University Press.
Congleton, R.D. and S. Lee (2009) 'Efficient Mercantilism? Revenue-Maximizing Monopolization Policies as Ramsey Taxation' (with Sanghack Lee). *European Journal of Political Economy* 25: 102–14.
Congleton, R.D., A.L. Hillman, and K.A. Konrad (eds.) (2008) *40 Years of Rent-Seeking Research*. Heidelberg: Springer.
De Soto, H. (2003) *The Mystery of Capital: Why Capitalism Triumphs in the West and Fails Everywhere Else*. New York: Basic Books.
Eckert, J.J., K. Lee, Y.I. Lew, M. Robinson, and E.W. Wagner (1990) *Korea: Old and New, A History*. Cambridge, MA: Harvard University Press.
Ekelund, R.B. and R.D. Tollison (1982) *Mercantilism as a Rent-Seeking Society: Economic Regulation in Historical Perspective*. College Station: Texas A&M Press.
Grossman, G.M. and E. Helpman (1994) 'Protection for Sale,' *American Economic Review* 84: 833–50.
Gupta, S., H. Davoodi, and R. Alonso-Terme (2002) 'Does Corruption Affect Income Inequality and Poverty?' *Economics of Governance* 3: 23–45.
Hillman, A.L. and E. Katz (1984) 'Risk-Averse Rent Seekers and the Social Cost of Monopoly,' *Economic Journal* 94: 104–10.
Hillman, A.L. and E. Katz (1987) 'Structure and the Social Costs of Bribes and Transfers,' *Journal of Public Economics* 34: 129–42.
Kang, D.C. (2002) *Crony Capitalism*. Cambridge: Cambridge University Press.

Krueger, A.O. (1974) 'The Political Economy of the Rent-Seeking Society,' *American Economic Review* 64: 291–303.

Krugman, P. (1983) 'New Theories of Trade among Industrialized Countries,' *American Economic Review* 73: 343–7.

Lee, P.H. and D. Baker (1996) *Sourcebook of Korean Civilization: From the Seventeenth Century to the Modern Period.* New York: Columbia University Press.

Lee, S. and K. Cheong (2010) 'The Political Economy of Financial Structure of Korean Firms,' *Journal of Developing Areas* 43: 221–32.

McChesney, F.S. (1997) *Money for Nothing: Politicians, Rent Extraction, and Political Extortion.* Cambridge, MA: Harvard University Press.

Mansfield, P. (2004) *A History of the Middle East.* New York: Penguin Books.

Mauro, P. (1995) 'Corruption and Growth,' *Quarterly Journal of Economics* 110: 681–712.

Mesquita, B.B. de, A. Smith, R.M. Silveson, and J.D. Morrow (2003) *The Logic of Political Survival.* Cambridge, MA: MIT Press.

Murphy, K.M., A. Shleifer, and R.W. Vishny (1991) 'Allocation of Talent: Implications for Growth,' *Quarterly Journal of Economics* 106: 503–30.

Ngo, T.W. and Y. Wu (eds.) (2009) *Rent Seeking in China.* London: Routledge.

Nitzan, S. (1991) 'Collective Rent Dissipation,' *Economic Journal* 101: 1522–34.

North, D.C., J.J. Wallis, and B.R. Weingast (2009) *Violence and Social Orders.* Cambridge: Cambridge University Press.

Olson, M. (1993) 'Dictatorship, Democracy, and Development,' *American Political Science Review* 87: 567–76.

Pei, M. (2007) 'Corruption Threatens China's Future,' *Policy Brief* 55. Carnegie Endowment for International Peace, Washington, DC.

Posner, R.A. (1975) 'The Social Costs of Monopoly and Regulation,' *Journal of Political Economy* 83: 807–27.

Rosser, J.B., M.V. Rosser, and E. Ahmed (2000) 'Income Inequality and the Informal Economy in Transition Economies,' *Journal of Comparative Economics* 28: 156–71.

Skaperdas, S. (1992). 'Cooperation, Conflict, and Power in the Absence of Property Rights,' *American Economic Review* 82: 720–39.

Schneider, F. and D.H. Enste (2002) *The Shadow Economy: An International Survey.* Cambridge: Cambridge University Press.

Tullock, G. (1967) 'The Welfare Costs of Monopolies, Tariffs, and Theft,' *Western Economic Journal* 5: 224–32.

Van Long, N. and N. Vousden (1987) 'Risk-Averse Rent Seeking with Shared Rents,' *Economic Journal* 97: 971–85.

4 Institutions for economic prosperity

An entrepreneurial perspective[1]

Young Back Choi

1 Introduction

Economic prosperity broadly defined is a universal human aspiration. Accordingly, numerous schemes for economic prosperity have been proposed. They include picking champions with positive external linkages to spearhead industrial development; protecting certain critical industries; cultivating industrial clusters for beneficial network effects; reforming institutions to assist, or to improve upon, the operation of the market; providing subsidies to assist the economy to migrate to higher-value-added industries through R&D; creating high-paying jobs; stimulating the economy through deficit spending to avert impending depression; providing a social safety net to diffuse political opposition from declining industries as a necessary evil to promote globalization; and even reducing inequality in income distribution in the belief that more equal distribution is consistent not only with industrial peace but with economic growth, and so forth.

The concept of national competitiveness, interpreted as a variant of industrial policy, has been soundly criticized by economists for overlooking the fact that international trade is a positive sum game, and for conflating the balance of trade of a national economy with the balance sheet of a business firm (Krugman 1994). In a charitable reading, however, the idea of national competitiveness reflects a universal aspiration for economic prosperity, based on an understanding that how one will fare in this life depends in no insignificant measure on where one lives, just as the fortune of the people on a ship depends on the fate of the ship.[2] The big question is: if the ship is listing, should one jump the ship or try to right it (Hirschman 1970)? For those who believe that the ship should be righted, what can be done individually and collectively? National competitiveness reflects this type of concerns.

The precondition for economic prosperity is the creation of wealth, the sum of what people value. A scheme for economic prosperity will succeed only to the extent that it leads to wealth creation. No matter how attractive, according to the prevailing opinion of the day, a proposed scheme for economic prosperity whose main goal is redistribution of existing wealth (or wealth yet to be created), for example, it will only lead to intensified competition for rent-seeking and wealth destruction; it is bound to fail, sooner or later. Therefore, the most fundamental criterion of judging a scheme for economic prosperity should be whether or not, and to what extent, it is conducive to wealth creation.

Wealth creation is the process of moving resources to higher-valued uses than hitherto thought possible, the very process by which profit is generated. Wealth creation, therefore, is necessarily driven by the entrepreneur, who discovers and exploits profitable opportunities.[3] Viewed in this way, any policy proposal for economic prosperity should be evaluated by the following question: will it promote or hinder entrepreneurship?

Unfortunately, most policy proposals for economic prosperity overlook the role of entrepreneurship in wealth creation. Often, entrepreneurship is assumed to be universally given, or the role of the entrepreneur is presumed by the policy-maker. That is, often the process of wealth creation is assumed to be automatic, or the policy-maker presumes to have the know-how of wealth creation. By ignoring the crucial issue of entrepreneurship in the process of learning and discovery, policy proposals overlook the issue of whether wealth creation is possible and whether there are incentives to capture profitable opportunities discovered, to policy-makers' later regret.

The main reason for these unfortunate practices is that traditional economics, with its exclusive focus on the efficient allocation of *given* resources, assumes that economic agents effectively know all there is to know, leaving no profitable opportunities unexploited. Traditional economics, instead, attributes all creation of value to productive inputs via the black box of the production function and any increase in wealth, first to the increase in inputs and then what remains to technological change, treated as an exogenous shock (Solow 1956).[4]

By ruling out the nitty-gritty of the market process, the discovery of profitable opportunities (by organizing efforts to move resources to higher-valued uses) and their dissemination through imitation as well as secondary discoveries, however, traditional economics is strangely powerless to explain the process of economic development.[5] Consequently, the static theoretical framework has led to many wasteful policy prescriptions, such as massive foreign aid for less-developed countries and shock therapy for transition economies, for example (Sachs 1994). Without a viable framework to understand the process of wealth creation, an attempt to evaluate a proposal for economic prosperity is like groping in the dark.

The aim of this chapter is to attempt to fill the lacuna by suggesting an entrepreneurial perspective on wealth creation, a perspective from which proposals for national competitiveness can be evaluated and, more broadly, institutions for economic prosperity can be explored. The outline of the chapter is as follows. First, I introduce a view on human action and decision-making in the face of radical uncertainty that departs considerably from the dominant tradition in economics. This view, in contrast to the neoclassical view, allows for (1) the limited (and subjective) understanding of human beings reflecting the individual experience of their particular circumstances, (2) the possibility of ignored opportunities to create greater value for some and their discoveries and exploitation by others with different understandings of the situation, and (3) the process of the discoveries becoming a commonplace as people learn from one another. This view of human action in the face of radical uncertainty is consistent with routines, dispositions, and the character of an individual, as well as conventions, norms, and institutions in organizations and society. Then, I discuss the role of entrepreneurship in the wealth-creation process, addressing the issue of the extent to which entrepreneurship is motivated by profit motives, as well as the issue of how institutional differences (politics, ideology, and legal framework) may impact entrepreneurship. Finally, I try to briefly comment, based on the entrepreneurial perspective, on some of the proposals for economic prosperity, including industrial policy, nominally free market policy resting on social insurance to compensate the losers, programs for job creation, and so on.

2 Human action in the face of radical uncertainty

Human beings are endowed with an ability to deal with radical uncertainty. It is the power of imagination that fills large gaps nature has created by hard-wiring human beings less thoroughly than other creatures. Life's demand for continuous action in the face of uncertainty is met by our guessing what the nature of the circumstance we are faced with is and what course of action would bring the most satisfactory outcomes. The manner in which human beings go about guessing and then acting on their guesses is not dissimilar to scientists' approach to their subject, hypothesizing about certain phenomena in which they are interested and subjecting the hypothesis to tests.[6] Human action is both experiential and experimental.

If the idea of human beings facing radical uncertainty and having to improvise every moment of their lives sounds farfetched, it is only because most of us live in a familiar setting, a setting with which we have grown familiar and comfortable. In the normal course of a day, by and large, we don't even have to think consciously about our lives; we manage our lives largely with familiar routines. Moreover, for the most part, people with whom we interact regularly act predictably, causing few surprises. We are usually so comfortable in our familiar settings that we feel that most of what we do makes eminent sense; we feel that we behave rationally and would not imagine doing things any differently. This, in part, explains why we find the economist's model of the rational actor sensible.

However, to think that the traditional economic model of rational choice captures the essence of the human condition is a mistake. The familiar surroundings in which we manage our affairs effortlessly have become so only through acclimatization. Just think about how uncertain we would be if we found ourselves in an unfamiliar setting. We would be genuinely puzzled – faced with radical uncertainty – though others who are already familiar with the situation would find the same situation not puzzling at all. Our individual system of routines, knowledge, and beliefs, which affords us a relatively easy life, has been acquired piece by piece, over time, in the course of our lives; it is highly individualized and idiosyncratic. Human beings are born with only certain biological capabilities and innate drives; the rest, including how we go about satisfying innate drives, are acquired individually over time, in the context of the society in which we live.

Let's call what we acquire to manage our lives since our birth – concepts, beliefs, skills, dexterity, and so forth – mental tools. Each piece of our mental tools (including the knowledge of their usage) is acquired through the process of decision-making in the face of radical uncertainty – the trial and error process of conjecturing the best course of action, putting it into practice, assessing the outcomes, making adjustments, trying again when the situation calls for it, and so forth. Only the kinds of practices that have brought satisfactory outcomes in our experiences are retained in our mental toolbox, as it were. Among the people with whom we interact, we are known by our habits and dispositions, by our mental tools.

Mental tools we accumulate include various rules concerning our relationships with others. In adopting certain rules, we in turn expect others to respect the rules, as we tend to think they are appropriate. Over time, people who interact regularly will have their individually observed rules adjusted sufficiently enough to have a semblance of mutual consistency in expectations about each other's behavior in order to maintain peace and afford a level of coordination and cooperation. Otherwise, perpetual frustration of expectations and mutual recrimination will ensue to the detriment of all.[7] Therefore, mental tools we accumulate over our lifetime include folkways, mores, customs, norms, conventions, and belief systems.

A larger society, beyond the possibility of frequent personal interactions and containing diverse groups of people, each with different sets of norms and conventions, will attain a degree of normalcy only when it develops, in one way or another, a set of more formal rules whose legitimacy is not constantly challenged. The reason for this tendency to adopt more formal rules such as laws is that having a rule is often better than having many (contending) rules, or having no (common) rules (observed by the majority), which is the same thing.

People equipped with their own idiosyncratic mental tools that are nevertheless so adjusted as to enable them carry on their lives doing their parts in the social division of labor and maintaining, more or less, mutually consistent expectations, would produce a state of the economy, aptly called the *stationary state*. In a stationary state, people behave in ways they deem satisfactory and have no incentive to behave differently. They are liable to think they are doing the very best they can, taking as given what they know and have. Indeed, the static equilibrium approach of the dominant tradition in economics is designed precisely to portray the stationary state (Schumpeter 1934).

3 Wealth-creation process and entrepreneurship

The stationary state is timeless and changeless. It is a snapshot of a changing world. In a stationary state, individuals try to do the best they can, given what they have (i.e., the mental tools they have acquired over their lifetime and have made mutually compatible to allow tolerably peaceful interactions with others.) Each individual's interest in taking up his or her respective station in the social division of labor is to produce the greatest (exchangeable) value possible, in combination with the values he or she can create from hobbies, leisure, and other 'household production.' Since each individual is doing the best he or she can, day in and day out, there would be no reason to alter his or her actions. If there is any change in several individuals' behavior and the pattern of economic activities, it must be in response to exogenous shocks. In making reactive adjustments to exogenous shocks, individuals' mental tools (what the resources are for, who has what resources, how they are to be valued, etc.) are assumed to remain the same. In a stationary state, in other words, there is no meaningful change; the only change is either proportional or adjustment within a given structure of know-how, broadly defined.

Nearly a century ago, Schumpeter pointed out the deficiency of the economic model of the stationary state as a tool for understanding the dynamic process of economic development. According to Schumpeter, changes in the capitalist economy are results of intermittent epoch-making innovations that create new industries and, at the same time, render obsolete many hitherto successful business practices. The success of entrepreneurial innovations invites imitation by others and soon renders the entrepreneurial innovation a commonplace. In the process, mental tools of individuals in society have corresponding changes. In Schumpeter's view, the entrepreneur is the dynamo of capitalism.

Though Schumpeter's theory of economic development, with its almost romantic portrayal of the entrepreneur, has made a considerable stir since its publication, the dominant tradition in economics has not changed much since. The main reason is that, despite Schumpeter's correct identification of the entrepreneur as the driving force of capitalism, his entrepreneur is a rather distinct breed from the economic man populating the economy in a stationary state. One can see this easily from Schumpeter's own characterization of the entrepreneur as driven by the desire to found an empire (a rather different kind of characterization than the economic man's mundane desire to maximize wealth). Schumpeter's entrepreneur might as well be a random exogenous shock. Indeed, upon examining what they could possibly learn from Schumpeter, economists have tended to conclude that Schumpeter offers no good way to alter or improve the received theoretical framework of static equilibrium and that Schumpeter's entrepreneurial innovation is largely a fancy way of talking about exogenous shocks to the economy that economists have been talking about all along.[8]

Indeed, from the perspective of the dominant tradition in economics, there is real difficulty in accommodating the Schumpeterian entrepreneur in the midst of economic man who populates the economy. How can there be profitable opportunities that the entrepreneur can grab when everyone is supposed to be doing the best they can?

The Austrian economist Kirzner (1973, 1979) allows for entrepreneurship by taking a rather different approach to economics as he views the economy in disequilibrium, constantly changing as people learn new things and adjust their actions accordingly. Kirzner has no problem with the Logic of Choice – that human beings try to do their best given their understanding of the situation. But he refuses to go along with the notion of mainstream economics that maintains that humans' understanding of their situation is fixed or shared with other humans. Rather, different individuals may have their own understanding of their own situations and, if their actions bring unsatisfactory results, they will try to revise their actions, necessarily reflecting a revision of their understanding. Even when several people act according to their understanding and they all deem the outcome satisfactory, another individual with a different perception (understanding) of the situation may see a profitable opportunity neglected by several people and capture it. That individual is the entrepreneur. The capture of the profit will move the economy a step closer to putative equilibrium, but equilibrium will never be reached because economic actors constantly become aware of new changes through their experiences, learn new things, and try to alter their actions accordingly.[9]

In the neoclassical economic framework, there cannot be, as it were, a 100-dollar bill lying on the sidewalk for someone to come by and pick it up. Why? It is because someone else would already have picked it up, leaving no trace of the 100-dollar bill (Arrow 1974). In the Kirznerian framework, however, it is the entrepreneur who notices the 100-dollar bill on the sidewalk that others somehow fail to notice. How? Everyone may be doing all they can to do further their interests based on their particular understanding of the situation and come to believe that there is no way to improve their lot. Only someone with a different understanding of the situation may notice a profitable opportunity, the proverbial 100-dollar bill, overlooked by others. Furthermore, the proverbial 100-dollar bill keeps on popping up, as people may not instantly realize the profit potential of various things that they learn in their experiences, the profit potential of which would become clearly visible with some additional experiences, or for someone with a different understanding. *The discovery and exploitation of profitable opportunities neglected by others is truly wealth creation that drives the economic development process.*

It appears that Schumpeter and Kirzner have different conceptions of entrepreneurship. Schumpeter talks about the entrepreneur as an *innovator* who creates a new industry while Kirzner talks about the entrepreneur as an *arbitrageur* who takes advantage of price differences in the market. The Schumpeterian entrepreneur drives the process of creative destruction, disturbing the economy in equilibrium; the Kirznerian entrepreneur moves the economy closer to equilibrium by closing price gaps through his or her arbitrage. Are they talking about two different kinds of entrepreneurship? Are there different kinds of entrepreneurship?

As there are different ways of capturing profits under different circumstances, and there are many, one is tempted to say that there are different kinds of entrepreneurship. At a higher level of abstraction, however, all entrepreneurship shares one feature – the discovery and exploitation of profitable opportunities ignored by others. Consider the Schumpeterian entrepreneur who is portrayed as disturbing the economy in equilibrium through innovation. The entrepreneur cannot create something out of nothing. All the necessary elements for his or her entrepreneurial success (in terms of manpower, technology, the market for his or her products, etc.) must be present in bits and pieces. Most people are so firmly convinced of the goodness of their own mental tools (their customary way of doing business) that they don't even entertain the possibility of profit from connecting the dots (differently). The Schumpeterian entrepreneur's innovation consists precisely of connecting the dots, offering a new combination (of what already exists). Apparently, the economy in so-called equilibrium in which the Schumpeterian entrepreneur introduces innovation already has unexploited profitable opportunities only to be noticed and captured.

In contrast to Schumpeter, Kirzner believes that the economy is never at equilibrium to begin with and that there are always profitable opportunities an alert entrepreneur can recognize.[10] In the market economy, profitable opportunities largely consist in arbitraging, that is, moving resources from their current lower-valued uses to higher-valued uses, or buying low and selling high.[11] In both cases, there exist profitable opportunities overlooked by others. The apparent difference between Schumpeter and Kirzner in their conception of entrepreneurship, therefore, is not substantial, but reflects differences in perspectives and styles (Choi 1995).

There still remains an important difference between Schumpeter and Kirzner in their conceptions of the entrepreneur. The Schumpterian entrepreneur is driven by his or her vision and by the ambition to found his or her own kingdom for personal glory. If he or she becomes the captain of an industry and becomes rich, the wealth is a byproduct, not necessarily his or her main goal. In this manner, Schumpeter emphasizes the un-economic-man-like quality of the entrepreneur. The Kirznerian entrepreneur is driven solely by the profit motive. Is it possible that the Schumpeterian entrepreneur is immune from incentives? Is the dynamism of the market economy possible without profit incentives?

In his eagerness to set the entrepreneur apart from the economic man in the stationary state – Schumpeter needs an agent who can shake the complacent stationary state – he portrays a romantic picture of the entrepreneur, a knight in search of the Holy Grail, as it were. Certainly, innovation can occur anywhere, any time, unpredictably. In overly emphasizing the distinctiveness of the entrepreneur from the rest, however, Schumpter fails to clarify the reasons that the market economy, relative to other types of institutions, has a much more rapid pace of innovation. Schumpeter, at times, seems to go out of his way to de-emphasize the differences in the pace of innovation under feudalism, socialism, and capitalism.[12]

Of course, in any human society, from time immemorial, there have been innovators who are consumed by ambition to chart their own course, deviate from the established conventions, and try new ways of doing things with fantastic successes. After all, all the things we use nowadays are the products of past innovations by someone, somewhere – fire, chipped stones and fish hooks, domesticated plants and animals, irrigation, pottery, iron, writing systems, paper, printing, algebra, ocean-going ships, banking, electricity, cars, airplanes, vaccinations, television, computers, and so forth, down to online shopping, GPS, and wireless phones. But is there any reason or rhyme to innovation or entrepreneurship? Do institutions make any difference in the pace of innovation?

Historically the pace of innovations (and their adaptations) has not been uniform. Some people hardly innovate and even stubbornly refuse to adopt innovations from elsewhere. Others innovate for a while at a vigorous pace, but the process of innovation eventually peters out. Yet others sustain and even accelerate the pace of innovation (Mokyr 1992). Over time, societies that continually innovate and eagerly adopt innovations from elsewhere become richer and stronger. Obviously, people in entrepreneurial/innovative societies tend to be more prosperous than people in other societies that are averse to adopting the innovations of others, let alone innovating on their own.[13]

4 Institutions for economic prosperity

What accounts for the difference in the pace of innovation and the fervor of entrepreneurship in different societies? The first step in answering this all-important question, I believe, is the Kirznerian entrepreneur, driven solely by profit. Profit, defined as the net above the next best realizable values, is possible only if the entrepreneur discovers that certain resources can be put to higher-valued uses than they are currently. The resources are put to their current low-valued uses because their owners, in their own understanding of things, know of no higher-valued use for them. The entrepreneur with a different understanding of the situation becomes aware that profit can be made by redeploying the resources to higher-valued uses.

Entrepreneurial alertness to profitable opportunities is further stimulated by incentives for gain. Suppose that a maverick introduces an outstanding innovation out of sheer ambition for personal glory and nothing else. The innovation would not have the same far-reaching impact on the economy if not for others who are not motivated by glory but solely by profit becoming entrepreneurs themselves by imitating, modifying, and extending the innovation in a variety of areas. In other words, if not for profit-motivated entrepreneurs, many innovations may remain singular testimonies to the audacity of isolated mavericks and geniuses. With the sweet smell of profit, many more individuals with less lofty goals or idiosyncrasies would be motivated to become the entrepreneur, accelerating the process of economic development.

Kirzner does not explicitly dwell on comparative institutions given his focus on the role of the entrepreneur in the *market process*. However, insofar as the entrepreneur is driven by profit incentives, we can examine different institutions in terms of profit incentives they provide for the entrepreneur. Institutions that provide sufficient incentive for entrepreneurship will be conducive to innovation, wealth creation, and economic prosperity. Those societies whose institutions do not provide sufficient incentive for the entrepreneur will not be as prosperous.

In the remainder of this section, I consider four essential features of institutions that impact entrepreneurship – freedom of action, channeling of actions to value creation, protection of fair gains thus created, and ideologies that encourage experimentation and pay due respect to entrepreneurship.

4.1 Freedom of action

The most important feature of institutions for economic prosperity is the freedom of thought and action. Wealth-creating entrepreneurship consists of discovering and exploiting profitable opportunities neglected by others, thereby creating values that would not exist otherwise. Wealth creation requires that the entrepreneur can freely experiment and seize profitable opportunities as he or she discovers them.

However, entrepreneurial freedom is not easily obtained because entrepreneurial innovation, by definition, is unconventional and could be hurtful to many, who may in turn react negatively to entrepreneurs (Choi 1993b). All economic actors conduct their affairs based on their own understanding. Often, many people, through repeated interactions, come to have a similar, or conventional, understanding of a situation. Actions rationalized based on conventional understanding will exhaust all *known* profit opportunities, leaving no more profit opportunity unexploited. However, there could be profitable opportunities unknown to the convention-bound; someone with a different, and superior, understanding of the situation may notice profitable opportunities ignored by others. Through his or her actions, when successful, the entrepreneur proves the shortcomings of conventional wisdom and forces others to change, however begrudgingly. For this to happen the entrepreneur should have the freedom to act, based on his or her own understanding, however unconventional or unorthodox that action may be.

Who would not like to come into possession of a superior way of doing things? Who would not like to become more innovative? Alas, there is no proven method of making people more entrepreneurial than they actually are. And there is no proven method of identifying who is more likely to be an entrepreneur or when and where entrepreneurship is feasible. The reason for this is that an entrepreneur possesses an understanding that is superior to that of others. Anyone who proposes to teach others how to become an entrepreneur, or who is likely to become an entrepreneur, or who knows when entrepreneurship is appropriate, presumes to possess the necessary understanding to be an entrepreneur. Isn't he or she like the numerologist who proposes to teach others how to pick a winning lottery number?

Any human being has the potential to learn from his or her experience and discover how things can be improved, or done better. The only thing required is freedom to act on one's imagination and understanding. Improvement in knowledge, the basis of wealth creation through entrepreneurial discoveries, comes, as in science, from new conjectures that outperform previously accepted conjectures. Other things being equal, the more freely individuals in society can explore different ideas with little inhibition and try them out in practice, however unconventional they may be, the higher the chance of improving knowledge and wealth in society. Likewise, all avenues of the discovery of profitable opportunities and their exploitation should be open. If individuals are discouraged from exploring new ideas (with a strict hierarchical ordering that severely censures any impertinence or deviance), not only will there be far fewer attempts to make discoveries, but even occasional discoveries may not be translated into wealth creation.

Freedom of action would mean little if there are restrictions on the redeployment of resources that the entrepreneur believes can be put to higher-valued uses than the current uses. Laws and regulations that unduly restrict voluntary transactions would restrict the freedom of entrepreneurial actions. Of course, there is room for laws and regulations to effectively deal with significant negative externalities, in addition to protecting minimally defined rights. By undue restrictions on voluntary transactions, I have in mind primarily those laws and regulations that are meant to create privileges for the interests of certain politically powerful groups, such as costly license requirements that make an entry into certain businesses difficult, if not impossible, especially for entrepreneurs with limited funding; labor and capital regulations that prohibit voluntary transactions that harm nobody (other than certain privileged interest groups); and so on.

4.2 Channeling actions to value creation

From an individual's point of view, a gain is a gain; he or she may not care whether the gain is through wealth creation or through redistribution at someone else's expense. The one who gains through wealth creation is the entrepreneur. The one who cleverly gains at others' expense by taking others' wealth without their consent is a thief, a scammer, or a rent seeker through various brazen or ingenious schemes of transfer using the machinery of the state (Baumol 1993). It should be noted that the acts of gaining at the expense of others diminish wealth not only in terms of the forgone opportunities of the grabbers (the value the grabbers could have created had they instead devoted their efforts to wealth creation), but also in encouraging others to try to do likewise (abandoning their wealth-creating activities) and inducing those who still wish to engage in value-creating activities to devote resources to avoid being hapless victims (Murphy *et al.* 1993).

If no distinction is made between different types of gains, the considerable talents of a society would be channeled to endeavors aimed at the redistribution of wealth. If enough people come to believe that the chance of success in life is greater through theft, scams, or rent seeking, the rank of entrepreneurship will be greatly diminished. Entrepreneurship can never be extinguished to the extent that people sometimes cannot help noticing how the current state of affairs falls far short of the potential. But many of those who are not desperately driven to cry out 'The emperor is naked!' will seek an easier way of making a living – taking from others.

One clear sign that a society is channeling talents to unproductive (and counterproductive) avenues is the eagerness with which people pursue government posts. The ultimate source of the prestige and attractiveness of government posts is the advantages afforded by them, namely, the combination of emolument, gifts (read bribes), and opportunities for extortion and grabbing.

For example, a not insignificant number of engineering students at Seoul National University, Korea's most prestigious university, take a leave of absence to prepare for the highly competitive (high-level) civil service exams, a gateway for a career in the government bureaucracy (including the judiciary branch), for wealth and prestige. This most unusual (and wasteful) practice, I believe, is evidence of the all-powerful government in Korea that can make or break fortunes and shower largess on favorites.[14]

The educational system in Korea shows symptoms of channeling talents to unproductive avenues as well. Koreans invest heavily in education. The rate of university enrollment is one of the highest in the world. Korean parents do whatever they can to make sure their children get the best education possible, by moving to neighborhoods with good schools (read expensive neighbors), enrolling them in costly cram schools, even sending a substantial number of children of tender age overseas. Considering the great effort expended on education, however, Korean achievement in science is relatively meager. The reason, I believe, is that a substantial portion of educational investment is devoted to relative positioning in the sorting process ultimately for government posts – a lot of cramming to outperform others in the relentless and competitive sorting processes for aspirants.

4.3 Protection of entrepreneurial profits

Entrepreneurship is stimulated by the prospect of profit. The incentive for entrepreneurship will be much diminished if gains from value creation are insecure, being subject to arbitrary seizure. Of course, most civilized societies have some protection for private property, without which freedom of action is meaningless and exchange of goods nearly impossible. But nominal property rights can be greatly attenuated through regulations, taxation, selective enforcement of laws, and arbitrary seizure by the government.

Entrepreneurial profit is especially prone to arbitrary seizure (for example, through targeted legislation or by decree). One reason, of course, is that when entrepreneurial profit is large, it is both noticeable and tempting for others to grab. Another reason is that the nature of profit is often misunderstood, rendering profit an object of social censure and envy. Recall that entrepreneurial profit is the proverbial 100-dollar bill lying on the street that no one noticed before. It is something anyone could have gotten, in hindsight. Unlike the quasi-rent accruing to entertainers people are fond of, or to inventors whose inventions people can easily appreciate, the source of entrepreneurial profit is often mundane, discovering profitable opportunities others somehow overlooked. Fantastic gains of the entrepreneur without easily appreciable reasons often arouse suspicion about

the legitimacy of profit (Hayek 1989). When general suspicion against the entrepreneur is stoked by resentments harbored by those whose livelihoods have been
disrupted by competition, the entrepreneur can become a target for pillory and
expropriation (Choi 1993a). Heightened resentment, in an unrestrained democracy, can be easily translated into mob-incited seizures through the power of
government, significantly compromising property rights and weakening entrepreneurial incentive.

How an entrepreneur's profit is protected depends greatly on how the masses
understand the nature of profit. For this reason, we now turn to consider how the
prevailing ideology portrays entrepreneurship.

4.4 Ideology of wealth creation

If entrepreneurs are envied and demonized and their properties subject to arbitrary seizures, they may survive the treacherous environment only with great difficulties. Even in the most inhospitable political milieu, of course, some
entrepreneurs may not be deterred as they cannot resist the lure of profit (a
1,000-dollar bill, as it were) and manage to secure sufficient protection for their
own properties, albeit at high costs. Lesser entrepreneurs, however, will be more
easily discouraged. If the ruling ideology of a society portrays the entrepreneur
negatively, the machinery of the state will be set against the entrepreneur. The
wealth-creation process will then be much dampened.

The ideology hostile to entrepreneurship contains some of the following
beliefs: no one can profit except at the expense of another; the rich got rich at the
expense of others; the poor are poor because they have been unfairly exploited
and victimized by the rich; the poor are innocent victims; the rich do not deserve
their wealth because they are merely lucky and it is unfair to those who have not
been lucky; the economic system is rigged against the poor; the rich get richer
and the poor get poorer; there is no mobility; the dominant force in the economy
is greed, when good wishes for all should be the ruling principle; everyone
should share equally; people, if they do not do it on their own, should be made
do what is good for all; and so on. It should be noted that many of these views,
based on a misunderstanding of the nature of the wealth-creation process through
entrepreneurial discoveries, are central to Marxism, socialism, and various forms
of the welfare state.

Economic programs based on ideologies hostile to entrepreneurship are self-
reinforcing. The government's attempts to redress the perceived inefficiency
and/or inequity of the market process cannot succeed in creating the promised
heaven on earth. Instead, they arbitrarily create winner and losers. Winners,
wishing to overlook the fact that they gain without creating value, will try to justify their gains and gain even more by further demonizing the victims (those
expropriated or disfranchised by arbitrary government programs violating their
property rights), further legitimizing hostile ideologies. The losers will have
reasons to believe that government programs are illegitimate and will try to do
their best to avoid being hapless victims, providing welcoming evidences of

'illegal' acts by victims to further justify and strengthen hostile ideologies. Repeated creation of winners and losers by the arbitrary government will greatly undermine the legitimacy of the state, so the rule of law breaks down, forcing all parties involved to resort to force and guile, trampling any remaining incentive to create value.

The ideology hospitable to entrepreneurship includes the following: one is responsible for one's life, for good or ill; one can succeed in this life through one's own effort; from shirtsleeves to shirtsleeves in three generations; one should live by one's own principles; one has the right to defend one's natural rights; it is possible to make an honest living; it is good to experiment and there is no shame in learning from others; people are free to do whatever they wish within their rights; if one does one's best one is likely to do well in this life; money is not everything; helping the unfortunate to get on their own feet is a moral duty of good people as individuals, but the state has no right to force people to do good as the state defines it; and so on.

Many civilized countries have developed various views hospitable to entrepreneurship as part of their cultural heritage (otherwise, they would not have become and remain civilized), but hospitable views are constantly put into question by hostile ideologues (motivated by the desire to redress the perceived inequities of the value-creation process) and are daily undermined by government programs that have been instituted based on hostile ideologies (sometimes further aided by nationalism and xenophobia).

The features of institutions discussed in this section – freedom, channeling talents to value-creating avenues, protecting the gains achieved with value creation, and hospitable ideologies – are criteria by which existing institutions can be assessed.[15]

Institutions with desirable properties cannot be created at will, however. To the extent that institutions are just the way people think and understand their situations, they cannot be willed by government decree, or by preaching by a group of well wishers, just as people cannot be made to think how or what someone else thinks they should. The most one can do, I believe, is to change *one's own actions*, make alliances with others with similar beliefs, and try to persuade others that they also can benefit from changing their views.

5 Evaluating schemes for economic prosperity

In this section, we will evaluate in most general terms various schemes for economic prosperity currently popular – job creation, encouraging investment for economic growth, social insurance to support globalization, and cultivating strategic industries to enhance national competitiveness.[16]

5.1 Job creation

Modern politicians of all stripes promise to create (well-paying) jobs; during an economic downturn, the promise of job creation is especially popular. But can the government create jobs? If any scheme by which one is paid money wages is called a job, the answer is, of course, 'yes.' But there are real jobs that create value and there are phony jobs that destroy value. Government-created jobs are largely value-destroying phony jobs.

The basis of a real job is value creation. If one knows a preferred way of creating value, one is self-employed. A variation of this is to be an entrepreneur – founding a business, offering jobs to others, persuading them that they can create more value working for the entrepreneur than they could manage either by working for another entrepreneur, or by becoming self-employed. When the entrepreneur realizes that the jobs he or she has offered fail to create anticipated values, naturally, he or she would withdraw the job offers, laying off employees. The formerly employed will now have to decide how to create value themselves, or hope that some other entrepreneurs will have a better idea of creating value. It may take some time for someone to figure out what the best way to create value would be.

When the unemployment rate is (deemed) high, when many entrepreneurs and the unemployed are uncertain about how to create more value, politicians, eager to deliver good tidings to people, embrace magicians offering a more appealing solution: the government should create jobs. There are basically three possible ways the government can make a difference on the level of unemployment statistics – government-created jobs, government-protected jobs, and jobs induced by expansionary macroeconomic policies.

1   Government-created jobs have steadily increased, including jobs in government bureaus, jobs in government-sponsored enterprises, as well as jobs in private enterprises doing business exclusively with governments. Beyond what is needed for the production of a minimal level of public goods, however, government-created jobs are not real jobs. They mostly destroy value. A society in which the majority of jobs are government created would be rather poor. Otherwise, the government should create jobs paying everyone good wages and solve all economic problems, once and for all!

2   The government may prevent the elimination of jobs at some firms, especially if they are regarded as 'too big to fail' or are 'too politically sensitive to let it fold,' by providing a privileged exemption from competition, or subsidies, or both. That a firm is on the verge of bankruptcy is a sign that the firm is destroying value. (Instead, its rivals are creating value.) By providing subsidies to struggling firms, for the sake of temporarily averting a large-scale layoff and keeping the rate of unemployment from rising, the government ends up prolonging value destruction by the 'jobs' so saved. The government is in fact conscripting taxpayers and consumers into the value-destruction process.

3   Keynesians advocate expansionary government policies to reduce unemployment, observing that if an economic downturn is left unattended, it may spiral downward into another Great Depression. The advocates of an expansionary policy don't seem to care whether a business downturn is a symptom of unsustainable previous business expansions (that destroy wealth) correcting themselves and searching for new profitable opportunities. They do not see that

widespread business failures represent innumerable profitable opportunities for other entrepreneurs, or that negative externalities of business failures (and the liquidation of value-destroying activities) would be more than made up by positive externalities of new ventures found in newly emerging value-creating opportunities. Nor do they realize that expansionary policies divert resources from other uses. They commit the fallacy of the broken window, focusing on the stimulus of expansionary policy (the seen), ignoring what it forecloses (the unseen) (Bastiat 1996). They scare the public with the possibility of an impending catastrophe and proffer their value-destroying scheme as an elixir.[17]

5.2 Encouraging investment

It is often argued that an economic downturn is caused by insufficient investment and that lowering interest rates and/or providing tax benefits for investors would remedy the situation. While those who stand to benefit from the measure would welcome such schemes, artificially stimulating investment leads to waste and value destruction, though the consequences may not be apparent for a while.

Often an economic downturn is a result of previous expansionary government policies, leading to overinvestment. The untenable business expansions that destroy wealth must be corrected sooner or later. The resultant business contractions and increase in unemployment, characterized as market failure, are direct consequence of incentive-distorting (and value-destroying) government policies. A general economic downturn of this type may be avoided only if the government refrains from pursuing expansionary policies as politically expedient. The short-term fix of throwing money randomly at economic downturns may seem to temporarily alleviate symptoms, or at least satisfy insistent and loud political demands of interested parties.[18] However, short-term fixes prolong the process of value destruction and create dependency, calling for more largess in the future, just as a drug addict craves increasing doses.

5.3 Providing social insurance to promote globalization

A popular scheme in the age of globalization is providing social insurance to ameliorate the plight of the losers in the face of global competition. Basically, the scheme is meant to effectuate the Kaldor-Hicks Efficiency of globalization, by actually compensating the losers by purchasing their assent to globalization (Rodrik 1997).

It sounds politically savvy (and humane too), but it is a variation of the traditional welfare state approach, which assumes that people have de facto rights to enjoy their customary level of standard of living. But to grant rights is to create obligations. Who will be obliged to bear the burden? If the value creator is forced to sustain the value destroyer, what will it do to the incentives to create values? For both the winners and losers of globalization, incentive to make an effort to discover further profit opportunities will be greatly diminished. The greater the attempts to ease the pain of the losers, the less desperate they will become to look for value-creating opportunities. Instead, the scheme will assist them in destroying much wealth created by others. The burden of supporting the losers who are in no hurry to abandon their value destruction will greatly diminish profitable opportunities. Only value-destroying government jobs that minister to the losers will proliferate. The liberal scheme of compensating the losers in the face of global competition will severely cripple the process of wealth creation.

A variation of this liberal scheme has been put to practice in the United States in recent decades with some grave consequences that are only beginning to be recognized. Instead of calling for higher taxes to finance ever-expanding social insurance, placing the burden of compensating the losers squarely on the winners and inviting their resistance, the US federal government has learned to circumvent the resistance of the public to higher taxes by borrowing money (from the public as well as government-sponsored pension programs, but now increasingly from foreigners) to fund much of the costs of social insurance schemes. Initially, it looked like a win–win proposal: increasingly generous (and expensive) social insurance programs have been introduced with applause from all interested parties; taxpayers have been spared, for the time being, from facing the true burden of the programs; investors have been made happy with easy credits; and a majority of politicians of all stripes get to sing the virtues of the free market and globalization, even as they are rapidly expanding the welfare state. This happy deception has lasted much longer than expected. Recently, however, the federal debt, which has mounted at an alarming rate, has put into question the long-term viability of the American welfare state and the future of the US standard of living.

The majority of Koreans seem to fully share the view that the losers from globalization should be compensated, especially when it comes to agricultural producers. When Korean agricultural producers feel that they are not fully protected against foreign imports, they take to the streets, waging violent protests. The recent nationwide protests against the importation of American beef, on the rumored mad cow disease contamination, are but an example. To the extent that agricultural producers are successful in enforcing their de facto rights to enjoy their customary living, with the blessing of other Koreans, much wealth will be destroyed.[19]

5.4 Cultivating strategic industries (national competitiveness)

Many believe that attaining the comparative advantage in certain industries is particularly advantageous for the prosperity of a nation. They include industries deemed to be high value adding, or to have significant network effects. On the drawing board, the ideas of cultivating strategic industries, or enhancing national competitiveness, sound good. If only they were so easy! Instead, we see many more failed cases of industrial policy than seemingly successful ones. Why?

The crucial reason for the difficulty of industrial policies is that the ideas of industrial promotion are *usually* based on the false assumption of the existence of wealth-creation potential, that is, certain profitable opportunities. The advocates of industrial promotion, if sincere, envision the promoted industries becoming profitable, sooner or later. In doing so, they presume that they have discovered profitable opportunities not exploited by others. Otherwise, if the profit opportunities were also seen by entrepreneurs, then the entrepreneurs would do their best to capture the profits. In that case, why should the government try to pre-empt the entrepreneurs? But how likely is it that politicians (or their advisors) discover profitable opportunities neglected by others when so many would-be entrepreneurs are racking their brains to find one? Would they have the alertness to opportunities (which usually comes from relevant experience in the field), or the incentive?

An industrial policy sponsored by the government can have an appearance of success in three ways:

1   There are *known* profitable opportunities that entrepreneurs are prevented from exploiting. A government-sponsored industrial policy may then succeed by exploiting the known profitable opportunities that others are *prevented* from exploiting. In this case, the industrial policy is superfluous; the success of the industrial policy could have been attained by merely *allowing* profit-seeking entrepreneurs to do what they are prone to do. All it takes is lessening restrictive regulations and allowing an easier entry.
2   Alternatively, *only* the policy-maker, not the entrepreneur in the private sector, sees (or thinks he or she sees) profitable opportunities. The supposed discovery of profitable opportunities could be genuine or false. If it is *genuine*, then the policy-maker is indeed the entrepreneur.[20] This may account for some of the successful cases of industrial policy. Even in this case, there will be questions about the legitimacy of the success of the industrial policy to the extent that the some of the policy-maker's actions are likely to be supra-legal. Moreover, if the policy-maker converts some of the profits from the policy into his or her own fortune, there will be suspicion of abusing his or her office, again raising questions about legitimacy. Furthermore, if the policy-maker succeeds once with an industrial policy, he or she is more likely to be emboldened and try again and again, soon moving into the area where he or she is less and less likely to discover profitable opportunities.
3   If the policy-maker's discovery of profitable opportunities is *false* and yet his or her policy seems to succeed, one should wonder about the real profitability of the policy. Just because a fabulous project is carried out and many people are hired, and so on, one cannot conclude that the project is genuinely wealth creating. The fabulous white elephant (the seen) may be built on many trampled profitable opportunities gone neglected (the unseen).

Of course, entrepreneurs in the private sector can make mistakes as well. But if their discoveries turn out to be false, they often cannot go on pursuing their dreams. They either go bankrupt, or their financial backers pull the plug. The policy-maker in charge of an industrial policy usually does not face the stern master the entrepreneur faces in the market and may end up destroying much wealth. It would have been better for the economy that such an industrial policy was never entertained.

6 Concluding remarks

I have tried to present an outline of a framework for examining various proposals for economic prosperity from an entrepreneurial perspective. This perspective emphasizes the entrepreneurial discovery of profitable opportunities as the process of wealth creation and the dynamo of economic development. The institutional requirements for wealth creation are freedom of action, channeling talents to productive avenues, protecting property rights, and combating hostile ideologies. The outlook that emerges from this perspective is generally consistent with classical liberalism, that a free market is most conducive to economic prosperity. The entrepreneurial perspective, built on the subjective nature of human *understanding* that guides human action, I believe, has the advantage of being less likely to be hijacked by the statist than is traditional economic theorizing about the market economy.

Notes

1 Earlier versions of the chapter were presented at the KIEA Conference on Institutions and National Competitiveness, August 17–20, 2009, Seoul, Korea, and at the Colloquium on Market Institutions and Market Processes, New York University, March 22, 2010.
2 Even in this age of globalization, citizenship is like a club membership. Membership in a certain club may be more beneficial than membership in another. Of course, everyone's initial membership is decided by the circumstance of his or her birth.
3 As the wealth-creation process is driven by the discovery of new ways of doing things, the entrepreneur is the agent of the social learning process, which has been variously characterized as a discovery mechanism (Hayek 1945), a social learning process (Choi 1993a), and an innovation process (Buchanan and Vanberg 1991).
4 Recent attempts to endogenize economic growth (Romer 1990) do not materially alter the view presented here (Parente 2001).
5 Schumpeter (1934, [1911]). Despite recent contributions by Baumol (1993, 2002), Schumpeter's criticism of the dominant tradition in economics still stands. It is because some really important insights into entrepreneurship, for example by Kirzner (1979), are still regarded as marginal to the main body of economics.
6 Smith (1982), Hayek (1952), Loasby (1991, 2002), and Choi (1993a, 1993b, 1999).
7 It is not that successful mutual adjustments are guaranteed, but that those who fail to make them will fare badly and become extinct.
8 Demsetz (1983: 275). Baumol (1993) treats entrepreneurship as a scarce resource. While his treatment allows for the analysis of different institutional contexts, it does not address the nature of entrepreneurship directly.
9 Kirzner (1973, 1979) insists that it is not for the economist to inquire into how or why people make specific decisions, or people learn from their environment, or the entrepreneur becomes alert to profitable opportunities.
10 What is the evidence? There are always entrepreneurs capturing profits!
11 Kirzner abstracts from the issue of organizing a firm to realize the perceived profit

opportunities and focuses on the market. But I do not believe that his view precludes any detailed discussion of business organizations.

12 Schumpeter (1934: 138–45).

13 In this chapter, I will focus on entrepreneurship, saving for future discussion the issues of diffusion of innovations. See Rogers (1983).

14 Korea ranks fortieth, along with Italy and Hungary, in the 2005 Transparency International Corruption Perception Index. Korea is behind Bahrain, Jordan, and Malaysia, and ahead of Tunisia, Kuwait, South Africa, Namibia, and El Salvador. Many Korean are incredulous and are prone to questioning the methodology of the survey, instead of engaging in self-examination. Korea is also ranked fortieth in the 2009 Index of Economic Freedom, just behind the Czech Republic, Uruguay, and St. Lucia, and just ahead of Trinidad and Tobago, Israel, and Oman.

15 Various indices exist attempting to measure the degree of institutional hospitality to entrepreneurship – *Economic Freedom Index*, *Corruption Perception Index*, *Global Competitiveness Index*, and *Ease of Doing Business Index*.

16 Nowadays few argue for the superiority of central planning as a means of economic prosperity, though for nearly a century its verity was an article of faith among many millions, many economists included.

17 Consider the recent massive bailout of financial firms in the United States.

18 There is a general conflation of *pro-business*, which seeks government-granted privileges, and *pro-market*, which seeks nothing more than the freedom of action and equality under law.

19 Some farmers may have some legitimate grievances concerning the government's restricting their land use and imposing unfair burdens on them. If so, the farmers should fight, through the political process for the lifting of the regulations, not through violence for their de facto rights as farmers.

20 One must wonder why he or she remains as the policy-maker, instead of going into his or her own business, capturing the alluring profit for himself or herself. There may be some barriers that prevent private entrepreneurs from capturing profit opportunities. In that case, the government could have accomplished the same results as the successful industrial policy by concentrating on removing the barriers.

Bibliography

Arrow, Kenneth. 'Limited Knowledge and Economic Analysis.' *American Economic Review*, 1974: 1–10.

Bastiat, F. *Economic Sophism.* Irvington-on-Hudson, NY: Foundation for Economic Education, 1996.

Baumol, William J. *Entrepreneurship, Management and the Structure of Payoffs.* Cambridge, MA: MIT Press, 1993.

Baumol, William J. *The Free Market Innovation Machine.* Princeton, NJ: Princeton University Press, 2002.

Buchanan, James M. *What Should Economists Do?* Indianapolis, IN: Liberty Fund Press, 1979.

Buchanan, James M. and Viktor J. Vanberg. 'The Market as a Creative Process.' *Economics and Philosophy*, 1991: 167–87.

Canadian Fraser Institute. 'Economic Freedom of the World.' 2009.

Choi, Young Back. *Paradigms and Conventions: Uncertainty, Decision Making, and Entrepreneurship.* Ann Arbor: Univeristy of Michigan Press, 1993a.

Choi, Young Back. 'Entrepreneurship and Envy.' *Constitutional Political Economy*, 1993b: 331–47.

Choi, Young Back. 'Industrial Policy as the Engine of Economic Growth in South Korea: Myth and Reality.' In *The Collapse of Development Planning*, ed. Pete Boettke, 231–55. New York: New York University Press, 1994.

Choi, Young Back. 'Entrepreneurship: Schumpeter vs Kirzner.' *Advances in Austrian Economics*, vol. 2A, 1995: 55–65.

Choi, Young Back. 'Conventions and Economic Change.' *Constitutional Political Economy*, 1999: 245–64.

Choi, Young Back. 'Misunderstanding Distribution.' *Social Philosophy and Public Policy*, 2002: 110–39.

Demsetz, Harold. 'The Neglect of the Entrepreneur.' In *Entrepreneurship*, ed. J. Ronen. Lexington, MA: Lexington Books, 1983.

Drucker, Peter. *Innovation and Entrepreneurship.* New York: HarperCollins, 1985.

Easterly, William. *The Elusive Quest for Growth.* Cambridge, MA: MIT Press, 2002.

Easterly, William. *The White Man's Burden.* London: Penguin, 2007.

Epstein, Richard A. *Simple Rules for a Complex World.* Cambridge, MA: Harvard Univeristy Press, 1995.

Hayek, Frederich A. 'The Use of Knowledge in Society.' *American Economic Review*, 1945: 516–30.

Hayek, Frederich A. *Sensory Order.* Chicago: University of Chicago Press, 1952.

Hayek, Frederich A. *Fatal Conceit.* Chicago: University of Chicago Press, 1989.

Heritage Foundation. 'Economic Freedom Index.' 2009.

Hirschman, Albert O. *Exit, Voice, and Loyalty.* Cambridge, MA: Harvard University Press, 1970.

Kirchhoff, Bruce A. *Entrepreneurship and Dynamic Capitalism.* Westport, CT: Praeger, 1994.

Kirzner, Israel M. *Competition and Entrepreneurship.* Chicago: University of Chicago Press, 1973.

Kirzner, Israel M. *Perception, Opportunity and Profit.* Chicago: University of Chicago Press, 1979.

Krugman, Paul. 'Competitiveness: A Dangerous Obsession.' *Foreign Affairs*, 1994.

Loasby, Brian J. *Equilibrium and Evolution.* Manchester: University of Manchester Press, 1991.

Loasby, Brian J. *Knowledge, Institutions and Evolution in Economics.* London: Routledge, 2002.

Mokyr, Joel. *The Lever of Riches.* Oxford: Oxford University Press, 1992.

Murphy, K.M., A. Shleifer, and R.W. Vishny. 'Why is Rent-Seeking So Costly to Growth?' *AEA Papers and Proceedings*, 1993: 409–14.

Parente, Stephen. 'The Failure of Endogenous Growth.' *Knowledge, Technology & Policy*, 2001: 49–58.

Rodrik, Dani. *Has Globalization Gone Too Far?* Washington, DC: Institute of International Economics, 1997.

Rodrik, Dani. *One Economics, Many Recipes: Gloabalization, Institutions and Economic Growth.* Princeton, NJ: Princeton University Press, 2008.

Rogers, E.M. *Diffusion of Innovations*, 3rd edn. New York: Free Press, 1983.

Romer, Paul. 'Endogenous Technological Change.' *Journal of Political Economy*, 1990: 71–102.

Sachs, J. *Poland's Jump to the Free Market Economy.* Cambridge: Cambridge University Press, 1994.

Sachs, J. *The End of Poverty.* London: Penguin, 2005.

Schumpeter, Joseph A. *The Theory of Economic Development.* Cambridge, MA: Harvard University Press, 1934.

Smith, Adam. *Essays on Philosophical Subjects.* Indianapolis, IN: Liberty Fund Press, 1982.

Smith, Adam. *Theory of Moral Sentiments.* Indianapolis, IN: Liberty Fund Press, 1984.

Solow, Robert M. 'A Contribution to the Theory of Economic Growth.' *Quarterly Journal of Economics*, 1956: 65–94.

Transparency International. 'Corruption Perception Index.' 2005.

World Bank. 'Ease of Doing Business Index.' 2009.

World Economic Forum. 'Global Competitiveness Index.' 2009.

5 Science, scientific institutions, and economic progress

Yong J. Yoon

1 Introduction

The premise of this chapter is that economic progress is made possible through discoveries, imitating and learning, and the creation of skills or knowledge, rather than by the accumulation of capital. It is argued that science is a systematic inquiry that is categorically different from the pre-scientific stage of useful knowledge or technical know-how. Useful knowledge acquired and transmitted in the pre-scientific stage was meager and lacked cumulative progress. Progress in knowledge became possible only when science developed into a social institution. The institution of science consists of specialists who interact regularly and can benefit from cumulative process. In this respect, progress in science shares the insights of Adam Smith in his theory of economic progress: that specialization and division of labor are limited by the extent of the market. However, as is discussed in this chapter, science as a social institution has aspects other than those of the market.

Section 2 discusses the role of technology in economic growth theory. Technology is a poorly understood term that is usually treated as a residual in growth accounts. Technology, science, and skills are used almost interchangeably in economics. Section 3 introduces Adam Smith's theory of economic progress. The idea of 'size matters' is extended to the process of skills transmission in non-market and pre-market societies. Anthropological studies of Tasmania are discussed as an illustration of 'demography matters' in technical change. Section 4 formulates the process of skills imitation and transmission, and provides a model for skills in economic progress. Section 5 discusses scientific institutions that developed and evolved with science. Section 6 provides concluding remarks.

2 Models for economic growth

In analyzing science as a market-like institution, I apply Adam Smith's theory of economic progress, especially his observation that size matters. By *size*, Smith means the size of the market, but we will consider the size question in pre-market society as well as in the modern industrial market economy. This approach is useful in understanding that progress in science cannot be explained by market process alone. To understand the significance of Smith's insight, we examine neoclassical growth theory and new growth theory, which considers endogenous growth or increasing returns.

Growth theory is concerned with the development of productivity in modern industrial economies. The importance of technical change in economic growth has been widely acknowledged by laypersons and economists. In this respect, Robert Solow's growth theory almost sounds like 'water falls downward.' Solow (1957) shows that economic growth, even in the short run, can be explained mostly by technical change or innovations rather than by capital accumulation. The significance of Solow's finding needs some justifications. In his 1956 *Quarterly Journal of Economics* paper, 'A Contribution to the Theory of Economic Growth,' he proposes a model in which outputs are produced by capital K and labor L and

$$Y = Af(K,L) = AK^{\alpha}L^{\beta} \tag{5.1}$$

where y is output and A is technology level. The production function assumes a Cobb-Douglas form, and exhibits constant returns to scale when $\beta = 1-\alpha$. The change in output, or economic growth, can be obtained by taking the logarithm of the production function and taking differentiation:

$$\ln y = \ln A + \alpha \ln K + \beta \ln L \tag{5.2}$$

$$dy/y = dA/A + \alpha dk/K + \beta dL/L. \tag{5.3}$$

Since population or employment is stable in the short run, economists believed that most of the growth is determined by capital accumulation, the term dK/K. But they were quite surprised when Solow (1957) showed that most of the changes in output can be explained by the unexplained residual term, technical change dA/A. Analyzing $A(t)$, the technology change, is the essence of endogenous growth theory by Lucas (1988) and Romer (1990). Once we have isolated technology as the engine of growth, we realize that technical change as the growth of knowledge or technological progress is a poorly defined or even indefinable term. We leave the exercise in neoclassical growth theory here, and examine Adam Smith's theory of economic progress. Smith's theory can be summarized by his proposition that specialization and division of labor is limited by the extent of the market. As the size of the exchange nexus increases, new specializations become economically viable and labor input becomes more productive through dexterity, saving switching time, and innovations.

3 Size matters

Smith's theory of economic progress can be summarized as 'the size [of the market] matters.' This is also the basis for his theory of free trade. In this discussion, I argue that size matters for the pre-market or non-market economy as well but the size in this case is demography rather than the extent of the market or purchasing power. Size, as well as the way science develops, matters in the transmission of skills in prehistoric human societies.

Smith believed that economic progress is inevitable. His theory of economic progress is summarized by the proposition that specialization and division of labor is limited by the extent of the market. Labor input in an economy becomes more productive as the size of the exchange nexus increases. Smith's theory of free trade is based on his theory of economic progress.

Specialization allows increasing returns by dexterity (skills and tacit knowledge), saving transition time (different tasks require different preparation so overkill has to be stored but will disappear fast), use of machines to simplify work, and innovations. The modern theory of increasing returns relies on Marshall's external economy (Lucas, Romer), monopolistic competition (Krugman), and the public good property of technology (Romer). These authors do not consider the extent to which the market influences growth potential. Exceptions are X. Yang, and Buchanan and Yoon, who extend Smith's theory to the modern theory of increasing returns.

Smith compares a savage chief and an ordinary worker in industrial-commercial England and notes that the ordinary English worker has more material comforts. As the size of the market increases, and purchasing power expands, there will be more kinds of goods produced by specialized workers, and each person will become more productive. Thus, the currently poor countries are poor because they are isolated, and when they leave their isolation and join the bigger world, they will also become prosperous. To Smith, economic growth and trade are the same phenomenon, while neoclassical trade theory and growth theory are separate and do not share Smith's insights.

About Smith's theory of economic progress we may raise two questions. Economic historians argue that the Smith theory explains economic growth only in the world of pre-Industrial Revolution. For instance, Wrigly and Deepak Lal think that there is a fundamental difference between the market economy before and after the industrial revolution. They consider the early one as based on organic resources and agriculture, while the later economy is based on inorganic resources and industry. The early stage can be explained by Smith's theory, but the latter requires a new theory.

Lucas (2004) also thinks that the pattern of economic growth changed after the industrial revolution. Growth before the Industrial Revolution was Malthusian growth, in which technical progress (in agriculture) was overtaken by population growth, and, as a result, the living standard had to remain stagnant. Lucas and others conjecture that the fundamental change was made possible through the accumulation of human capital. Increasing returns enter through human-capital accumulation that interacts with accumulated capital goods. To answer these questions and criticisms related to Smith's theory of economic progress, we need a theory of skills, and I will use the term *skill* to represent the concept of useful knowledge for production, technology, or know-how. Smith was fully aware of the role of technology and science in economic progress. Specialization allows innovation and use of machines. Philosophers in the university (i.e., scientists) may invent a steam engine that is useful for production. However, he did not provide a separate theory of knowledge or technology per se for economic progress.

Another question that I am raising concerns the transition from primitive society to the modern market world. The primitive society consisted of groups or tribes with 50 or fewer members. The hunter-gatherers looked for what they needed when the need arose. There was limited preparation or storage. Some groups roamed, while other groups stayed closer to certain regions. In a primitive society, each person or a small group of hunters and gatherers produced everything they needed. Imitation was the major behavioral pattern, and there was no specialization and no exchange, although there must have been some kind of limited barter between groups and tribes. There were minimal social exchanges between groups.

Archaeologist show that changes in population size can explain the pattern of acquisition and loss of culturally transmitted skills. Henrich (2004) and Powell *et al.* (2009) show that small populations were more likely to lose complex skills. Size matters. Individuals live in groups and learn skills from other members or by contact due to migration between groups. The density of the interacting groups and the degree of migration between them explain the accumulation of cultural skills better than the length of time since first occupation of a region. This finding is related to the modern human behavior characterized by symbolic behavior, systematically produced tools, and an increase in long-distance transfer of raw materials.

Archaeologists compare tribal societies according to their cultural diversity, which includes language, diet, toolkits, and long-distance travel for exchanges. In such societies, skills were an important part of cultural diversity. Productivity was totally determined by skills acquired by the tribal members, and useful knowledge was discovered accidentally and randomly by luck. The discovered skill practiced by the discoverer was imitated by others, especially by the younger members. The imitation of a successful skill is part of human psychology and proclivity. However, the learning or imitation could be incomplete and the learned skill could be improved upon. Archaeological studies of Tasmania by Henrich (2004) and others demonstrate that size, measured by demography, matters.

3.1 Demography and Tasmania

Tasmania is an island about one-third the size of the Korean peninsula (68,000 km^2), located 240 km southeast of Australia. Humans arrived in Tasmania about 34,000 years ago. About 10,000 years ago, the Tasmanians were cut off from Australia by rising ocean levels at the end of the last glacial epoch. Archaeologists find interesting facts about Tasmania from diggings. Toolkits before and after the geological separation reveal that there was less cultural diversity after the separation. (Cultural diversity is measured by toolkits.)

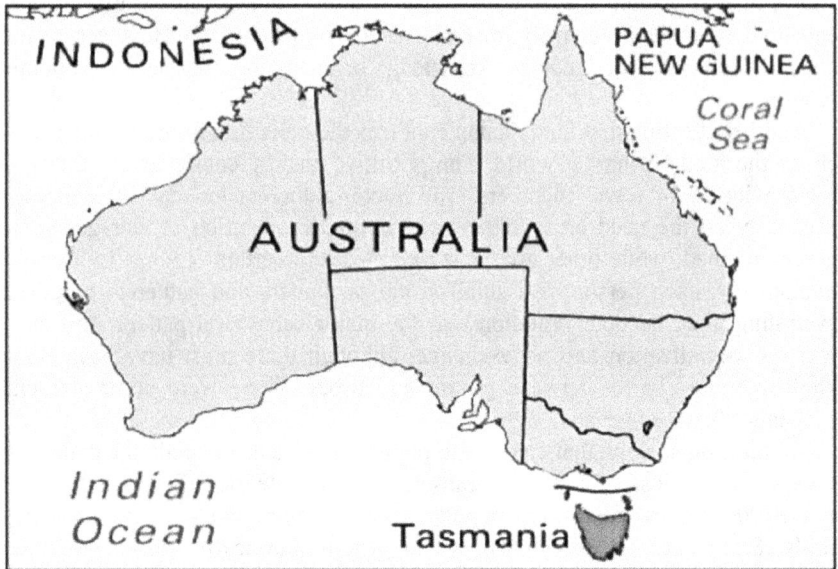

Tasmanian technology was simple compared to their contemporaries in Australia and to their own ancestors. At the time of European discovery, the Tasmanian toolkit consisted of only 24 items, while aboriginal Australians possessed the entire Tasmanian toolkit plus additional specialized tools. Some 7,000 years ago, the ratio of stone to bone tools was 3:1. Then, 3,000 years later it was 15:1, and 3,500 years ago bone tools disappeared.

4 Models for skills

In the earlier state of civilizations, skills, which include knowledge and technical know-how, were discovered accidentally and thus randomly. The discoverers became skillful and others wanted to learn from those who were skillful. At this stage, we can imagine skills were transferred by social exchange, not by market exchange. It is part of human psychology to imitate those who are skillful and successful. But, learning from imitation can be imperfect, and what is learned can be modified by innovation or experiments or even by accident. Unlike the market for goods and services, imitation was a rather imperfect way to exchange skills. Even today, the market for knowledge or skills is imperfect and quite different from the market for goods and services. Education does not guarantee skills will be transferred in exchanges. Students pay tuition but the way skills are learned cannot be controlled by the price.

Society consists of groups, and the group members interact closely. They compare skill levels of others and imitate the one with the highest skill level. The groups also interact among themselves, perhaps through intermarriage, though most groups are suspicious of each other. To be more formal, consider the skill level of a master in a group of workers. Let z be the skill level of the master, the highest level of skill among the members of the group. Individuals in the group try to imitate z. Individual i will acquire skill level $z - \alpha_i$, and add innovation, which will change his skill level to $z_i = (z - \alpha_i) + \beta_i$. Both α_i and β_i are random variables with means α and β. If the distribution of β_i dominates that of α_i, skills will develop over time. If the distribution of α_i dominates that of β_i, then gradually skill will decline. The highest level of skill for the next period will be $z' = \max \{z_i\}$. This model of skill transmission implies that, as the interacting groups become bigger, there is a high chance that skills will improve in society.

As a scientific method of experiment is introduced, the probability of discovery will increase. This will be considered as innovation. The experiments will shift the distribution of βi for the experimenter and the group members. The next step is the institution of science. The method of persuasion is introduced. Experimental results are objective, but individuals may have different theories to explain the experiments, so a method of persuasion must develop. The basic premise is that there is objective truth which can be understood by reasoning, but individuals have their own prejudices and make their own errors. However, personal errors and prejudices are uncorrelated among individuals, while truth is common to different opinions because we share reasoning. Thus, by free communication, we may reach the truth. The institution of science or institutions will agree on premises or the grammar of our effort for innovation. Under these premises, specializations and exchange will increase our knowledge in a cumulative process, and the quantity and quality of knowledge will depend on the extent of the interaction among members.

4.1 A model for random discovery

Consider an economy in which the kinds of goods produced are fixed. Imagine a community of 100 hunters who are natural equals, being identical in all relevant dimensions. Each hunts deer and beavers for his own consumption. There are two goods in this economy: deer meat and beaver skin. Each hunter divides his hunting time equally between deer hunting and beaver hunting, and he catches one deer and one beaver during the period. In this environment, there is no incentive for exchange and each person lives in autarky.

Now, each hunter is randomly visited by the good luck of discovering useful knowledge, a better way of hunting either beavers or deer. Say, with probability 0.1, he discovers useful knowledge for deer hunting or beaver hunting. The discovered knowledge enhances his skill by 100 percent. He can now kill either two deer or two beavers. Each hunter faces an expected growth of 10 percent deer meat or 10 percent beaver skins. Or, using deer meat as a *numeraire*, each person in autarky expects a 5 percent increase in living standard.

Hunters may specialize and exchange. Hunters who discover useful knowledge for deer hunting specialize in deer, and we expect over time half of the people, or about 50 hunters, will become deer hunters. Likewise, about 50 people discover useful knowledge for beaver hunting and become beaver hunters. (This process may happen rather rapidly if people imitate the skillful deer hunters and beaver hunters.) Each deer hunter produces four deer and each beaver hunter produces four beavers. After specialization and exchange, each person will consume two deer and two beavers. Since the probability of discovering useful knowledge is 10 percent, the expected consumption of each person will be 2.1 deer and 2.1 beavers. This means a 10 percent increase in their standard of living.

This simple exercise reveals that, even for the same rate of discovery, the economy can grow faster through specialization and exchange. However, doubling the size of the community, now 200 hunters, would make no difference in their expected growth in living standard. Again, half of the hunters will specialize in deer hunting and half in beaver hunting. Each person faces the same random luck of discovering useful knowledge with probability 0.1. After specialization and exchange, the living standard is expected to increase by the same 10 percent, while in autarky the expected increase was only 5 percent.

Perhaps a model like this influences the mindset of protectionist sentiments we face in public opinion and political debates. However, the result may change if some of the goods are nonrival. In addition to deer meat and beaver skin, we introduce a third good, 'bell ringing,' which is a public good or a collective consumption good. One person can ring the bell for the whole community. Then, a bigger community will reduce the cost per person for the provision of the good.

For a fuller analysis of this insight, we introduce a sea of goods and of technologies. The sea of goods is not necessarily specified or fully known ahead of time. It is a collection of goods that are imagined, and the collection may increase as discoveries are made. The production of each good is by constant returns and labor is the only input. Furthermore, we assume that production requires a lead time. Thus, production decisions must be made before preferences are revealed. The Smithian theorem is examined in this environment with stochastic demand, precommitment in production, and discoveries of knowledge for production.

In this environment, the extent of the market plays two roles for economic progress. The larger nexus will increase the probability of discovering useful knowledge. The second role of the economic nexus is that, in the stochastic sense, a new good becomes nonrival. As the market nexus extends, more new goods with stochastic demand will become economically viable. The new good may be a standard private consumption good, but demand by one person does not diminish the availability to other potential consumers. All potential consumers, in fact all consumers, conspire to make new goods become accessible. This argument applies to knowledge yet to be discovered that might be useful in producing a new good. People tend to agree unanimously about future need, perhaps because of the argument exposed here. Indeed, people tend to be cooperative about the future by encouraging other people to discover useful knowledge and produce new goods; even if it may turn out to be a private consumption good, they cheer each other as if it is a public good. This logic is analogous to 'behind the veil of uncertainty' in *Calculus of Consent* by Buchanan and Tullock (1963).

To be formal, consider a community consisting of N persons. Each person has one unit of labor per period that can be input for producing one unit of any good. Production knowledge is required to produce a good. For a simple illustration, consider a two-period economy with two kinds of goods: X is the standard private consumption good of certain demand, and Z is the stochastic good whose production knowledge has to be discovered at the beginning of period 1. The demand for Z, as in option demand (Weisbrod), is infrequent and uncertain. Let q be the probability that a person, any person, will discover useful knowledge for producing a new good Z. Then, the probability that at least one person in the community has the production knowledge is qN.

Preferences are revealed at the beginning of period 2, but the production decision has to be made at the end of period 1. Each person expects a preference for good Z with probability p. With probability $1-p$, they will have no preference for good Z, and their utility is $u(X)$ from the consumption of X. After the realization of preference for good Z, the utility from the consumption of Z is $v(Z)$; and $v(Z)>v(X)$. This person's expected utility when a new good is available is

$$(1-p)u(X)+pv(Z) \tag{5.4}$$

which will be compared with the utility when the new good is not provided,

$$(1-p)u(X)+pv(X) < (1-p)u(X)+pv(Z). \tag{5.5}$$

Let z denote the expected demand for good Z by an individual. The aggregate demand is zN and the specialization is economically viable if $zN>1$. Specialization of Z requires the production knowledge that has to be discovered, and, for sufficient demand, the probability qN has to be greater than 1. As the size of the exchange nexus increases from N to M ($M>N$), the chance of discovery increases and good Z will become economically viable. Thus, the extent of the market limits the kinds of specializations for new goods, as Smith's theorem predicts.

5 Scientific institutions

We have already noted the similarity between the market and science. To specialize and exchange is the way the market works. Science develops by interactions among specialized workers, and the specialization depends on the extent of the social exchange nexus. While specialization is also inevitable in science, exchange is not necessarily like the market exchange. Knowledge is discovered and the discoverer specializes in it for production of further knowledge. Others imitate and learn the skill and improve upon it, which is what economists call 'learning by doing.' But the price system is not the way the scientific social nexus works. It is costly to learn knowledge and skill, but the ultimate cost is the subjective cost of understanding the other's knowledge. Knowledge is also unique in that ideas can be made public.

The institution of science is formulated as an exchange system in which discovered knowledge is embodied into a specialized task. The institution of science in this respect is a virtual club, much as the market is a virtual club. On the other hand, the scientific institutions – journals, universities, and other scientific organizations – work very much like the loan-making process of banks. The contribution of commercial banks to the national product is the production of information. Through the loan-making process, banks evaluate loan applications and select profitable ones. In this process, banks produce economically useful information. By the same token, journals and universities produce information regarding promising scientific projects.

6 Conclusion

In a primitive society, individuals learned skills from those around them who had the best skills. The progress of skills depended on the size of the group and the intensity of interaction among the groups. Even in modern days, the progress of science and technology depends on the size of the groups of interacting specialists. However, the cumulative process of knowledge became possible only after science emerged as a social institution.

Institution is a formal pattern that evolves largely unintended as Hayek claims, but institutions can develop with the help of intended effort. The role of institutions noted in this chapter is their role in reducing uncertainties. The origin of institutions is human nature and the capacity for persuasion, which is mobilized in truck, barter, and exchange. In any exchange of goods and services and ideas, persuasion is what humans use, but persuasion can be inefficient and ineffective without rules for interaction, just as language has rules to construct ideas and communicate with minimum misunderstanding. In this respect, science is an organized system of knowledge, designed to be efficiently communicated. Science is an institution of persuasion, and persuasion is done by logic and experiment and inevitably relies on conjectures and presumptions. Science, as Lord Kelvin said, is measurement, and as Heisenberg said, is ultimately based on experiments.

We may examine another proposition of Adam Smith. Smith proposed that the economic progress of a nation depends on the relative proportion of people involved in market-like and science-like employments as opposed to non-market and non-scientific work. I may discuss this theorem by comparing two scientific and technological breakthroughs. One is the introduction of the printing press to England in the fifteenth century. The other is Chu His's new Confucian philosophy in the twelfth century in China. According to Geoffrey Hughes (1988), the rate of coining of new words accelerated sharply with the coming of the printing press. Around 1500 CE, the growth of vocabulary was about 50 new words per year. A century later, it was 350 words per year. This massive change must have disturbed the former equilibrium of the language and greatly influenced economic conditions. Chu Hi's brilliant philosophy has influenced Chinese and East Asian literati for 1,000 years. But the impact of the English language had more market-like and science-like impacts, while Chu Hi's system was about moral philosophy. Perhaps this provides a partial story about the different paths the East and the West have taken for many hundreds of years. Of course, this is my speculation and I am willing to listen to your criticism.

Bibliography

Buchanan, J. and Y. Yoon (1994) *The Return to Increasing Returns*. Ann Arbor: University of Michigan Press.

Buchanan, J. and Y. Yoon (2002) 'Globalization as Framed by the Two Logics of Trade.' *The Independent Review* 6, 399–405.

Friedman, M. (1953) *The Methodology of Positive Economics*. Chicago: University of Chicago Press.

Henrich, J. (2004) 'Demography and Cultural Evolution: How Adaptive Cultural Process Can Produce Maladaptive Losses – The Tasmanian Case.' *American Antiquity* 69, 197.

Hu Shih (1967) 'The Scientific Spirit and Method in Chinese Philosophy.' in Charles Moore (ed.), *The Chinese Mind: Essentials of Chinese Philosophy and Culture*. Honolulu: University of Hawaii Press.

Hughes, Geoffrey (1988) *Words in Time: A Social History of the English Vocabulary*. New York: Basil Blackwell.

Keynes, John Neville (1963 [1890]) *The Scope and Method of Political Economy*. New York: Augustus M. Kelley.

Krugman, P. (1979) 'Increasing Returns, Monopolistic Competition, and International Trade.' *Journal of International Economics* 9, 469–79.

Lal, Deepak (1998) *Unintended Consequeces*. Cambridge, MA: MIT Press.

Lucas, Robert E. (1988) 'On the Mechanics of Economic Development.' *Journal of Monetary Economics* 22: 3–42.

Lucas, Robert E. (2004) 'The Industrial Revolution: Past and Future.' *Region*, May.

Powell, A., S. Shennan, and M. Thomas (2009) 'Late Pleistocene Demography and Appearance of Modern Human Behavior.' *Science* 324, 1298.

Romer, Paul M. (1990) 'Endogenous Technical Change.' *Journal of Political Economy*, 98: S71–S102.

Smith, A. (1776) *An Inquiry into the Nature and Causes of the Wealth of Nations*. Oxford: Oxford University Press. 1976 edn.

Solow, Robert M. (1957) 'The Technical Change and the Aggregate Production Function.' *Review of Economics and Statistics* 39: 312–20.

Solow, Robert (2000) *Growth Theory*. Oxford: Oxford University Press.

Stigler, George 'The Process and Progress of Economics.' Nobel lecture, December 8, 1982.

Weil, David (2000) *Economic Growth*. Reading, MA: Addison Wesley.

Weisbrod, B. (1964) 'Collective-consumption Services of Individual-consumpotion Goods.' *Quarterly Journal of Economics* 77, 71–7.

Yang, X. (2001) *Economics: New Classical versus Neoclassical Framework*. Malden, MA: Blackwell Publishing.

Yoon, Y.J. (2008) 'Stochastic Demand, Specialization, and Increasing Returns.' *Journal of the Divison of Labour and Transaction Costs*, June 1.

6 University and industry linkages

The case of Korea[1]

Joon-Mo Yang

1 Introduction

Korea has been known as one of the countries that enjoyed a most remarkable economic growth. Behind this high economic growth, there have been impressive technological advances in Korean industries. In the 1960s, iron ore, tungsten, and raw silk were Korea's major export goods. In the 1970s, the major export goods changed to textiles, clothing, plywood, and wigs, but those goods still did not require high technology with a broad science base. In the 2000s, high-technology industries have led the Korean economy. What made this transition in technology possible? A clue can be found from 'learning by doing,' but did the institutions and policies matter?

This chapter will focus on innovation policies and institutions, especially concerning the linkage between universities and industries. The linkage is essential in finding another clue to the miracle, and for documenting Korean policies in building up institutions for strengthening the linkage. It is not clear how universities contributed to this transition process from a low-technology-based economy to high-technology-based economy. Even though there has been controversy over how much Korean universities have contributed to the Korean miracle, there are many stories that higher education and its research indirectly played an important role in the transition process.

The contribution of Korea's universities to technology development and economic growth tends to be underestimated because of its indirect characteristics. In terms of research, Korea's universities could not measure up to advanced counterparts. Rather, government research institutes and the research laboratories of leading companies have been famous for their performances in research and development (R&D) as well as technology adaptations.

One of the most important functions played by universities is to supply well-trained human resources to private companies. While most companies have actually run their own research institutes, and spend 7.7 times as much as universities do on R&D, as of 2006, universities were the main source of science and technology support to private companies. Korean professors also contributed to the Korea's innovation system by participating in R&D projects individually or by acting as policy advisers either for the government or for private companies.

Traditionally the connection between basic research and industrial innovation is explained by a linear model of knowledge production and transfer. The linear model is a framework for understanding the process of knowledge creation from basic science or theories to development and commercialization. Even though it is epistemologically correct, the linear model fails to help us understand the economic and social determinants of knowledge creation. Steinmueller (1994) argued that the linear model had been criticized because it made little account of the role of technology in shaping the aims, methods, and productivity of science and neglected the non-scientific origins of many technological developments, even though it was useful as a heuristic for examining basic research and industrial innovation. Rosenberg (1992) suggested that the emergence and diffusion of new technologies instrumentation was central but neglected the consequences of basic university research.

The major role of universities is unarguably to perform scientific research, but Korea's universities are not as strong as universities in advanced countries on the frontier of research. Fransman (1994) observed that Japanese universities have often been an important source of intra-frontier research for Japanese companies. This observation can also be made in Korea's case. Professors at top research universities have been connected to private companies. They have conducted research projects personally for private companies in developing technologies either from science knowledge or from applications of technologies to commercialization. However, these activities were not institutionalized and the relationship between universities and the private sector had a tendency to rely on informal connections. The Korean government recognized the importance of cooperation between universities and the private sector and provided a legal framework and incentive mechanisms in order to make universities play more active roles in the technology development process.

The linkage between universities and industry is rather complex. As Pavitt (1984) put it, most technological knowledge is not generally applicable and easily reproducible. It is specific to firms and applications. Moreover it is cumulative in development and varied among sectors in source and direction. Therefore universities and private firms should have long-term relationships so that they can accumulate technological knowledge in the dynamic technical trajectory.

As globalization prevails and competition intensifies, people tend to be convinced that more value can be created from knowledge and that the transition to a knowledge-based economy is essential for sustainable economic growth. Even though leading companies are investing more money in R&D than before, more than any other institutions, they tend to ask more help from universities and complain more frequently about universities' performance. Ironically, this tendency tells us how important the role of universities is. The remaining question is how we can change the system so that the economy can be upgraded.

The purpose of this chapter is to introduce the essential ingredients of the Korean model for university and industry linkage and to review the efforts for upgrading the linkages. Section 2 underscores the importance of the ecosystem of technology development. Even though the linkage models are similar, the performance would be very different due to different ecosystems. In this section, the theoretical aspect of the innovation ecosystem is discussed and the Korean case is represented. Section 3 focuses mainly on the Korean model of university and industry linkage and explains the effort of the government in upgrading the linkages. Section 4 evaluates the performance of the Korean model, and Section 5 concludes the chapter.

2 The ecosystem of technology development

2.1 Tripartite interactions: the government, industry, and university

The ecosystem of technology development consists of human resource providers, capital providers, science and technology providers, and policy-makers. Interactions among those agents produce talented researchers and R&D results. Moreover, R&D can be commercialized and its value can be realized through those interactions. The self-sustaining ecosystem of innovation is such that all agents in the system can benefit from the activities and that innovators and entrepreneurs can expect opportunities to be compensated in the system without endless exogenous or public support.

In order for the science and technology provider to take advantage of capital inflows either from firms or from capital markets, there should be a chance of commercialization. Without commercialization, the only source of capital input is public money, which lacks in self-sustaining circular capital flows. The human resource provider should also have an incentive to produce more qualified human resources within an interactive system. Policy-makers must design the incentive mechanism so that all agents can perform their own responsibilities without pumping in a huge amount of public money.

In the ecosystem of innovation, universities are essential. In the period from the 1960s to the 1970s, private firms in Korea did not pay attention to developing new and advanced technology; instead they made more efforts to bridge the technology gap between advanced countries and Korea. As a result, a major breakthrough occurred in process technology rather than in new-product technology. Process technology enhances the efficiency of producing commodities rather making new commodities. One of the main reasons Korean firms concentrated on process technology was because they didn't have enough capital. Actually, they were heavily indebted. In fact, they had to rely on process technology because the capital required for process technology is small, and because its payback period is short.

After Korean firms accumulated their capital and the stock market responded to the technological ability of the firms, the firms began to put their money into developing new products and basic science due to the changed environment as well as global competition.

Technology development requires time and money. Any sustainable technology development process needs a cashing-out process. Firms are accustomed to thinking of marketability when they begin to develop new technology and new products. However, universities usually have a different incentive mechanism. Most researchers in universities do not have a concrete understanding of the marketability of their research, and they are inclined to publish academic papers, which are usually far from commercialization. Even though commercialization of technology is very important for sustainable technology development, universities have not been very active in this area until recently. Therefore, universities have enjoyed their own autonomy in the technology ecosystem. Exogenous input such as public research funds is a major resource to strengthen the research capabilities of universities.

In Korea, universities have the most valuable research resources and environments for creativeness and innovation, and they have contributed to building up knowledge in the academic sense, but their main agenda is mostly about education. Many success stories of university-oriented technology development and commercialization in developed countries have influenced policy-makers and professors for a decade. Ventures and stock market listings, and commercialization of technologies, are perceived as essential elements to improve the innovative environment and universities' capacity. Now many policy measures are in place to transform universities' incentive mechanisms, but still universities contribute to expanding the knowledge base mainly by producing human resources.

The linkage between universities and industry is very important from a couple of viewpoints. The first viewpoint is that the linkage itself makes the ecosystem sustainable; the second is that the linkage is a way of contributing to making society more innovative.

Universities have contributed to industry by supplying talented human resources. This indirect conduit of the linkage should not be belittled. Direct linkages are various: performing joint R&D projects with industry, nurturing venture firms in university incubators, consulting firms on an individual basis, turning universities into business entities for selling their R&D results, and spinoffs are a few examples.

There are two basic issues in the discussion of university–industry cooperation. One of the issues concerns changing the incentive mechanisms of universities. Universities have traditionally been educational institutions. As such

Table 6.1 Major players in technology development

Players	Role	Characteristics	Incentive transformation
University	Science and technology Provider	Exogenous	Organizational restructuring
	Human Resource Provider	Passive	
Firm	Science and technology Provider	Endogenous	Capital market enhancement
	Capital Provider	Active	
Government	Policy maker	Exogenous	Incentive compatible policy-making
	Capital Provider	Passive	

institutions, universities have been independent in providing curricula for a long time. However, there are many criticisms about the competitiveness of university education in terms of how well university education meets the needs of a competitive economy. Because higher education is too professional and too academic, others outside the ivory tower cannot intervene in changing the curriculum in response to a firm's needs. Moreover, Korean professors have enjoyed privilege and respect, so that the university has been very slow in changing in response to outside demand. Even though there have been concerns about laggard higher education, the results of reform efforts are promising.

Since 1994, the Ministry of Education, Science, and Technology and the Korean Council for University Education have conducted a comprehensive evaluation of university education; the categories of the evaluation are university management innovation, education quality, educator capacity, student support systems, infrastructure, university–industry cooperation, and strategic specialization. Alongside the evaluation, there have been many financial support programs for university R&D and human resource development. For example, the government spent 4,488 billion won in 2005. The amount was 2.29 percent of the total government budget and 0.56 percent of GDP. As of 2005, the budget to enhance educational competitiveness was 9.5 percent of total financial support, which was much smaller than the budget for R&D. The largest share of the budget allocated to universities was spent on current expenditures, so there has not been much room for universities to change their governance and meet the needs of the business sector.

Even though many policies have been implemented, Korea's universities need more efforts to increase their educational competitiveness. Moreover, universities must find an incentive mechanism by which the curricula and other educational provisions are to be adjusted to meet the demand of the economy and to contribute more to developing the economy.

The other issue is to build up the R&D capability of universities. According to the 2007 assessment, in terms of the number of publications in journals listed by the Science Citation Index, only Seoul National University and Yonsei University are ranked among the top 100 universities in the world. Considering the economic size and the number of universities in Korea (there are 195 universities and 107 junior colleges as of 2007), this shows the level of global competitiveness of Korean universities.

The Korean government addressed this issue and has tried to enhance the core ability of each university. The Ministry of Education enacted a law that could establish an advisory committee for university specialization. The committee could coordinate financial support for universities from various ministries so that each university can focus on its core competency.

Compared to other countries, Korean universities spend relatively less on R&D investment, and private companies spend relatively more. Korean universities have spent approximately 21 trillion won (2.5 percent of GDP) as of 2005. The government spent 4.5 trillion won, which is 22.7 percent of the total budget, on universities, that is, far less than the OECD average (78.1 percent as of 2005).

Therefore, the Korean government has to spend more in order to improve the R&D capability of Korean universities, which is a basis for industry upgrade under the condition that those investments must be more efficient.

The policies for changing the incentive mechanism and improving the R&D capability of universities are continuously implemented. These policies are also necessary for enhancing universities and industry linkage. At the same time, more importantly, the ecosystem of technology development should be effective and sustainable. Therefore, the Korean government has provided a legal framework and incentives so that universities can have their own mechanisms to accumulate capital by appropriating their R&D results. Tripartite interactions among three agents form the technology development trajectory. It is the government that can build up the institutions and make the interactions in the early stages.

Recognizing the essential needs, the government emphasized universities' role in industrial development via R&D. In other words, universities became the most important tool for the government to improve industries. This is because universities have the most knowledge capital and largest science base in Korea. Universities have well-trained researchers, and relatively good R&D facilities. The companies in basic industries have already established innovative capacity, and they are leading innovators.

Table 6.2 shows two facts: one is that the Korean ecosystem becomes more privately oriented and self-sustaining and the other is that universities become more active in cooperating with industries. In the 2000s, firms have more patents as a result of the cooperation between private firms than the cooperation between

Table 6.2 Joint patents distribution by cooperating institutions

Cooperative agents	1990–4	1995–9	2000–4	1990–9 annual average	2000–5 annual average
A with A	281	914	1,752	120	301
A with B	521	2,138	928	266	156
A with D	20	155	312	18	62
A with C	848	1,281	427	213	72
A with E	1	10	43	2	9
B with B	1	10	72	2	18
B with D	5	16	4	3	1
B with C	10	63	136	8	23
B with E	0	1	10	1	2
D with D	2	0	3	1	2
D with C	2	64	269	9	45
D with E	0	0	2	0	1
C with C	2	23	34	4	7
C with E	771	2,663	4,521	343	767
E with E	156	1,056	2,637	121	454

Source: Author's calculation from the data of Ministry of Education, Science and Technology (www.mest.go.kr).

Notes
A: private firms B: public institutions C: non-profit organization D: university E: individual.

firms and universities. In the 1990s, public institutes contributed the most joint patents with private firms, but the number of joint patents decreased in the 2000s. Instead, the number of joint patents between universities and private firms has increased tremendously.

2.2 For a self-sustaining system

As industries develop, the innovation policies change. The policy changed toward increasing self-sustainability of innovations in terms of funding. Co-evolutionary industrial policies worked out successfully, and the technologies have been embodied in industry. In this process, universities have been involved in indirect ways: supplying human resources, influencing science and technology policies through related government committees, and participating in national or private R&D projects. In the 1990s, there was a tendency to expect lucrative new business related to new technologies and innovation.

The most important advance in innovation systems in Korea is that the government opened the door for venture capitalists to cash out their investments and for small firms and technological firms to be able to raise capital. The Ministry of Finance announced 'Plans for organizing the market for revitalizing the stock transactions of the small and medium sized firms' in 1986 and established the over-the-counter market in the Korea Securities Dealers Association in 1987. In 1996, the Korea Securities Dealers Association established the KOSDAQ (Korea Securities Dealers Automated Quotation) market. In 1997, the government amended the Securities and Exchange Act in such a way that investors can be protected from unfair activities and transactions can be promoted on the basis of accountability and stability. The stock market has played an important role for

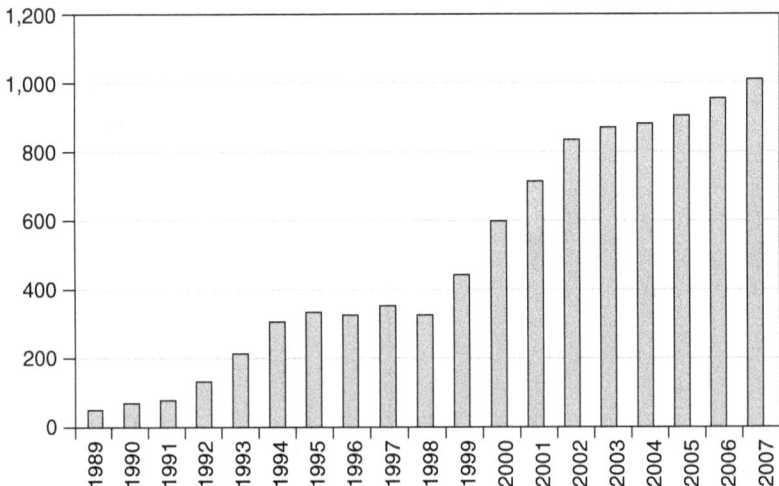

Figure 6.1 The number of firms listed in KOSDAQ (source: author's graph from the data from the Bank of Korea (http://ecos.bok.or.kr/).

mobilizing capital for R&D. After the introduction of KOSDAQ, the number of firms listed on KOSDAQ has increased tremendously from 47 in 1989 to 1,022 in 2007. Even though there were booms and busts, the capital market contributed to promoting many venture firms in the 2000s.

There were fundamental changes in the 1990s. Before the 1990s, the linkages between universities and industries were rather indirect. Even though the Korean ecosystem is moving toward a more self-sustaining system, the system needs more impact from science-based knowledge in order to upgrade.

The increasing tendency of university and industry cooperation resulted from government efforts. The list of those efforts is as follows even though it is not comprehensive:

- Establishing institutions for a self-sustaining ecosystem;
- Enhancing universities' innovation capacity;
- Changing incentive mechanisms of universities;
- Providing diffusion channels for universities' technologies;
- Encouraging joint R&D with industries;
- Making universities play an important role in the regional innovation system and regional development;
- Providing a Legal Framework and institutions to implement the above measures.

These efforts will be discussed in the following sections. As the Korean ecosystem for innovation is moving toward a more self-sustaining system, universities are playing more important roles in the system.

3 The Korean model of strengthening university and industry linkage

3.1 The generic model

3.1.1 Incentive mechanism reforms

University and industry linkages are complex. In order to strengthen the linkages, there should be a comprehensive approach rather than a step-by-step or piecewise approach. Tripartite relationships among universities, business, and government involve various organizations, which have different incentive mechanisms for themselves. Therefore, a legal framework and government actions should be provided in order to change incentive mechanisms so that those institutions can actively participate in cooperative efforts and have so-called win–win results.

The relationship between university and industry has long been established on a personal basis. In Korea, a university professor has been respected by the general public as a kind of social mentor rather than a technology provider. Traditionally, the business activities of selling knowledge or providing knowledge were regarded as something that intellectuals should not do. However, in reality, there were societal needs, and many professors, ironically, actively participated in the government as members of various committees, consulted with firms, and participated in R&D projects. Recognizing that this practice had limitations in strengthening the linkage systematically, the government has tried to change the system and practice of university and industry linkages.

Before the government addressed this issue, the relationship was rather indirect. Students paid tuition to a university, and took the courses that professors provided. In this practice, the relationship between students and professors remained a traditional and ethical one. There was no incentive mechanism that encouraged professors to take care of students' needs and care for the industrial education demand. After students graduated from universities, they worked in industries with limited knowledge about the real business world, and they had to adapt themselves to new environments. While professors had contact with industries through mentoring relationships with former students, professors had no incentive to delve into the reality of industry. Industries had many social mentors but it was very difficult for them to find technicians and troubleshooters that could help them to solve their specific problems, including technology development and strategies.

The previous system had the following problems: first, there was no mechanism that gave professors any incentives to meet the demands of students and society and to change their curricula for industrial demands; second, there was no incentive that enabled universities to invest more in R&D for their benefit; third, there was no direct liaison organization for deepening the relationship between universities and industries; and fourth, there was no flexibility in governance of universities for facilitating cooperation with industries. In order to address these problems, the government has implemented policies which can be classified as incentive mechanism reforms, the providing of linkage support systems, and competence building.

Incentive mechanisms are very important for establishing ethical cycles that enhance cooperation between universities and industries. First of all, the government has recognized the importance of assessing universities' performance since 1994 and differentiating financial support. In particular, public and national universities had long remained autonomous entities because society believed that universities had to be free from all political influences and remain as a social guardian against political dictatorship and for democracy. When most Koreans believed that a certain level of democracy had been established and that the performance evaluation had nothing to do with political independence, the government implemented a nationwide evaluation of universities and differentiated the salaries of professors according to their performance. Most private universities also followed the government reform policy. At first, the professors' performance evaluation focused on the areas of teaching and academic research, but it is changing toward emphasizing research funds, patents, and joint work with private firms. The incentive to publish academic papers has become much stronger because of the professors' performance evaluation.

According to the Ministry of Education, Science, and Technology (2008), the number of publications in the Scientific Citation Indexed Journals by Korean researchers has increased to 25,494 in 2007 from 9,854 in 1998. The number of publications was 11,332 in 1999, 23,099 in 2005, and 23,297 in 2006. This steady increase in the number of publications is partly due to the performance evaluation and a strict tenure-review process.

Moreover, most universities have implemented professors' performance evaluations that put more emphasis on university and industry cooperation. In 2007, 116 universities out of 140 surveyed included domestic patent registration performance criteria, and 114 universities included international patent registration criteria in their performance review process. The weights of these criteria in the evaluation were on average from 14 percent to 22 percent of the weight on academic paper publication in SCI journals. Table 6.3 illustrates how universities approach the issue of cooperation. This changed attitude is due to the changed social demand and the changed laws, such as the Industrial Education Promotion and Industry Cooperation Promotion Act in 1995 and the Special Act for Venture Business Promotion in 1997.

Especially for public and national universities, the changes in the legal framework for university and industry cooperation were more essential. It has been customary for most universities to follow the national universities' policies for their instructors.

According to legal reform for cooperation, for example, universities were able to provide the facilities and land for venture business, and university professors became able to participate in venture businesses for a longer time than university regulations and the tertiary education law permitted them to. National universities could even utilize the revenues from renting their facilities without contributing the money to the treasury. These efforts were expected to change the incentive mechanism for promoting cooperation with industry.

3.1.2 Linkage supporting system

The second stream of policies for cooperation promotion is to build up the linkage supporting system. Because the Korean government has long emphasized the important of science and technology development, the applied areas of cooperation between universities and industries have been wide and comprehensive. The government used cooperation as a policy tool in areas such as regional economic development, industrial complex development, and industrial human resource development, as well as science and technology development. Therefore, there should be a coordinating body to govern these activities across ministries, government agencies, industries, and universities.

The National Science and Technology Council (NSTC) was established in January 1999 as the nation's highest decision-making body for science and technology policies. The President of the Republic of Korea is the chairman of NSTC. NSTC has subordinate committees for preparing strategic goals and their action plans. Among the ministries, the Ministry of Education, Science, and

Table 6.3 Relative weight of university and industry cooperation activities compared to SCI publications in annual university instructors' evaluation

Classification	2006		2007	
	Number of universities	Average ratio (%)	Number of universities	Average ratio (%)
Domestic patent submission	29	9.8	41	14.0
Domestic patent registration	97	17.4	116	22.0
Foreign patent submission	29	10.4	41	17.5
Foreign patent registration	99	15.9	114	20.8
Technology transfer cases	10	5.2	19	12.6
Technology transfer revenue	22	14.8	32	12.1
Technology consulting cases	19	4.5	28	7.9
Technology consulting revenue	–	–	14	11.9
University and industry joint research cases	30	19.6	28	14.1
University and industry joint research funds	–	–	48	21.3
Professors startups	13	3.5	16	8.1

Source: Korea Research Foundation (2007, 2008).

Technology, and its agencies, are basically the most important bodies for strengthening the linkages. However, other ministries focused on linkage because they want to use the capacity of universities as leverage.

First of all, it was an urgent policy agenda to establish a system to improve industrial technology and human resource development for better competitiveness. In order to address this issue, the government proposed the act for promoting industrial and energy technology in 1994. This act showed the change in the policy. The previous government policy was to target a specific industry and to support the industries, which was a so-called picking-the-winners policy. In the new act, even though the government still maintained a strategic approach, it abandoned a targeting approach, and instead adopted a functioning approach to industrial policy. In the act, there were many articles to establish the infrastructure of technology development and to promote joint R&D among public research institutes, universities, and private firms internationally and domestically. The act specified an article that enabled the government to plan specific promoting programs. The law was changed to the Act for Industrial Technology Infrastructure Building in 1999 and to the Industrial Technology Innovation Promoting Act in 2006.

There are articles to allow the government to establish an Industrial Technology Development Committee and to make the government responsible for the funds that will be needed for promotion. The law also provides the legal basis for important government agencies that will implement strategic policies. The Korea Science and Engineering Foundation (KOSEF) and the Korea Research Foundation (KRF) have supported various joint research projects between universities and industries. Those foundations have also contributed to human resource development by strategically designing evaluation criteria for emphasizing the participating researchers' capabilities and the human resource development aspects of the projects. In addition to these supports, KOSEF runs the program that supports universities that hire those who have extensive experience in the public sector. This program aims at giving college students opportunities to learn practical skills in fields outside academia.

More importantly, the government addressed the direct channel for intensifying linkages. Many governmental agencies and foundations have been established to address this issue. With the Industrial Technology Innovation Promotion Act, the Korea Industrial Technology Foundation (KOTEF) was established in 2001. In order to reinforce future growth potential through technological innovation, the government recognized the need to foster competence in schools, companies, the government, and other entities to initiate technological innovation and to create and spread an environment of technological innovation across the nation. KOTEF is to play a pivotal role in the course of promoting knowledge-based technological innovation. As a major mission, KOTEF will build an interlinked network where technological innovation-initiating entities can participate and seek cooperation with international entities to promote industrial technology development.

The Industrial Education and Industrial–Academic Cooperation Promotion Act is the most important law governing industry and university linkage as well as cooperation between industries and vocational schools. The law basically specifies the roles of the government and various committees, and industry–university linkage organizations; it also provides the legal basis for establishing technology holding companies of universities and other appropriate treatments for promoting industry–university linkages.

The Korea Research Institute for Vocational Education and Training (KRIVET) was established in September 1997 to support a national policy on human resources development and the development of the vocational capacity of Koreans through lifelong learning. KRIVET has maintained a close partnership with two ministries in particular – the Ministry of Education, Science, and Technology and the Ministry of Labor. KRIVET advises the two ministries regarding vocational education, training, and human resource development policies, and supports policy implementation. KRIVET implemented various projects for promoting industrial cooperation, such as the Industrial Cooperation Center University Program, the Industrial Cooperation Organization Support Program, and the Local Firms Tailored Education Support Program.

Universities responded quickly to the changes. They established industry–university cooperation offices in the independent incorporated bodies. For example, Seoul National University established the SNU R&DB Foundation in 2003, and Yonsei University established the Yonsei University Industry–Academic Cooperation Foundation (IACF) in 2004. Both were offices of research affairs before they became incorporated entities. Most universities followed this kind of transformation of internal organization according to the changed law, the Industrial Education and Industrial–Academic Cooperation Promotion Act.

Those offices are the centers of the industry and university cooperation; they perform tasks such as technology transfer, joint R&D, consulting, and providing tailored curricula for private firms' specific needs. They are the centers for maintaining the patents that have been achieved as a result of professors' research. The law provides the necessary measures for the sustainability of those organizations, including revenue-handling procedures and property rights management. Every university can establish a legal entity without any approval procedure.

By law, in principle, the property rights belong to the corporation or the foundation, which is subordinate to the university. The president of the university reserves the right to appoint the board members of the foundation. The Invention Promotion Act specifies that an employee's invention in the private sector belongs to the person who actually did the inventing, but the Industrial Education and Industrial–Academic Cooperation Promotion Act specifies that the property rights belong to the corporation in a national university. Therefore universities can handle all the details related to property rights, including application, dispute settlement, and transfers.

The government provided a linkage supporting system by changing laws and supporting the reforms of the university organization financially, and changing practices in various supporting projects. Currently, most universities have established a linkage supporting organization. Some of them have proved successful while most universities are still waiting for evidence that they are performing well.

Another goal is to make universities involved in direct business and to build a technology transfer and commercialization system. The office of university and industry cooperation is the core center which manages the university–industry linkage and handles university research budgets. The offices began to be established in 2003. Most of them take the form of a foundation as a legal entity. In 2003, only 12 universities had established an office or foundation, but in 2004, 117 universities had established the office. Its revenue comes from various activities of industry-related work. As in Table 6.4, most of the revenue comes from overhead from government research projects, and the second source of budget is the overhead cost paid by industry research projects. Other activities such as technology transfer and business incubators do not create a large amount of budget revenue.

One of the conduits of technology diffusion is university-related venture business, which can be defined as follows: (1) the case when professors start a business, (2) the case when universities or institutes related with universities invest, (3) the case when students are involved in university research projects, (4) the case when a business incubates in a university for a period of less than five years, (5) the case when five-year-old-or-less firms have joint projects with universities, (6) the case when a five-year-old-or-less firm receives a technology transfer from a university in developing the current business.

The number of university-related venture businesses reached 1,473 by the end of April 2005. On average, each university has 6.6 venture firms if it has any. Most university-related venture firms were established out of joint research projects with universities, while the number of the firms that professors or students started for themselves is only 245, which is relatively low. This shows that professors and students have less incentive to devote themselves in the business

Table 6.4 The revenue of the university–industry cooperation foundations (unit: million won, %)

	A	B	C	D	E	F	G	H	I	J	K
Average amount	53.4	2.5	19.0	38.0	62.3	249.1	814.7	27.9	182.2	52.9	1,502.1
Class 1	3.56	0.16	1.27	2.53	4.14	16.58	54.24	1.86	12.13	3.52	100
Class 2	11.67	70.82	1.86	12.13	3.52	100					
Class 3	28.25	54.24	1.86	12.13	3.52	100					

Source: Korea Research Foundation (2007: 69).

Note
A: technology transfer, B: consulting, C: university firms, D: business incubator, E: other cooperation with industries, F: overhead cost from industry projects, G: overhead cost from government projects, H: operational budget allocation, I: from previous accounts, J: contributions, K: total sum, class 1: ratio to the total revenue, class 2: ratio of research cooperation to non-research cooperation in terms of total average revenue, class 3: ratio to the total revenue when the funds of joint R&D with firms are included in industry–university cooperation activities.

area. Hong and Kim (2006) surveyed university-related venture firms concerning the strategy of listing on the stock exchange, but only 4.2 percent were listed, and 13.1 percent were in the process of listing. Some 49.4 percent responded that they will not list and 26.6 percent want to list on the stock exchange. Most university-related venture firms regarded financing problems as a major barrier. Judging from these observations, universities are still separated from business; therefore, support policies are necessary for stronger linkages.

3.1.3 Competence building

The most important thing in cooperation with industry is the competence of universities, either from academic perspectives or from business perspectives. Universities have their own goals, which have lasted for a century in Korea; professors are free from any de facto obligation, and respected by Korean society. Excellent scientists want to join the faculty club for a cozy life, and there have been increasing concerns over this tradition in Korea. The government has two goals for transforming universities into competitive institutes that can play a core role for upgrading Korea. One goal is to introduce competition in an academic society through evaluating universities by an academic standard of, especially, education and research. The government announces every year how many articles are published in SCI journals and how each university performs in the evaluation, for example. This will, hopefully, enhance the innovative capacity of universities.

The other goal is to enable universities to participate in the business sector. The government provides the legal framework and actions for this goal. Universities are allowed to do business by establishing offices of cooperation between universities and industry. Professors can leave to do venture business while maintaining academic positions.

These two goals are seemingly contradictory; good academic performance does not necessarily mean good business achievement. In practice, however, these two goals seem to work well and have synergetic effects. Industries have an incentive to invest in education as human resource management, and the government allows private universities to establish special classes as a way of university–industry cooperation. The curricula of those classes tend to meet industry demand.

There were other policies that influenced professors to change their curricula. For example, there was the NURI project from 2004 to 2008. NURI is the acronym for New University for Regional Innovation. The goal of the project was to make local universities specialized and to nurture human resources readily adaptable to local industry. The budget of the project was US$260 million per year, US$1.3 billion total; 109 local universities, 130 project units, and 170,000 students participated in the project; and 20,000 trainees participated in on-site training programs at major companies.

There are synergistic effects not only in education but also in research because the government distributes research funds to only those who have cooperative projects with industries. Since 1999, the policy named Brain Korea 21 has been implemented, and the government poured into the budget approximately US$290 million per year. The policy's goal is to select top ten research-oriented universities in key fields, and to rank them in the world's top ten in terms of SCI-paper publications. Thereby, Korea can aim to become one of the world's top ten advanced countries in terms of technology transfer from university to industry (from 10 percent in 2004 to 20 percent by 2012). As a result, cooperation with industries as well as publications in academic journals increased. Industries have invested more than US$100 million for joint work with universities participating in this project.

Generally speaking, the Korean model of strengthening university and industry linkages consists of three categories. One is to reform the incentive mechanism so that both universities and private firms may actively, voluntarily, and sustainably participate in sharing knowledge. Education, research, and business activities can achieve their maximum level of contribution to society by these synergetic effects. The second one is to provide the legal and financial basis for preparing the linkage system. The last one is to build up the competence of universities so that they can meet the demand of industry either in education or in research. Figure 6.2 summarizes three categories of government policies.

3.2 Legal framework and government policies for university–industry cooperation

3.2.1 Characteristics of the legal framework

The government has provided comprehensive support to promote industry and university cooperation. In order to implement those policies, the government had

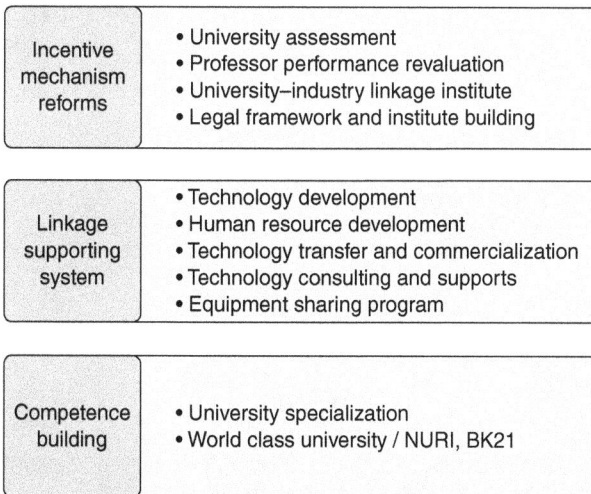

Figure 6.2 Categories of government policies.

to have a legal basis. There have been many revisions of laws and many newly enacted laws regarding the enhancement of cooperation. The main law directly related with linkage is the Industrial Education and Industrial–Academic Cooperation Promotion Act, but there are various laws that use the university and industry linkage to pursue their own goals.

Lee and Koh (2007) described the stages of Korean university and industry linkage policies. The concept of linkage was introduced in the 1960s. The Industrial Education Promotion Act, which was changed to the Industrial Education and Industrial–Academic Cooperation Promotion Act, was enacted in 1963, and the Vocational Training Act was enacted in 1967. These laws focused on training technicians the firms needed on the job. After Korea succeeded in upgrading industry, the government tried to enhance industry and university linkages. The Ministry of Science and Technology supported Specific R&D Projects beginning in 1982, and supported Mid-term Core Technology Development Projects and Outstanding Research Center Development Projects in the 1990s. Since 1998, universities have led linkage by strengthening the competitiveness of universities, and the infrastructure system was set up. In this period, university and industry linkage had its full-fledged system. Since 2003, the government has tried to use linkage as the foundation for improving regional innovation systems and the development of regional economies. The Special Act for National Balanced Development was enacted in 2004. In this special law, there are many articles to support local universities' capacities and their cooperation with industry.

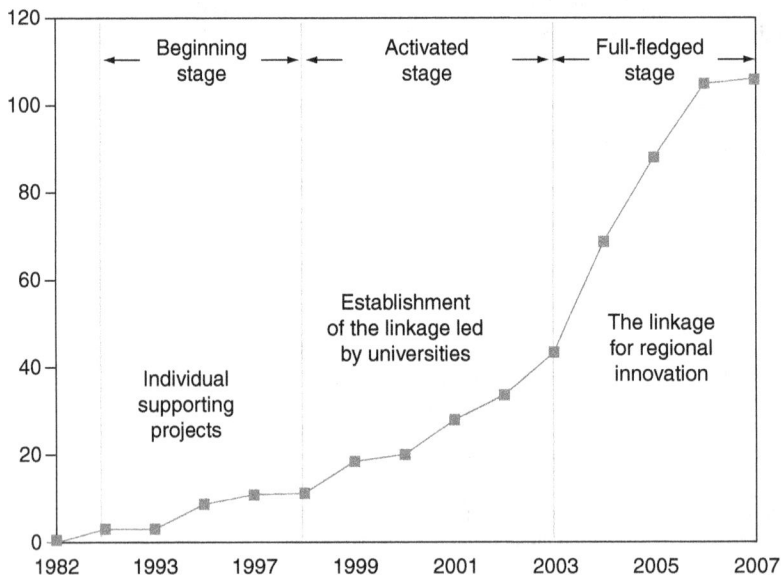

Figure 6.3 University–industry cooperation support projects by stages (unit: cases) (source: Lee and Koh 2007: 64).

There are many policies that can be categorized as system building, legal bases for government planning, job-oriented education programs, equipment and facility support, human resource exchanges, joint R&D and business operations, database building and sharing, business startups in universities, and specialized organizations for linkages. Various laws include many articles governing these categorized supporting functions.

The most interesting thing that can be observed in Table 6.5 is that most laws establish the legal base for government planning and support. With this base, the government can approach strategically, or with a roadmap to enhance linkages. Even though the market is the most important selection mechanism, there has been room for the government to steer the movement of the market. It might be controversial as to whether the plans or the strategies proved to be successful, but the strategic thinking and allocation of resources according to the strategies are better than intervention without any strategies.

3.2.2 Government policies

Based on the legal framework, the government has actively supported cooperation between universities and industries. Because the government has been convinced that cooperation is the most important factor for upgrading industries and maintaining competitiveness, it implemented comprehensive projects for enhancing linkage. The policy spectrum contained the major elements related with the linkages as follows:

- Human resource development;
- Technology development;
- Technology transfer;
- Technology support;
- Equipment sharing and infrastructure building.

The budget for university–industry cooperation in 2006 showed that technology development is key for cooperation. The total budget for technology development was 1,718.1 billion won in 2006. The next largest budget of 730.7 billion won was allocated to improve human resource development. As we can see in the budget allocation, actual cooperation between universities and industries comes from both technology development and educational areas.

The Ministry of Education, Science, and Technology has paid more attention to fostering the competency of universities' R&D capacities and education, while the Ministry of Knowledge Economy has implemented policies from industrial perspectives. Other ministries have implemented policies for their own goals.

As do most countries, Korea has many government agencies. The performance of the policies actually depends on the capacity and intent of the agencies. Many agencies have been established for a long time, and even though the names changed, the history of the agencies has lasted more than a decade on average.

Table 6.5 University–industry cooperation related legal framework

Classification	A	B	C	D	E	F	G	H	I	J
System building	2	24, 25–35			5, 11			8		
Legal base for government planning	10	4	3	4	4	6	3		4–5	
Job-oriented education program	12		7–9, 12, 14		6				6	
Equipment and facility support		11, 13, 18, 19		17, 23				18(4)		
Human resource exchange		9, 12(2)	21		8	10	11, 17, 19	16	8, 15	
Joint R&D and business operation		37		12, 13, 14, 15, 16	9	10	21	18(2)		5
DB building and sharing				21	7			16(2)	7	
Business start-ups in school			23				14	18(3)		
Specialized organization	22, 28	14, 25, 38	16, 18	5–10				23		

Source: Lee and Koh (2007, p. 23).

Notes
A Special Act for National Balanced Development
B Industrial Education and Industrial–Academic Cooperation Promotion Act
C Job Training Promotion Act
D Technology Transfer Promotion Act
E Joint R&D Promotion Act
F Act for Industrial Technology Infrastructure Building
G Act for Industrial Technology Complex Support
H Special Act for Venture Business Promotion
I Special Act for Small and Medium-sized Firms Manpower Support
J Act for Industrial Technology R&D Corporation Support
The number of the table indicates the article number of the law and the number inside parentheses indicates the number of sub-clauses of the article.

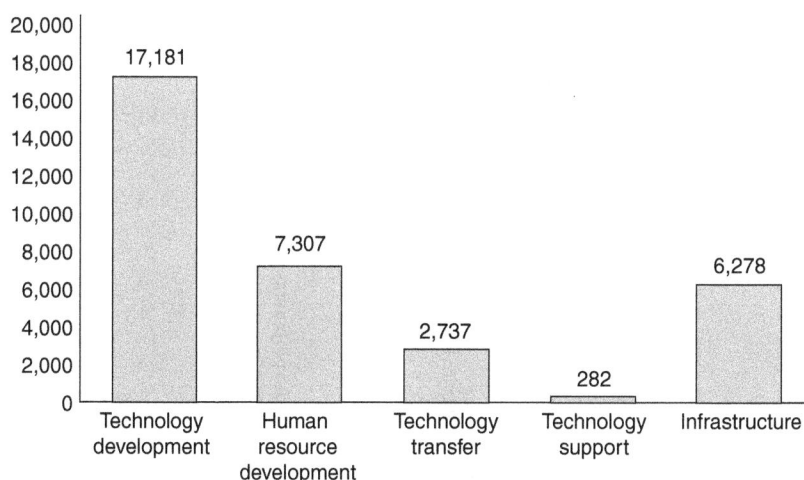

Figure 6.4 The budget for university–industry cooperation by types as of 2006 (unit: 0.1 billion won) (source: Lee and Koh 2007: 68).

Therefore, there have been systematic implementations for those policies. The Board of Audit and Inspection of Korea (BAI) has the comprehensive right to audit and inspect government agencies. In 2005, for example, BAI inspected the operation of support programs to universities. The government spent 5 trillion won every year (5.5 trillion won in 2003) on R&D and about 20 percent of the spending went to universities. There were a few cases of mishandling the research funds of professors, but in the inspection report, the Korea Research Foundation and the Korea Science and Engineering Foundation used a pool of 25,000 referees each, and the system turned out to be appropriate with stronger post-audits. This kind of regular audit and inspection of the agencies and the agencies' operation and practice has helped the agencies to improve their accountability and capacity for policy implementation.

Table 6.6 shows examples of industry and university linkage programs. The Ministry of Education, Science, and Technology spent a relatively larger amount of its budget for establishing linkage and making the linkage much stronger.

The Ministry also spent more on human resource development and capacity building of universities. The different aspects of the spending strategy were that even in human resource development programs, the programs should address the issues of the industry and university linkages. That is, the programs required universities to educate students in a way that their graduates meet the demand of industries. The Ministry of Knowledge Economy focuses more on technology development and technology transfer for industries. The large conglomerates have built up their independent R&D capacities. So the Ministry of Knowledge Economy addresses three issues: one is concerned with frontier pathfinding projects, which need the talents and gurus of universities; the second one is

Table 6.6 Government agencies and their linkage programs

(a) Programs related to the Ministry of Education, Science, and Technology

Institute	Program	Main support area	Budget 2006 (0.1 billlion Won/ 0.1 million USD)
Korea Research Foundation	Special purpose program	HRD	76.7
	BK21 (Research University)	HRD	2,900
	NURI (local university specialization)	HRD	2,600
	Connect Korea (TLO, patent search, tech. export etc.)	Technology transfer	287.7
Korea Research Institute for Vocational Education and Training	University–industry cooperation core college and HRD university program etc.	450	
Other	College and university specialization programs	HRD	2,300
Korean Science and Engineering Foundation	Specific R&D program	Technology development/equipment and infrastructure	2,366
	Basic science research program	Infrastructure	820
Korea Industrial Technology Association	University–Industry Cooperation Personnel Training Program	HRD	
Other	Science park development program etc.	Infrastructure	340

(b) Programs related to the Ministry of Knowledge Economy

Institute	Program	Main support area	Budget
Korea Institute of Industrial Technology Evaluation and Planning	Growth engine technology development program etc. (all programs are the type of consortium among universities, research institute, and firms)	Technology development	3,169
	University–industry cooperation linkage program etc.	Equipment and infrastructure	451
	Center for comprehensive electronic parts	Technology support	9
	Promotion of technology transfer and commercialization	Technology transfer	405
	Regional industry promotion program etc.	Technology development/technology support/ infrastructure	3,572
	Regional innovation industry base building program	Technology development transfer and commercialization/technology support/ infrastructure	515
	Techno park building program	Equipment and infrastructure	200
	Industrial complex innovation cluster program	Technology support (for providing solutions by networking)	462.5
	Regional Innovation Center	Equipment and infrastructure	480
	Regional Innovation System specialization program (RIS)	Technology development/technology support (supporting for more region-specific industries)	591
	Regional technology innovation program	Technology development/technology support/ equipment and infrastructure	335
Korea Industrial Technology Foundation	University–industry cooperation specialized university support program/etc.	Technology development/technology support/ HRD	848
	High valued industry human resource specialized development program etc.	HRD	217.5
	Region innovative human resource development program	HRD	240.8
	Regional innovation industry base building program (human resource development program)	HRD	10

continued

Table 6.6 continued

Korea Industrial Technology Association	Program for Search and Transfer of Technologies unused by universities and research institutes	Technology transfer	20
Korea Technology Transfer Center	TBI etc.	Technology transfer	
Institute for Information Technology Advancement	New Growth Engine Core Technology Development Program	Technology development	4,846
	Information and communication human resource development program	HRD	727.5
	Regional IT specialized research institute establishment and operation program	Infrastructure	65
	Business incubation center program	Infrastructure	
Korea SW Industry Promotion Agency	Information and communication human resource development program	HRD	149.4
	IT technology management specialists education program (KAIST) etc.	HRD	89.4
Small and Medium Business Administration	Industry University Research Institute Joint R&D projects	Technology development	426
	Industry–University Cooperation Office Support Program	Technology development/HRD	70
	Business Start-up Graduate School	HRD	100
	Support Program for Firm's Research Institute on Campus	Equipment and infrastructure	34
	Business Incubator Program	Equipment and Infrastructure	153
	Other programs		152

(c) Other ministries' programs

Ministry	Agency	Program	Main support area
Ministry of Maritime Affairs and Fisheries	Korea Institute of Marine Science and Technology Promotion	Marine-Bio 21 Program, etc.	Technology development
Ministry of Environment	Korea Institute of Environmental Science and Technology	Next Generation Core Environmental Technology Development Project etc.	Technology development
Ministry of Labor	Human Resource Development Service of Korea	Growth Engine Specialized University Support Program, etc.	HRD
Korean Intellectual Property Office	Korea Invention Promotion Association	Patent Commercialization Support program	Technology development transfer and commercialization/technology support
Ministry of Health, Welfare, and Family Affairs	Korea Health Industry Development Institute	Bio-Commercialization Technology Development Program, etc.	Technology development
Ministry of Agriculture and Food		Core Strategic Technology Development etc.	Technology development

Source: Author adapted the contents from Lee and Koh (2007: 69–71).

concerned with small and medium-sized firms; and the last one is concerned with regional development.

Regional development was politically popular issue. Since 2003, the government has had a comprehensive plan for regional development. The purpose of NURI21 was to enhance capacity building for local universities, for example. NURI21 was concerned with fostering educational capacity under the condition that universities restructure themselves by specializing in areas that regional industries demand. The Regional Industry Promotion Program, the Regional Innovation Industry Base Building Program, the Regional Innovation Center, the Regional Innovation System Specialization Program (RIS), the Regional Innovative Human Resource Development Program, and the Techno Park Program were implemented for regional development with the concepts of clusters and regional innovation systems.

There was even a massive investment in this area, but there is criticism about the efficiency of the investment. One of the success stories is the case of Yonsei University and the Wonju Medical Equipment Industry, which shows the possible application for other developing countries' regional development. The complete understanding of these policies has yet to come, and the regional development outcome is not yet obvious to everyone. Due to global competition, the regional economy cannot survive if the backup technology is not globally competitive.

4 The performance review of the model

4.1 SWOT review

4.1.1 Strengths

The government used industry and university linkage as a core hinge across a wide range of development strategies. In fact, private firms and market forces have been the major factors in the development of the Korean economy and industrial upgrade. Government policies were effective in several important ways when the Korean economy took on the responsibility of upgrading industries. The technologies that professors and researchers in public and private institutes jointly developed became globally competitive. However, Korea is experimenting with a new approach; the government is placing universities in the lead of the development process and opening the future. The most important strength is the fact that the Korean government recognizes the importance of the linkage.

Because of the economic success of the last 40 years, the Korean economy has begun to build strong pillars to support the knowledge economy. As Suh and Chen (2007: 9) showed, the results of knowledge assessment methodology (KAM) by the World Bank show that Korea's performance in terms of the basic scorecard of knowledge indicators is strong.

Table 6.7 shows R&D expenditure by types. Companies spend 76.9 percent of their total R&D expenditure and universities spend only 9.9 percent as of

Table 6.7 R&D expenditure by institutes (unit: 100 million won, %)

Type		1997	1998	1999	2000	2001	2002	2003	2004	2005
Total	Expenditure	121,858	113,366	19,218	138,485	161,105	173,251	190,687	221,853	41,554
	Ratio	100	100	100	100	100	100	100	100	100
	Growth	12	7	5.2	16.2	16.3	7.5	10.1	16.3	8.9
Public institutes	Expenditure	20,689	20,994	19,792	20,320	21,602	25,526	26,264	29,646	31,929
	Ratio	17	18.5	16.6	14.7	13.4	14.7	13.8	13.4	13.2
	Growth	9.1	1.5	−5.7	2.7	6.3	18.2	2.9	12.9	7.7
Universities	Expenditure	12,716	12,651	14,314	15,619	16,768	17,971	19,327	22,009	23,983
	Ratio	10.4	11.2	12	11.3	10.4	10.4	10.1	9.9	9.9
	Growth	24.8	0.5	13.1	9.1	7.4	7.2	7.5	13.9	9
Companies	Expenditure	88,453	79,721	85,112	102,547	122,736	129,754	145,097	170,198	185,642
	Ratio	72.6	70.3	71.4	74	76.2	74.9	76.1	76.7	76.9
	Growth	11.1	9.9	6.8	20.5	19.7	5.7	11.8	17.3	9.1

Source: Ministry of Education, Science, and Technology (http://english.mest.go.kr).

2005. This ratio has been stable for a long time. However, the absolute amount of R&D spent by universities has increased annually by 10.2 percent on average since 1997.

Universities generally have a high quality of researchers in various fields. Korea's R&D expenditure structure is led by private companies so that the number of researchers employed by companies is larger than that of researchers in universities. The growth rate of the number of researchers in universities is 4.5 percent on average since 1997. Considering research funds and the number of researchers, universities are a good source of innovation and research.

In addition to funds and researchers, universities have usually been indirectly related to the central government and local governments, and to industries. Therefore, it is not surprising that cooperation among government, industries, and universities is emphasized. Furthermore, through economic development, universities have played an important role by providing talented graduates and participating specific researchers. Therefore, the time has come to link universities and industries more systematically.

4.1.2 Weaknesses

The major weakness of linkage was the incentive mechanism of universities. In addition to the incentive mechanism, the competence of universities was in question. In globalization, the technology that companies need is the most updated one, but sometimes professors lag behind the trend because of academic tradition and the teaching load.

The competence of universities is very important because it can create trust and an innovation capacity, which are needed most in long-term relationships that lead to technology development. Even though universities have shown potential, the potential has not been realized to its full capacity. R&D expenditure is heavily concentrated on a group of exceptionally large companies, while other small and medium-sized companies have no resources to invest in R&D.

As for the concentration rate of the total industrial R&D expenditure in 2005, the top five companies took up 42 percent, the top ten companies used 48.4 percent, and those in the top 20 expended 55.6 percent. In terms of the number of researchers, the concentration rate of the top five companies was 30.6 percent. The data on the concentration of researchers by company type in 2005 showed that large corporations took up 59.3 percent with 91,514 researchers, small and medium-sized companies 19.8 percent with 30,619 researchers, and venture businesses 20.9 percent with 32,173 researchers.

This concentration created the problem that those who have the money and resources have less incentive to cooperate with universities, and those who need cooperation have no resources to invest money in cooperative projects with universities. This is one of the reasons that the government must address this issue.

R&D investments by region have been concentrated in specific regions, such as Daejeon, where the Korean government built the R&D cluster so that there

Table 6.8 The number of researchers by institute (unit: person, %)

Type		1997	1998	1999	2000	2001	2002	2003	2004	2005
Total	Researcher	138,438	129,767	134,568	159,973	178,937	189,888	198,171	209,979	234,702
	Ratio	100	100	100	100	100	100	100	100	100
	Growth rate	4.5	6.3	3.7	18.9	11.9	6.1	4.4	6	11.8
Public Institutes	Researcher	15,185	12,587	13,986	13,913	13,921	14,094	14,395	15,722	15,501
	Ratio	11	9.7	10.4	8.7	7.8	7.4	7.3	7.5	6.6
	Growth rate	−2.2	−17.1	11.1	−0.5	0.1	1.2	2.1	9.2	1.4
Universities	Researcher	48,588	51,162	50,151	51,727	53,717	57,634	59,746	59,957	64,895
	Ratio	35.1	39.4	37.3	32.3	30	30.4	30.1	28.5	27.6
	Growth rate	7.2	5.3	−2.0	3.1	3.8	7.3	3.7	0.4	8.2
Companies	Researcher	74,665	66,018	70,431	94,333	111,299	118,160	124,030	134,300	154,306
	Ratio	53.9	50.9	52.3	59	62.2	62.2	62.7	64	65.7
	Growth rate	4.9	−11.6	6.7	33.9	18	6.2	5.1	8.3	14.9

Source: Ministry of Education, Science, and Technology (http://english.mest.go.kr).

are many public research institutes in the region. Other than the Daejeon area, the Seoul and Gyeonggi provinces show much higher ratios than any other provinces. This concentration was pointed out as a barrier to developing regional economies other than the Seoul and Gyeonggi provinces. The debate was about nationally balanced development. The proponents argued that support to strengthen the innovative capacity of other regions was essential for regional

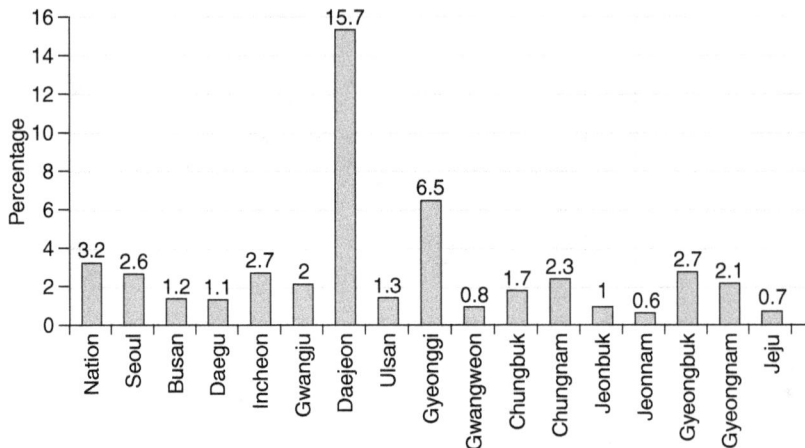

Figure 6.5 R&D per GRDP as of 2006 (source: the data are available from database in www.rsid.or.kr (http://renet.go.kr/index.do).

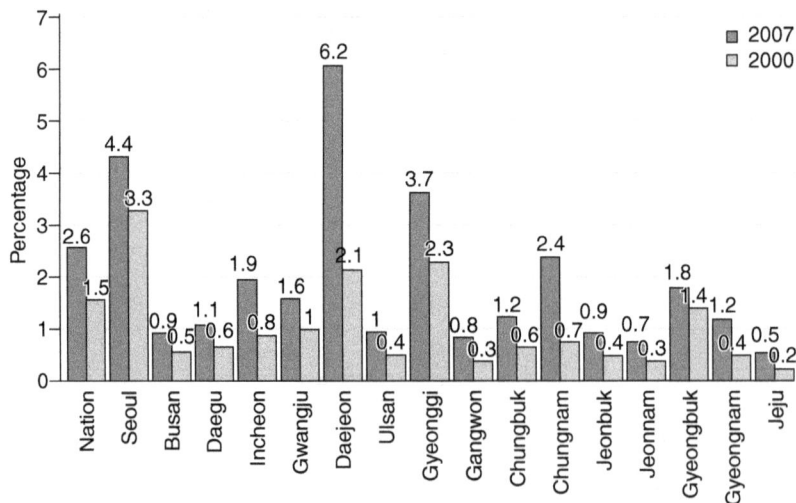

Figure 6.6 IPR per population by regions: comparison between as of 2007 and 2000 (source: the data are available from database in www.rsid.or.kr (http://renet. go.kr/index.do)).

development. Others complained that the emphasis on using regional innovators and universities would weaken developmental momentum because of the competition between the innovative capacity and the effectiveness of the support.

4.1.3 Opportunities

The ecosystem of technology development has been upgraded in the last two decades. In 1986, the government enacted two laws: one is the Small and Medium Business Start-ups Support Law, and the other one is the Financial Assistance to New Technology Business Law. Under these laws, venture capital can invest in small and medium business startups with new technologies. The government can also support those startups by using the Small Business Corporation's funds. The Small Business Corporation was established in 1979 as a government agency to implement policies for the promotion of small and medium-sized firms. Korean small and medium-sized manufacturers with high potential and knowledge-based businesses or venture firms can access financial loan packages.

Moreover, in 1996, the Korea Securities Dealers Association and securities companies established the KOSDAQ market. Before its establishment, venture capitalists had difficulty cashing out their investments. In 1999, the government eased the conditions of listing on the KOSDAQ market so that many lucrative firms such as telecommunication firms had opportunities to raise capital through KOSDAQ.

Capital markets opened new channels for venture capitals and startups. The number of venture firms has increased steadily even though there have been fluctuations due to stock market volatility. The number of venture firms was 2,042 in 1998, and increased to 11,392 in 2001. As the stock market plummeted in 2002, the number decreased to 8,778. However, the number was 15,008 in 2008. This increase was partly due to venture capitals including Kibo Technology Funds.

The most important source of capital has been from non-profit institutions initiated by the government. Kibo was founded in 1989 by the Korean government as a non-profit guarantee institution under the special enactment, the Financial Assistance to New Technology Businesses Act, which was revised and titled the Kibo Technology Fund Act in 2002. Kibo has contributed to the national economy by providing credit guarantees to facilitate financing for new technology-based enterprises while promoting the growth of technologically strong small and medium enterprises (SMEs) and venture businesses.

As Table 6.11 shows, the government contributed US$634 million, and other financial institutions contributed US$159 million as of January 2006. With this, Kibo Technology Funds provided US$11,599 to venture firms. Some 78.1 percent of venture firms received this guarantee and could borrow the operating capital from banks. Generally speaking, these government efforts and preferential treatments for venture business have created opportunities.

With a financial support system, Korea can have a sustaining and viable ecosystem of innovation. Technology development and the realization of its value

Table 6.9 The venture capital outstanding (unit: billion won, number)

Year	2000	2001	2002	2003	2004	2005	2006	2007	2008.6
Venture capital companies	147	145	128	117	105	102	104	101	100
(Paid-in capital)	2,139.1	2,219.4	1,965.1	1,865.1	1,652.8	1,536.8	1,553.7	1,555.8	1,571.4
Venture capital association (funds)	326	396	412	430	424	400	350	332	326
(Amount of funds)	2,463.4	3,051.2	3,269.8	3,578.7	3,817.2	3,936.4	3,833.6	3,947.9	3,991.8

Source: Small and Medium Business Association (2008: 78).

Table 6.10 Kibo technology fund's major services

Technology guarantee	Guarantees for monetary liabilities to financial institutions • Guarantees given to new technology businesses • Obligation to provide at least three-quarters of the total technology guarantees under the Kibo Act
	Guarantees given to innovation-leading SMEs • SMEs with excellent technologies, the nation's top 10 next generation growth engine industries, as well as six promising industries for future growth (6T) and knowledge-based service businesses
	Technology appraisal guarantees • Guarantees to qualified businesses through Technology Appraisal Certification System
Technology appraisal	Adoption and utilization of the Technology Appraisal Certification System • Future-centered value appraisal of businesses for loans, guarantees, and investment
	Technology Value Appraisal • Appraise intellectual properties • Evaluate collateral value of technology • Assess monetary value for technology transfer
	Feasibility Assessment of Technology • Certify venture enterprises • Select the beneficiaries of government project funds • Appraise technology for extending technology guarantees
	Comprehensive Technology Appraisal • Appraise corporate value for investment • Designate 'superior-technology' companies • Support venture businesses for KOSDAQ-listing
Technological and managerial advisory service	Business consultation • Help SMEs rationalize management • Facilitate technology development • Clear managerial and technological obstacles
	Support for company restructuring and technology transfer • Provide financial and legal advice for restructuring • Formulate business strategies for technology transfer • Provide match-making service between sellers and buyers
Management of guarantee defaults and claims	Investigation of debtor's properties Subrogation Payments Legal Procedure for Debt Collection

Source: Kibo Technology Funds (http://eng.kibo.or.kr/).

Table 6.11 Kibo technology funds' capital fund formation and its performance (unit: US$ million)

	2006.1	2005	2004	2003	2002
Guarantee outstanding (A)	11,599	11,244	12,941	13,981	13,764
Contributions	793	946	819	427	415
From the government	634	342	593	246	262
From the financial institutions	159	604	226	181	153
Capital funds (B)	1,172	788	756	872	1,318
Leverage ratio (A/B)	9.9	14.3	17.1	16	10.4

Source: Kibo Technology Funds (http://eng.kibo.or.kr).

have become routine for entrepreneurs. The linkages between universities and industries open new opportunities in the globally competitive business environment.

4.1.4 Threats

Even though linkages are important in developing economy and upgrading industries, they have been treated as auxiliary and even as unnecessary. The linkages have usually been weak and lacking in sustainability. The cash flows to venture business and R&D are not enough. Value creation requires a relatively longer time horizon and uncertainty is relatively high. University and industry linkage is faced with a new risk.

The previous linkage was rather weak and indirect. In the past, those firms who had specific R&D needs had to rely on outside resources such as public research institutes and universities. Now many private firms have the capacity to develop new technology. The previous approach of cooperation remains effective, but a new era needs a more aggressive approach that is much riskier in order to turn the tide. Venture business and R&D commercialization from universities are imminent issues, but due to global competition, the competitiveness of linkage and market conditions have become more important. The chance of success will sharply decrease unless there are enough supporting funds for these activities.

IBM (2007) claimed that Korean venture businesses were plunged into a death valley. That is, many venture business firms are experiencing difficulties financing sufficient working capital in a timely manner. Usually, venture capital tends to invest in those firms that last for three to seven years in business. As of 2005, only 20.9 percent of firms that had a venture capital investment had been in business less than three years. Venture capital does not invest in real venture firms. The number of invested firms is decreasing, while the amount of investment has increased because of global competition and the risk of failure.

Business cycles also affect venture capital and linkage activities. Industry and university linkage requires a longer horizon to see the results, but investment depends on the current economic situation. The worldwide financial crisis and

Table 6.12 Venture businesses' source of funds (unit: cases, %)

Source of funds	Venture capital	Technology appraisal guarantees	Technology appraisal loans	R&D firms	New technology support	Pre-venture business	Total
The number of firms	605	11,920	346	2,354	0	34	15,259
Ratio (%)	4.0	78.1	2.3	15.4	0	0.2	100.0

Source: Kibo Technology Funds (http://eng.kibo.or.kr).

economic depression will affect R&D activity and cooperation just when cooperation is needed most.

The government role to fill the gap between the intended investment and the necessary investment is very important. Kibo Technology Funds or other non-profit supporting funds are important, and their capital for the guarantee and lending for venture business firms has played a crucial role.

4.2 Linkage offices' capabilities

The most important government policy to promote cooperation between industries and universities is to establish and promote linkage offices. There are various types of linkage offices; linkage offices in joint organizations of government and the private sector such as Techno Park, in cluster promotion organizations, and university linkage offices. After the revision of the law, most universities established industry–university cooperation offices. In 2003, ten universities had a linkage office, and in 2004, 87.1 percent of 140 surveyed universities had established them as independent corporations according to the Korea Research Foundation (2008). The average size of the office staff was 16.9 in 2007, and among them, half of the staff were university staff members and the other half were independently hired for the linkage corporation. The staff in the largest office in the surveyed universities numbered 80 persons, and there were cases where only university staff worked for the linkage office and there were no other independent staff members.

The sources of revenue in university–industry cooperation offices are not diversified and the disparity of the revenues across universities is large. Compared to the survey results in 2006, the average of revenue has increased. The main source of revenue, however, is the overhead cost paid by public and government research projects. This means that the sustainability of the linkage is not strong, and the government role is still important.

The good news is that the revenue from industrial cooperation is increasing. The average revenue was 98.5 million won in 2005 and 175.2 million won in

Table 6.13 The revenue of industry–university cooperation offices as of 2007 (unit: million won)

Sources of revenue	Average	Minimum	Maximum
Technology transfer	151.6	0	6,595
Consulting	48.6	0	4,659
University firms	28.2	0	980
Business incubation	55.9	0	388
Education by commissioning	140.1	0	5,789
Other cooperation	68.1	0	799
Overhead cost for private research	341.2	0	9,079
Overhead cost for public research	1,155.9	2	12,991
Contribution	367.9	0	9,687

Source: Korea Research Foundation (2008: 41).

2006, and it increased to 492.5 million won in 2007. There are a few universities that created value added beyond expectation, but on average there are many universities that cannot cover their cost considering the average revenue and average number of staff. Generally speaking, the system and the performance of the office improved. Success will depend on the universities' ability to cooperate with industries, and on R&D and technology development capacity.

4.3 Competency improvement of the university

It is a core issue to build up competency and to change the orientation to more cooperation with industries. Academic abilities such as academic publications are actually linked with the capability for industrial cooperation. However, orientation is also an important factor because it requires time and effort to apply R&D results and science knowledge to a specific application for industrial needs.

According to IMD's 2006 *World Competitiveness Yearbook*, Korea's ranking in terms of university education was fiftieth, which was lower than Turkey and Japan (forty-ninth). University competency is important, because only excellent research will be commercialized and be an engine of economic growth.

Recognizing the importance of universities' capacity, the government supported many programs to improve the competitiveness of universities. For example, the purpose of the Brain Korea 21 program is to nurture world-class research universities. During the period from 1999 to 2005, the program of the first phase benefited 89,366 researchers and 20,000 graduate students. In 1998, the number of articles published in SCI journals was 9,444, and increased to 23,515 in 2005. Of the articles published in SCI journals, 34 percent were funded by the Brain Korea 21 program.

The second phase, from 2006 to 2012, will spend 2.3 trillion won. By 2012, ten research-oriented universities with global competitiveness will be established, and Korea will become one of the ten most advanced countries in the world in knowledge transfer from universities to industries (Korea ranked twenty-first in 2005, according to IMD). In 2006 alone, the program participants submitted 3,709 domestic patent applications and 845 international patent applications. There are other programs such as NURI and World Class University that focus on the improvement of university competitiveness.

4.4 Technology transfer

To promote technology transfers, there have been various policies. Since 2006, the purpose of the Connect Korea program has been to support technology liaison offices (TLO). The concept of the program is to establish Core TLO as a consortium of TLOs for universities in the region. Eighteen universities are selected as core TLO center universities in the four regions. This program aims to provide opportunities for connecting technology providers and technology demanders: networks of researchers in the universities, venture capitalists and

Table 6.14 The patent registration as of 2007

Ranking	Industry	Patent	Ranking	University	Domestic	International
1	Samsung Electronics Co., Ltd.	11,033	1	KAIST	1,780	558
2	LG Electronics	7,871	2	Seoul National University	1,430	110
3	Samsung SDI	3,916	3	Yonsei University	1,103	266
4	Hynix Semiconductor	2,558	4	Korea University	914	60
5	Hyundai Motor Company	1,847	5	Postech	866	170
6	Dongbu Electronics	1,706	6	Hanyang University	704	26
7	Posco	1,671	7	Inha University	59	15
8	Samsung Electro-Mechanics	1,372	8	GIST	488	74
9	SK Telecom	1,248	9	Sungkyunkwan University	427	22
10	Daewoo Electronics	1,184	10	Pusan National University	403	16

Source: KRF (2008: 149) for university patent holdings, and Korean Intellectual Patent Office homepage (www.kipo.go.kr/en).

firms, local government officials, and business service providers. From this program, the government expects to build an ethical cycle: technology development, transfer, and investment for R&D. This program is similar to UCSD's CONNECT in the United States. In 1985, UCSD established a TLO (called CONNECT). Some 900 technologies have been commercialized, and US$1.1 billion was invested. Recognizing this successful performance of a TLO, the government supported TLOs by 3 billion won in 2006 and will support them with 7.5 billion won per year for the next five years.

The implementation of Connect Korea is as follows. First, the government will select core TLOs by enlisting the help of local governments in selecting the core university. By evaluating regional R&D capabilities, regional industrial structures, the distribution of technology demanders, and so forth, the government will select and establish the consortiums with the help of a core university in forming consortiums with other neighboring universities. The major tasks are as follows:

- Building DB for their technologies, and patent information;
- Establishing nationwide innovative networks;
- Developing nationwide technology search engines;
- Implementing evaluations on the technology level, marketability, and so forth.

From these activities, the government expects that universities will have the incentive to do more technological development and to find opportunities for commercialization and transferring of technology more actively. This program will strengthen the connectivity of the regional innovation system so that it will contribute to regional industrial development.

The performance of technology transfer is remarkable. In 2003, technology transfer contracts numbered 210, and increased to 951 in 2007. The revenue from the transfers was about 2.0 billion won, and increased to 16.4 billion won.

4.5 Human resource development with industrial cooperation

One of the issues in upgrading industrial clusters is how to improve the quality of workforces in regional industrial complexes. The industrial cooperation core

Table 6.15 Technology transfer and commercialization

Classification		2003	2004	2005	2006	2007	Total
Number of contracts	Cases	210	243	587	563	951	2,554
	Changes (%)	–	15.7	141.6	–4.1	66.9	–
Revenue from transfer	Revenue (mil. won)	1,973	3,184	6,323	9,033	16,415	36,928
	Changes (%)	–	61.4	98.6	42.9	81.7	–

Source: KRF (2008: 222).

college and university program addressed this issue. The program provided policy packages in order to promote linkages between industries and universities as well as developing human resources. Basically, two ministries provided the budget for this purpose. Table 6.16 shows the budget allocation for the last five years.

The target schools are eight universities and five industry colleges. The support areas are (1) joint R&D with local firms and consulting, technology transfer, and R&D centers tailored to local firms; (2) equipment-sharing programs that support equipment sharing with local firms and provide the equipment and facility for training employees of local firms and students of vocational schools; (3) changing the university operation system for industrial cooperation, including changing the incentive mechanisms for professor recruiting and performance evaluation; (4) human resource development for meeting the demands of local firms and local industries that include educational programs for the employees of local industries, seminars, and conferences.

The performance of the program for the last three years was evaluated as satisfactory. The specialized curriculum trained 50,108 persons and the tailored department's enrollment was 1,604 students. The university employees trained on commission was 4,603 persons. The number of technology transfers was 237, and the number of consultations was 10,105. The number of patent applications was 756, and the cases of equipment sharing were 38,717. The numbers showed the increasing tendencies.

4.6 The case of Yonsei University and the Wonju Medical Equipment Industry

The Wonju Medical Equipment Industry has developed as a result of cooperation among the university and central and local governments, and it is one of the successful stories of the government policy. It started from the efforts of the Biomedical Engineering faculty, Yonsei University Wonju Campus. The Biomedical Engineering faculty applied for the Techno Park project of the Ministry of Commerce and Trade in 1997, but it failed to receive the support. In 1998, the Wonju city government helped to establish a university incubator for medical electronics. The incubator started on very small scale, which was only $660\,m^2$; 11 firms moved into the incubator. Those firms' technologies originated with the professors of the Department of Biomedical Engineering; they began to produce

Table 6.16 Financial support for industrial cooperation core college and university program (unit: billion won)

Classification	2004	2005	2006	2007	2008	Total
Ministry of Knowledge Economy	20	22	22	20	23.5	107.5
Ministry of Education, Science, and Technology	20	22	22	22	22	108.0
Total	40	44	44	42	45.5	215.5

test products in 1999, and displayed their products at Korea International Medical and Hotel Equipment (KIMES). These activities enabled Yonsei University Wonju Campus to be designated as a Technology Innovation Center (TIC) by the Ministry of Commerce, Industry, and Energy. Wonju city provided a factory site in the industrial complex, and those firms from the incubator had a production system for their products.

In 1999, the Ministry of Education, Science, and Technology recognized the Research Institute for Medical Instruments (now the Institute of Medical Engineering, Yonsei University) as a Regional Research Center (now changed to Regional Innovation Center, RIC). The purpose of the RIC program was to transfer university technologies to the industries the region specialized in.

The Small and Medium Business Administration supported the incubator for medical instruments of Yonsei University. The university had three elements for medical industry development, which are the R&D support function (RRC), business incubator (TIC and Incubator center), and production function (industrial complex provided by the local government).

In 2000, Yonsei University Wonju Campus was designated a Venture Business Cultivation Promotion Region by the Small and Medium Business Administration. Wonju City and Yonsei University Wonju Campus made efforts to build the Wonju Medical Electronic Industry Promotion Center into which the Medical Measurement and Rehabilitation Engineering Research Center and the Advanced Medical Appliance Technology Innovation Center and other supporting facilities could move. Yonsei University provided the land, and Wonju City and the central government provided 7 billion won for the construction. The construction of the center began in 2000 and finished in 2002. Since 2003, the government has supported the Wonju Medical Equipment Industry in various ways.

In 2003, the Wonju Medical Equipment Industry Techno Valley was founded and was to support R&D, operate the facilities, and promote the Wonju Medical Equipment Industry by educating and advertising. In 2004, Wonju received Innovative Cluster Promotion Support.

In 2004, Yonsei University Wonju Campus received NURI, a program supporting medical appliance engineering education for five years, and it received BK21 in 2006. With these supports, Yonsei University Wonju Campus became a hub for supplying technology, education, and necessary consultation to the Wonju Medical Equipment Industry.

Yonsei University Wonju Campus received Regional Innovation Center Support (RIC) for nine years from 1999 to 2008 (Wonju campus received RRC and TIC, but RRC and TIC were merged into RIC). The total fund was 8.5 billion won. The first step was to develop the basic technologies that firms needed most. That period was from 1999 to 2002. Most Wonju medical firms were small and did not have enough capital to catch up to the advanced technology in the current market. In the period from 2003 to 2005, after the university succeeded in providing technologies, it provided a core technology for global competition, and since 2005, the technology has been commercialized. With the support of RIC, Yonsei Universities incubated 11 firms and conducted 40 research projects. The joint R&Ds with firms succeeded in commercialization. For example, the joint R&D with Mediana produced the items and sold 17 billion won worth of products in 2007 alone. The joint R&D with HumanTech was successfully commercialized and earned 4.8 billion won from 1999 to 2007. In total, nine joint R&Ds were commercialized, and many others are to be commercialized. During the period 1999–2008, 24 R&D results were submitted for patents, and 17 were registered as patents; nine items registered as utilities; and 57 university technologies were transferred to firms.

Table 6.17 shows the number of firms and their performance. Before Yonsei University Wonju Campus made an effort to develop a medical industry in Wonju city, no one recognized the existence of the medical industry in Wonju. It started with 11 venture firms in incubators, and now Wonju medical cluster has 74 firms and employs 1,729 persons. Still, compared to large companies' employment and sales scales, those of Wonju are relatively small, but the efforts showed a so-called can-do spirit and the possibilities for developing regional economies with universities' efforts.

It is very difficult to judge which factor is the most important, because the case of Wonju enjoyed comprehensive support. Every source of support was identified through selection procedures based on evaluation and competition. However, success depends not only on support but also on entrepreneurship. Professors were not sitting on the R&D money; instead they struggled to survive and succeed. The decade-long struggle of the transition from nothing to something was key to the successful story. We can say that the seed was self-generated entrepreneurship, and that it prospered with the help of local and central governments.

5 Conclusion

Behind the remarkable economic growth, there have been many talented people from universities, but universities have been behind the scenes until recently. Samsung Electronics alone has more patents than several major universities have combined. Basically, Korea has a private sector leading the ecosystem of technology development, which is gaining its self-sustaining momentum. Now that Korea has entered into a new phase of development in the globalized world economy, Korea needs more innovative people who think creatively. We do hope that universities can handle this challenge. Korea is experimenting with the transformation of universities so they can be more directly involved in the innovation and technology development process.

On the basis of Korean experiences, three propositions can be presented as follows:

- Proposition 1: There is no easy way to jump from low technology to high technology;
- Proposition 2: There is always a gap between business needs and professors' incentives;

Table 6.17 Firms and products in Wonju cluster pilot complex

	The number of firms	Amount				New products		Employment
		Total amount	Domestic	Export	Ratio	2005	2006	
Wonju	65	153,631	69,861	83,770	43	29	74	994
Hongcheon	5	182,148	32,042	150,106	51	2	6	536
Heongseong	1	15,911	15,911	2,075	4.4			168
Chuncheon	3	5,621	2,588	3,033	1.6			31
Total	74	357,311	106,566	250,745	100			1,729

- Proposition 3: The success of projects depends on how they are implemented, and successful implementation depends on thorough evaluations, and the comprehensiveness and the duration of support.

The policies to promote industry and university cooperation should be comprehensive. Otherwise the effectiveness of the policies will be diminished. Proposition 1 suggests that the policy horizon should be long, and the strategies should be prepared according to the current situation by step-by-step approaches. For the regional development of Wonju by using linkage, it took a decade to glimpse the successful performance and share the results, even in the successful cases.

Proposition 2 explains why the Korean government relied on government-funded research institutes rather than universities when they implemented industry support policies. However, this does not suggest that university and industry cooperation is not important. Rather, it suggests that it is a difficult task to build up linkages and to promote collaboration and that there should be different strategies according to the development stage of the ecosystem.

The recent data, however, shows an optimistic sign of change. Some professors successfully became CEOs of their own venture firms, which produced world-first products. A decade-long relationship with firms helped universities to produce competitive technologies ready for commercialization. Some doctors in university hospitals established venture firms with their technology. The atmosphere of the ecosystem has changed because of the success stories.

Still, universities and industrial linkages in the ecosystem of technology development are exogenous and not sustainable unless the government supports linkages. Therefore, proposition 3 remains important because it reminds us of the importance of implementation. The government agencies' capacity is key for efficient implementation. International cooperation as well as full usage of domestic resources will be helpful for evaluation and assessment.

I would like to reiterate the importance of the ecosystem of the NIS. Entrepreneurship is a necessary condition for a successful system, but it is dependent on social and legal institutions. It is also important to point out that government funding is not a sufficient factor for success and that it should be considered as auxiliary support. One of the reforms made in Korea is that the revised law allows universities to run technology holding companies. There should be a channel for venture firms to be listed in a stock market like KOSDAQ.

Building a self-sustaining ecosystem of innovation is a difficult task. The system led by the private sector may lack long-term vision. In this respect, the government is expected to provide longer-term R&D investments, such as R&D expenditures on basic science, and investment in future industrial transition. Therefore, the system should consist of many different institutes and institutions which are incentive compatible and are fully synergetic.

Note

1 This is a revised version of chapter 3 of the report 'Science and Industry Linkages: Partnership between University & Business – The case of Wonju Medical Device Cluster' as a part of the research project on 'Developing National Technology and Innovation Capacity: Lessons from Korea and Application to Turkey,' with KDI, and the paper presented at the 2009 KEA-KIEA-GRI International Conference.

Bibliography

Booz Allen & Hamilton (1997) *Korea Report*, Seoul: Maeil Economic Newspaper.

Choi, Youngrak (2003) *Evolution of Science and Technology Policy in Korea*, Seoul: STEPI (Science and Technology Policy Institute).

Dasgupta, P. and David, P. (1994) 'Toward a New Economics of Science,' *Research Policy*, 23, 5: 487–521.

ETRI (2007) *ETRI 30 Years, IT Korea 30 Years*, Seoul: ETRI.

Fransman, Martin (1994) 'The Japanese Innovation System: How Does it Work?' in Mark Dodgson and Roy Rothwell (eds.) *The Handbook of Industrial Innovation*, Northampton: Edward Elgar.

Hong, Seoung-min and Kim, Gap-su (2006) *The Comparison of University Venture Firms in Korea, Japan, and China, Korea Industry Technology Foundation*, Seoul: KOTEF.

IBM (2007) *Korea Report 2007*, Seoul: Korea Herald.

IMD (2006) *IMD World Competitiveness Yearbook*, Lausanne: IMD.

Korea Institute of Intellectual Property (2008) *Report on Technology Commercialization Measurement*, Seoul: Korea Technology Transfer Center.

Korea Research Foundation (2007) *White Paper on the Industry and University Cooperation*, Seoul: Korea Research Foundation.

Korea Research Foundation (2008) *White Paper on the Industry and University Cooperation*, Seoul: Korea Research Foundation.

Krugman, Paul R. (1994) 'The Myth of Asia's Miracle,' *Foreign Affairs*, 73: 62–78.

Kwon, Jene (1994) 'The East Asia Challenge to Neoclassical Orthodoxy,' *World Development*, 22, 4: 635–44.

Lee, J. and Koh, S.J. (2007) *Study on the Policy Measurement for Promoting the Industry and University Cooperation*, Seoul: KITF.

List, F. (1845) *Das Nationale System der Politischen Oekonomie*, trans. G.A. Matile (1856) *National system of Political Economy*, Philadelphia: J.B. Lippincott & Co.

Ministry of Education, Science, and Technology (2008) News Briefing, unpublished news briefing.

Pavitt, Keith (1984) 'Sectoral Patterns of Technical Change: Towards a Taxonomy and a Theory,' *Research Policy*, 13, 6: 343–73.

Pavitt, Keith (1994) 'Key Characteristics of Large Innovation Firms,' in Mark Dodgson and Roy Rothwell (eds.) *The Handbook of Industrial Innovation*, Northampton: Edward Elgar.

Porter, M.E., Takeuchi, H., and Sakibara, M. (2000) *Can Japan Compete?* Basingstoke: Macmillan.

Rosenberg, N. (1992) 'Scientific Instrumentation and University Research,' *Research Policy*, 21: 381–90.

Small and Medium Business Administration (2008) *Annual Report on Small and Medium Business*, Seoul: Small and Medium Business Administration.

Steinmueller, W. Edward (1994) 'Basic Research and Industrial Innovation,' in Mark Dodgson and Roy Rothwell (eds.) *The Handbook of Industrial Innovation*, Northampton: Edward Elgar.

Suh, Joonghae and Chen, Dereck H.C. (2007) *Korea as a Knowledge Economy: Evolutionary Process and Lessons Learned*, Korea Development Institute and World Bank Institute, WBI Development Studies, Washington, DC: The World Bank.

Yang, Joon-Mo, Kim, Tae-Wan, and Han, Hyun-Ok (2006) 'Understanding the Economic Development of Korea from a Co-evolutionary Perspective,' *Journal of Asian Economics*, 17: 601–21.

7 Institutions and industrial policy

The case of heavy-chemical industries
in Korea (1973–9)

Sung Sup Rhee

1 Introduction

Industrial policies have long been a contentious issue among economists. Although the debate has been revived on and off since the time of Friedrich List (1827), it still remains unresolved. Pros and cons are wrangled through restless debates, but no new theoretical dimension has been proposed to bring together opposite camps into an integrated theoretical framework (Chang 2009; Thurow 1993; Yoo *et al.* 1995).

This chapter intends to propose institutions as a dependent variable in the theoretical structure as a new dimension by which to embrace both sides of the debate. In this study, the long-run model is proposed to include institutions as a new endogenous element of the variables to explain the progress of economic development. At the same time, the short-run view of economy is proposed to explain the validity of the argument for the government's role in economic policy implementation. In the theoretical structure in which institutions become a strategic variable, the government's control of policy science begins to impact economic development.

In the long-run model of institutions, the role of government does not exist. Institutional change follows an evolutionary process (Ostrom 1990; Rhee 2007). However, once institutions become embedded in the analytical structure, they offer a niche in which to lay the groundwork for introducing the strategic factor of policy governance by the strategic means of institutional change. Of course, the ultimate impetus should come from entrepreneurship or policy innovation in the public sector, which should be supported by political motivation. However, this does not pertain to the topic of a rational choice model. Section 2 of this chapter unveils an institutionalist model of economic development, the salient contribution of which is to identify institutions as a dependent variable which contributes directly to economic growth. In Section 3, a new mechanism of public choice is introduced, which offers room for the intervention of public policy, which has an authentic impact on investment decisions. Section 4 introduces the summing up of the master plan of the Heavy-Chemical Industrial Promotion Policy (HCIPP for short). In Section 5, the importance of innovative attributes and public or political entrepreneurship is underscored in the presentation of a character classification and chronicle of the HCIPP implementation steps. In Section 6, the HCIPP performances are assessed. In Section 7, the case of financial market policies is introduced as an example that highlights the significance of the relationship between economic development and policy intervention. Section 8 summarizes and concludes the chapter.

2 An institutionalist model of economic development

It is embarrassing to acknowledge that the market, a central concept of economics, is only loosely conceptualized in the sense that the role of institutions is not well recognized or positioned in the analytical structure of orthodox economics.

The market should be defined by its underpinning institutions. In particular, the conceptual configuration of a property right is defined and determined by a range of related institutions. What is idiosyncratic in this connection is that institutions are imperfect in their ability to protect property rights. It is particularly true in the case of business models that introduce new categories of business enterprise that depend on multiple properties, or in the case of innovative concepts of business that combine new categories of properties. Frequently, legal disputes arise prompted by conflicts of interest, which become complicated among stakeholders. Industrial policy addresses the problem of businesses that deal with industrial activities in newly introduced categories of industry.

The clarity of legal rights becomes blurred by the interruption of opportunistic behavior: holdouts, moral hazards, and so on. Sometimes, relational contracts, like the establishment of a good neighborhood, are an effective instrument for the protection of property rights. An introduction of new legislation may change the legal environment, which impacts the property rights relationship. Political climate affects the direction of legislation. The imperfection of institutions offers room for opportunities for long-run economic development and short-run policy intervention of the government at the same time. The recursive process of the evolutionary development of institutions establishes renewed institutional environments, which facilitate the introduction of new business models. Such a cycle of interaction between business models and institutional development presents a recursive institutional model of economic development.

In the short run, the imperfection of institutions presents a chance to invite public intervention for creating institutional changes through the political process of legal legislation, or allows the executive administration to implement public policies.

Figure 7.1 reveals that economic growth does not merely give rise to the accumulation of capital and technology, but also operates to attain institutional development. Through the repeated use of market institutions, economic growth catalyzes the development of social institutions, which extends and deepens operational fields of market activities. Hence, the development of market institutions follows.

For instance, in the early 1960s when export businesses were new, they were not familiar to administrative public authorities, such as banks (credit rationing

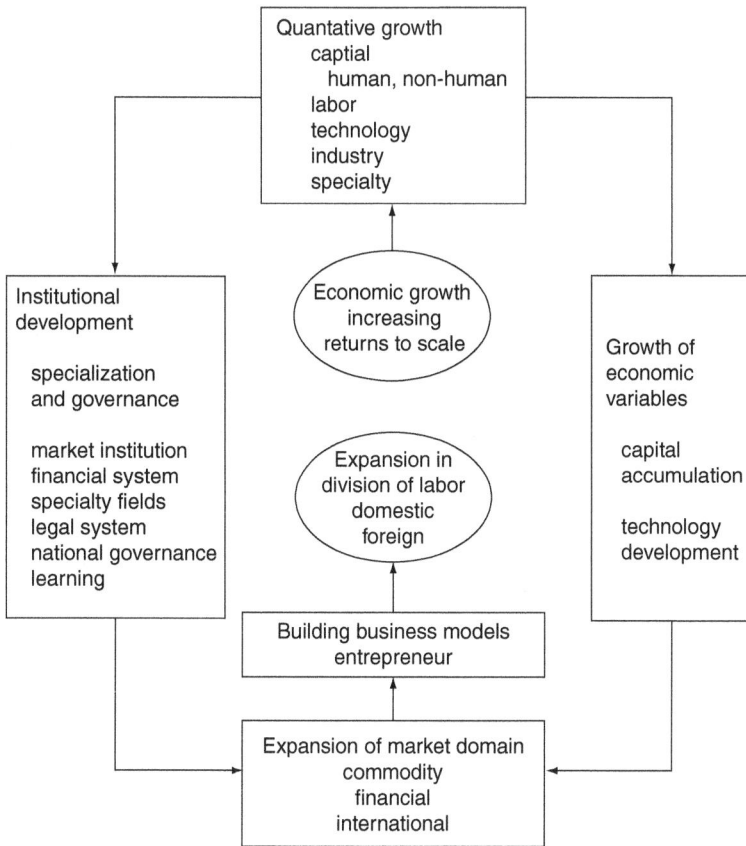

Figure 7.1 An institutionalist model of economic development.

helped build powerful authority), customs offices, or the Ministry of Commerce and Industry (it had the authority to grant permission to import). Authoritative institutions' administrative procedures for exports often involved, by intention or not, slow and painful permission processes, which sometimes required sitting for a license examination. However, as export volume expanded, administration became routine work and achieved progress in procedural steps. Now, administrative procedures for exporting businesses tend to be more rational and efficient.

In this way, economic growth induced institutional development. So, in the next period of Korean history, the same economic activities were conducted in a more developed environment of market institutions. In the fulfillment of economic activities for the same purpose, the choice of more advantageous business models became available. Therefore, exchange activities became lively, and the division of labor expanded. Such vigorous exchange activities spurred a new cycle of economic growth.

The cycle of capital accumulation, technological progress, and institutional development began a new recursive development process. This is the story disclosed in Figure 7.1. Taking such institutional elements into consideration, each economy situated in respectively different stages of development, even though dealing with the same items of goods, produces those items in differentiated environments with regard to institutional development, capital accumulation, or technological stock. Respectively, different environmental conditions facing the same commodities production but located in different stages of development, which is depicted in Figure 7.2, precisely confirms the story of Figure 7.1.

3   Government initative for cost retrenchment

Figure 7.3 breaks up the unit costs of investment into three components: (1) transaction costs for consent-making among stakeholders, (2) transaction costs due to underdeveloped market institutions, and (3) interest costs of capital. The sum of the two transaction costs (1) and (2) is denoted *OC*.

The point is that the size of the OC differs substantially in accordance with the modal difference of legal institutions, which is determined by the direction

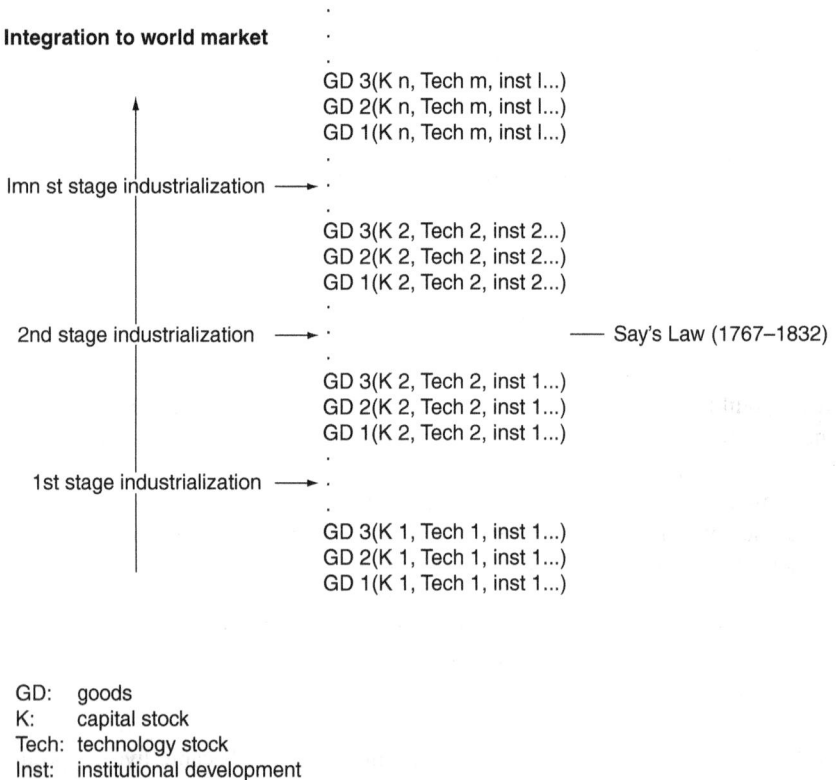

Integration to world market

GD 3(K n, Tech m, inst I...)
GD 2(K n, Tech m, inst I...)
GD 1(K n, Tech m, inst I...)

Imn st stage industrialization ⟶

GD 3(K 2, Tech 2, inst 2...)
GD 2(K 2, Tech 2, inst 2...)
GD 1(K 2, Tech 2, inst 2...)

2nd stage industrialization ⟶ ⎯⎯ Say's Law (1767–1832)

GD 3(K 2, Tech 2, inst 1...)
GD 2(K 2, Tech 2, inst 1...)
GD 1(K 2, Tech 2, inst 1...)

1st stage industrialization ⟶

GD 3(K 1, Tech 1, inst 1...)
GD 2(K 1, Tech 1, inst 1...)
GD 1(K 1, Tech 1, inst 1...)

GD: goods
K: capital stock
Tech: technology stock
Inst: institutional development

Figure 7.2 Stages approach to industrialization.

Expected profit rate
of individual project

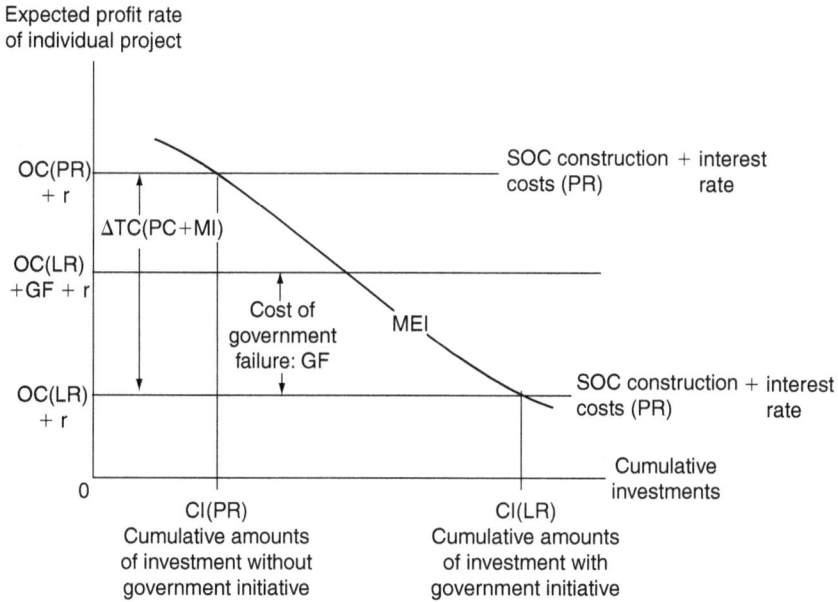

Figure 7.3 Retrenchment of SOC construction costs by government initiative and investment stirring-up.

MEI:	marginal efficiency of investments
PR:	property rule
LR:	liability rule
r:	interest rate
TC:	transaction cost
GF:	governmnet failure
CI:	cumulative investments
OC:	PC+MI
PC:	transaction cost (difficulty of consent-making among stake holders)
MI	transaction cost (underdeveloped market institutions)
ΔTC(PC + MI):	incremental transaction cost (difficulty of consent-making among stake holders + underdeveloped market institutions)

of government policy. In developing countries, as contrasted with developed countries, undeveloped market institutions magnify the transaction cost components (1) as well as (2), which raise the size of the OC as well. Due to the underdevelopment of market institutions, corruption grows out of the absence of advanced institutions or the inefficiency of public administration and adds to the difficulty of consent making among stakeholders so as to possibly give rise to tremendous SOC construction costs.

As a nation moves toward industrialization, market institutions improve so that the inefficiency of public administration or corruption costs drops, though consent-making costs remain resilient. On the contrary, individuals' enhanced consciousness of private property rights may incur treacherous holdout costs to the consent-making procedure. Despite just compensation being presumed, the treatment mode of legal liability, when administering public-taking measures, changes transaction cost (1) significantly.

In the event that the jurisprudence chooses to place priority on the property rights of stakeholders among alternative jurisprudential modes of legal liability patterns when public use must be made of stakeholders' private properties for the fulfillment of industrialization projects, such as property rule (PR), property owners' unyielding stand on claims of rights or opportunistic behavior may make arbitration and settlement more arduous, which is indicated by the OC (PR) in Figure 7.3.

However, if jurisprudential priority is placed on the public authority's right to exercise public taking, such as liability rule (LR), stakeholders' persistence or opportunistic behavior will surely be blockaded so that arbitration and settlement costs drop, which is indicated by the OC (LR) in Figure 7.3.

Of course, just compensation is presumed in either case. In other words, the difference comes not from a lack of compensational justice, but from a difference between the negotiation stands of the respective parties, public authority versus private property owners, under different jurisprudential modes. In general, the differential between the OC (LR) and the OC (PR) is substantially large.

If industrialization is pursued by government initiative, the parties promoting public projects will possibly be at an advantage in the choice of jurisprudential rule among alternative modes. The change from PR rule to LR rule sharply reduces conflict settlement costs among stakeholders – in other words, reduces transaction costs.

In a case involving government initiative compared to a case not involving government initiative, the amounts of investment surely reveal a striking difference.

Of course, such an outcome presumes a condition – that the government will succeed in public decisions in the direction of industrialization policy measures. However, this is a strong presumption. It indicates the extent of the difficulty in conditional fulfillment. More often than not, government initiatives accompany frequent failures in policy decisions because of the inefficiency of public services or corruption due to incompetence in public administration.

4 Implementation programs of HCIPP

The main contents of the HCIPP master plan may be summarized as the following five items.[1]

1   Leading sectors of the heavy-chemical industry, which would be intensively fostered, were selected. Iron and steel, nonferrous metal, ship building, machine tools, electronics, and chemicals were selected as leading industrial sectors.

2   The goal of the promotion policy for selected industries was to build international competitiveness. Despite the unprecedented venture of business into

heavy-chemical industries, this plan is distinctive in that the export of products was targeted from the beginning. To pursue the objective, a large-scale production system was pursued to achieve economies of scale. With respect to technology, the upgrading of the industrial structure to a technology-intensive composition was pursued.

3 Policies directed to increase technical manpower were pursued as a national program. An industrial high school system was introduced to produce technical manpower through a regular education program. Additional registration quotas were granted to the science and engineering departments of universities. Educational curricula were remodeled from a focus on theoretical education to practical hands-on education. Programs of practical technology-priority policies were pursued: reinforcement of vocational education institutions, establishment of technical proficiency certification schools, establishment of a technician proficiency certificate system, socially preferential treatment of engineers and technicians, and the active participation in the International Vocational Training Competition.

Also, nationwide science-technology enhancement movements were pursued, such as the establishment of the government's sponsoring of research institutes and the construction of the Daeduk Research Estate, promoting science-technology development in private research institutes.

4 Integrated national land development plans were established in accordance with industrial sites to be constructed. Heavy-chemical industry is a large-scale plant industry, which requires spacious land and has far-reaching forward and backward linkage effects. Thus, it is efficient to concentrate the location of related plants into a single site and then transform it into an industrial complex. The geomorphologic regions, which meet tough conditions of location pertinent to heavy-chemical industries, are likely limited to a few places in the entire country. Therefore, the choice of industrial sites should be preceded by the ordinance of integrated national land development plans.

The development of large-scale industrial sites requires not only land development, but also the provision of SOCs, such as roads, ports, industrial water, and electricity. In addition, the location of schools, research institutes, office of public administration, banks, hospitals, and other public service institutes should be taken into consideration. Dormitory towns, which provide residents' housing facilities, should be constructed. A heavy-chemical industrial site plan is the backbone of the HCIPP. Figure 7.4[2] discloses the shape of the industrial site construction plan of the HCIPP.

5 The total government promotion system was prepared with respect to financial resources, tax incentives, and public administration. Investment financing was the biggest obstacle for the HCIPP. A scheme to settle this financing problem was a joint venture with foreign investors, mostly at an advised joint ratio of $50:50$, from which source foreign capital as well as technology was to be drawn out. In the event that domestic financial resources were not able to be supplied from the firm's internal resources, long-term, low-interest-rate policy financing funds, such as the industry rationalization fund, were built up. The National

Industrial site plan

First chemical industrial site expansion	→	Ulsan
Second chemical industrial site	→	Yeosu
Third chemical industrial site (reserved)	→	Samchuk, Bukpyeong
First free trade export zone expansion	→	Masan
Second free trade export zone	→	Beein, Koonsan
First steel industrial site	→	Pohang
Second steel industrial site (reserved)	→	Downstream basin of Nakdong River
Electronics industrial site	→	Kumi
Machine tool industrial site	→	Changwon
Shipbuilding industrial site	→	Ulsan, Pusan, Kuhje

———————————————————— Incompletion ———

Heavy (smeltering) industrial export zone	→	Onsan
Mid-land integrated industrial site	→	Asan Bay area

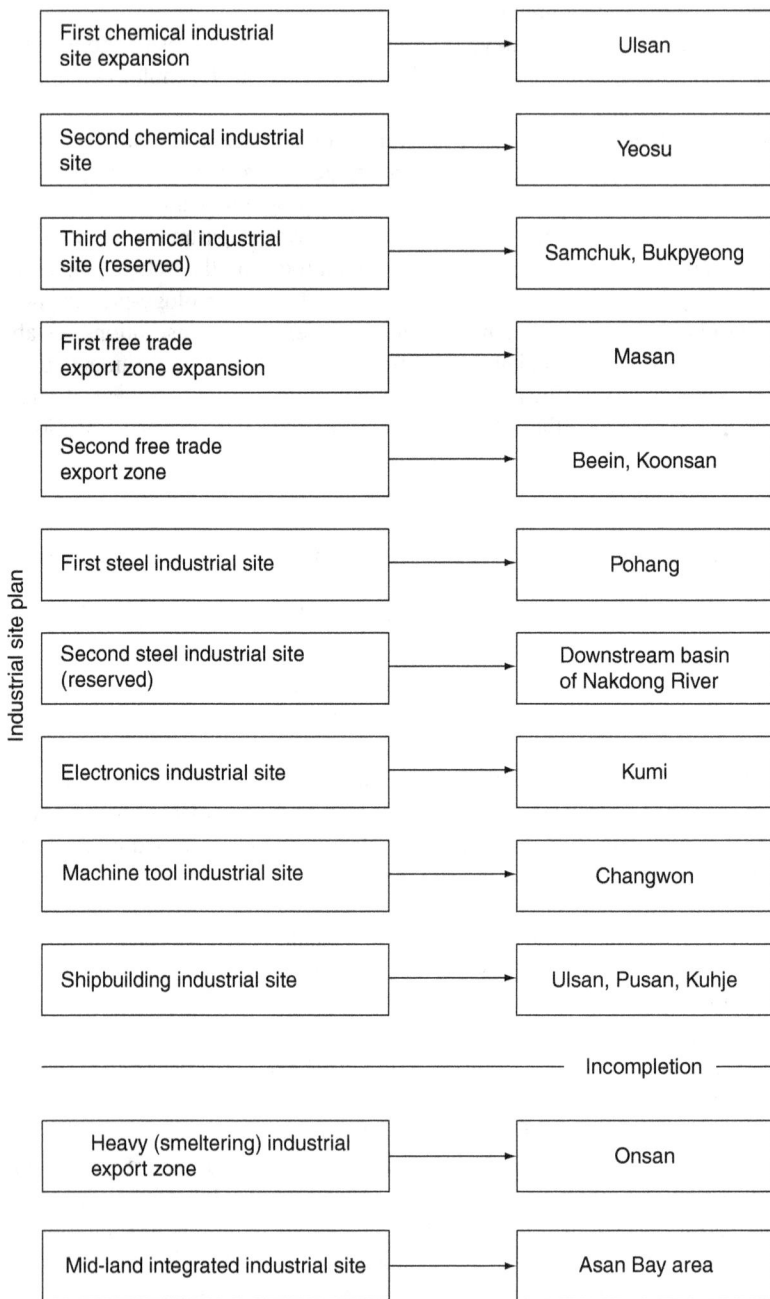

Figure 7.4 Heavy-chemical industrial site construction plan.

Investment Fund was established to provide financial resources to heavy-chemical and defense industry firms.

5 Character classification and policy implementation steps

Figure 7.5 marks the implementation steps of the HCIPP in the abscissa of the time dimension of the table. However, policy measures are classified into three different groups according to the institutional attributes of individual policy measures. First, the HCIPP, at its outset, was launched by the political leadership so that the policy measures, which were able to be introduced because of the determination of the political leadership, are identified as the first group classification. Second, in the implementation stage, a group of engineers-turned-technocrats performed the leading role in the steps of policy design and program implementation so that the policy measures launched in this stage are

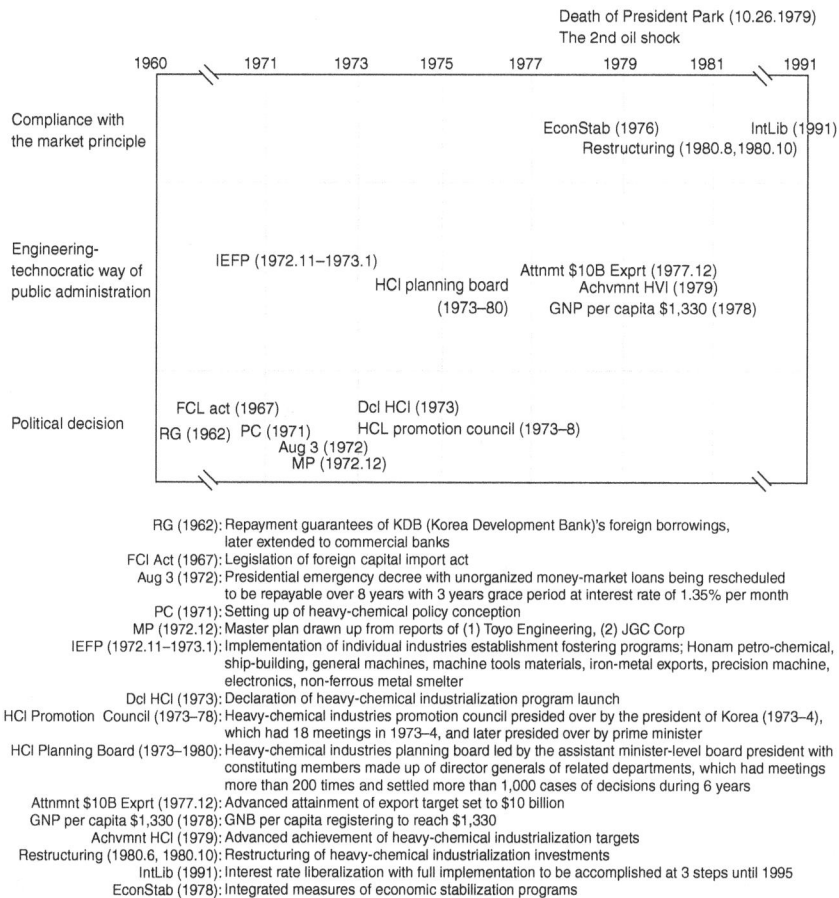

Death of President Park (10.26.1979)
The 2nd oil shock

	1960	1971	1973	1975	1977	1979	1981	1991
Compliance with the market principle						EconStab (1976) Restructuring (1980.8,1980.10)		IntLib (1991)
Engineering-technocratic way of public administration		IEFP (1972.11–1973.1)		HCI planning board (1973–80)		Attnmt $10B Exprt (1977.12) Achvmnt HVI (1979) GNP per capita $1,330 (1978)		
Political decision		FCL act (1967) RG (1962) PC (1971) Aug 3 (1972) MP (1972.12)	Dcl HCI (1973) HCL promotion council (1973–8)					

RG (1962): Repayment guarantees of KDB (Korea Development Bank)'s foreign borrowings, later extended to commercial banks
FCI Act (1967): Legislation of foreign capital import act
Aug 3 (1972): Presidential emergency decree with unorganized money-market loans being rescheduled to be repayable over 8 years with 3 years grace period at interest rate of 1.35% per month
PC (1971): Setting up of heavy-chemical policy conception
MP (1972.12): Master plan drawn up from reports of (1) Toyo Engineering, (2) JGC Corp
IEFP (1972.11–1973.1): Implementation of individual industries establishment fostering programs; Honam petro-chemical, ship-building, general machines, machine tools materials, iron-metal exports, precision machine, electronics, non-ferrous metal smelter
Dcl HCI (1973): Declaration of heavy-chemical industrialization program launch
HCI Promotion Council (1973–78): Heavy-chemical industries promotion council presided over by the president of Korea (1973–4), which had 18 meetings in 1973–4, and later presided over by prime minister
HCI Planning Board (1973–1980): Heavy-chemical industries planning board led by the assistant minister-level board president with constituting members made up of director generals of related departments, which had meetings more than 200 times and settled more than 1,000 cases of decisions during 6 years
Attnmt $10B Exprt (1977.12): Advanced attainment of export target set to $10 billion
GNP per capita $1,330 (1978): GNB per capita registering to reach $1,330
Achvmnt HCI (1979): Advanced achievement of heavy-chemical industrialization targets
Restructuring (1980.6, 1980.10): Restructuring of heavy-chemical industrialization investments
IntLib (1991): Interest rate liberalization with full implementation to be accomplished at 3 steps until 1995
EconStab (1978): Integrated measures of economic stabilization programs

Figure 7.5 Chronicle of implementation steps of heavy-chemical industrialization policy.

distinguished as being affiliated with the second group classification.[3] Third, the market principle was invoked and applied as a rule to deal with individual non-performing projects in the industrial restructuring stage when overcapacity became a problem due to excessive investments. The policy measures used in this stage are pertinent to the third group classification.

First of all, the important steps of a program launch could begin due mainly to the determination of the political leadership, which was equipped with a futuristic vision: outlining the concept of the HCIPP (PC 1971), seeking professional advice from consultants to translate the policy vision into the Master Plan (MP 1972), and delivering a declaration of the HCIPP (Dcl HC 1973).

The political leadership was most salient in the policy decisions of the early stage, which placed prior settlements before the launching of the HCIPP: Repayment Guarantees of the Korea Development Bank's foreign borrowings, which were later extended to commercial banks (RG 1962), legislation of the Foreign Capital Import Act (FCI Act 1967), and the Presidential Emergency Decree, which dictated the arrangements for unorganized money-market loans to be rescheduled to be repaid over eight years with three years' grace period at an interest rate of 1.35 percent per month (August 3, 1972).

However, the most critical step of policy implementation was the organization, formation, and operation of the Heavy-Chemical Industries Promotion Council (HCI Promotion Council 1973–8). Although the official president of the council was the prime minister, the council had been presided over by the president of Korea for the first two years. The council had 18 meetings during this period and settled 66 cases of agenda lists so that the difficulties arising from the process of implementing the HCIPP at the beginning stage were directly resolved by the president himself.[4]

The HCIPP, which was launched by political decision, could be effectively implemented by public administration because the plan could successfully mobilize professional workforces, which had practical professional knowledge as well as the administrative competence of execution in public administration. For instance, as the Individual Industries Establishment Fostering Program (IEFP 1972.11–1973.1) was enacted, the Heavy-Chemical Industries Planning Board was established as the executive organization of the HCI Promotion Council (HCI Planning Board (1973–80) and continued to hold the position to perform a pivotal role in implementing the measures of public administration until the program could be completely fulfilled.

In consequence, the goals of the HCIPP were achieved by 1979 (Achvmnt HCI 1979). The targets of $10 billion exports (Attnmnt $10B Exprt (1977.12)) and $1,000 per capita GNP (GNP per capita $1,330 (1978)) were attained ahead of schedule.

From the outset, the HCIPP aimed at creating export industries. Although the industrialization program was designed and promoted by government initiative, it may not be considered an outright violation of market principles since the exporting of industrial products was targeted. Though unintended at the beginning, as the program approached its completion, the government-led heavy-chemical industrialization policy was replaced by the market principles of private initiative (EconStab 1978). The excessive amount of equipment, which turned up in the implementation process of the program, was sold and restructured (Restructuring 1980.8, 1980.10). Through the interest-rate liberalization policy in place only in 1991 the market principle of private initiative became established as the main mechanism of the economy, so that not much room remained for the justification of government-run industrialization policies such as the HCIPP.

6 Performance of heavy-chemical industries

The composition of light industrial products in total exports was 52.7 percent in 1977 but dropped to 8.3 percent by 2006. On the contrary, the compositional weight of heavy-chemical industrial products, which was 32.8 percent in 1977, continuously increased to 83.1 percent by 2006. Korean exports turned to a structure unambiguously lopsided toward heavy-chemical industries.[5] The industrial structure of exports was been dramatically upgraded.

Figure 7.6 reveals the trend of the industrial composition of light versus heavy-chemical industries in exports. Since the early 1980s, heavy-chemical industrial products have become the mainstay of exports, a trend which has continued to grow ever since. The exports of light industrial products fell to an unparalleled minor share after the year 2000.[6]

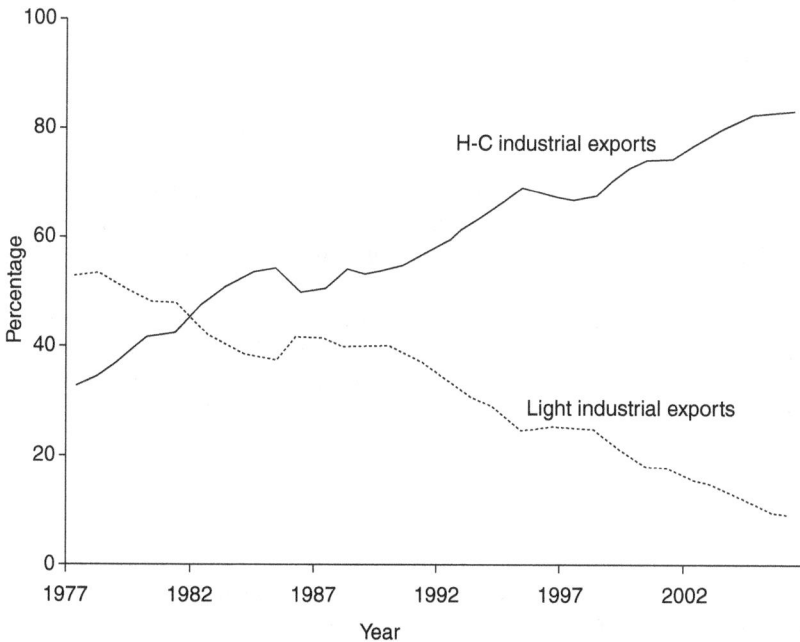

Figure 7.6 Export composition of light vs. H-C industrial products.

7 Financial market policies

The financial market develops gradually in conjunction with the progress of economic growth. The financial market cannot attain the level of advancement of developed countries while the economy remains in a state of backwardness, as it does in many underdeveloped countries.

According to Bloomfield and Jensen's reform (1951), which recommended policies for the private autonomy of bank management built upon private ownership, the return to government policy intervention may be unavoidable in the process of constructing the structure of financial institutions in order to attain the financing of targeted policy activities. In other words, such retrogression may be considered the self-expression of the unrealistic limit of the reform policy, which aimed at autonomy and liberalization in an economy still staggering due to the backwardness of economic development.[7]

The extent to which the government interferes in the autonomous operation of the financial market is gauged in the vertical axis, whereas the horizontal axis gauges the extent of the innovativeness of the government in achieving each policy of institutional change. Important policies of institutional change in the financial market since the 1960s are identified and plotted in Figure 7.7.

In a condition where the institutional development of the financial market did not make enough progress to serve the financial demands of society, which swelled as the economy grew, the doctrine of private autonomy and private initiative failed to provide settlement in the financial impasse. The innovativeness of the horizontal axis in Figure 7.7 indicates the effectiveness of ad hoc policies to break the impasse.

Figure 7.7 reveals that early policies in the 1960s locate largely in the first quadrant, which indicates heavy government intervention and high innovativeness of policies, whereas the policies in the later period are clustered in the third quadrant, which indicates dwindling government intervention, representing the support of private autonomy and private initiative, but indicating diminished innovativeness of policies. In other words, the path of financial policies seems to move along a diagonal from a northeast to southwest direction.

However, there were exceptional cases of heavy government intervention but meager innovativeness, such as a standstill of financial assets in 1961 (FFA (1961) or currency denomination in 1962 (CD 1962). These policies are located far from the diagonal line. It is intriguing that such off-diagonal policies are assessed as failures.[8]

8 Concluding remarks

Industrial policy has been a contentious issue in economics. The discussion arguing for it has been regarded as heresy by orthodox economics. In this chapter, a new institutionalist model of development economics is introduced to lay the ground for acknowledging institutions as part of the evolutionary process

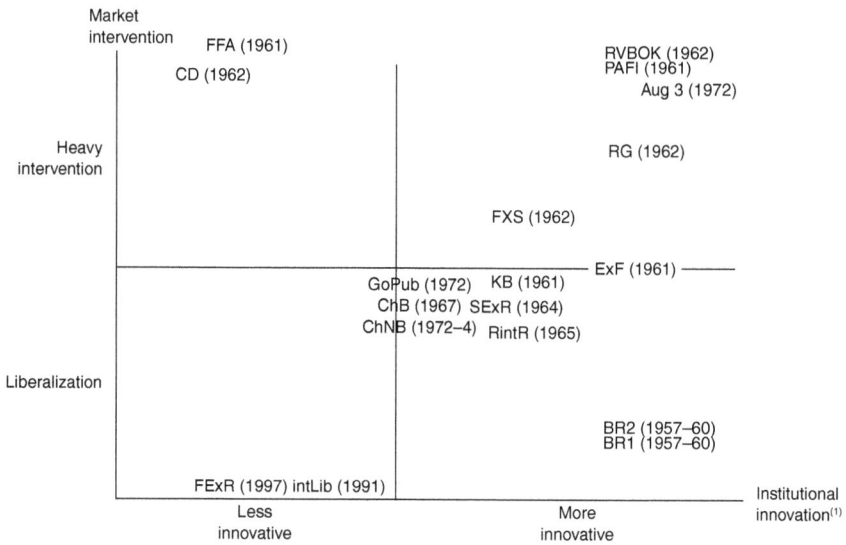

Market
intervention   FFA (1961)   RVBOK (1962)
                                                  PAFI (1961)
            CD (1962)   Aug 3 (1972)

Heavy   RG (1962)
intervention

                                    FXS (1962)

                                                ─ ExF (1961) ───────

                        GoPub (1972) KB (1961)
                        ChB (1967) SExR (1964)
                      ChNB (1972–4) RintR (1965)

Liberalization

                                                BR2 (1957–60)
                                                BR1 (1957–60)

            FExR (1997) intLib (1991)   Institutional
                Less   More   innovation[1]
              innovative   innovative

Notes
[1] 'innovative' indicates the power of policy measures to break the ice of institutional inertia.

Abbreviations

BR1 (1957–60): Bloomfield & Jensen Recommendation 1 – autonomous central banking and price stability
BR2 (1957–60): Bloomfield & Jensen Recommendation 2 – transfer of commercial banks to private ownership
ExF (1961):   Introduction of Export Financing Ordinance
FFA (1961):   Freezing Activities in All Financial Institutions – freezing financial assets in all financial institutions (1961,5,16–8,24)
PAFK (1961):   Provisional Act on the Operation of Financial Institutions – restrictions on management rights of dominant
               stockholders of commercial banks: repudiating the philosophy of BR2 (1957–60)
KB (1961):   Legislation of Kookmin Bank Act
FXS (1962):   Legislation of Foreign Exchange Supervising Act
RVBOK (1962): Revision of the Bank of Korea Law – repudiation of BRI (1957–60)
CD (1962):   Currency Denomination
RG (1962):   Repayment Guarantees of KDB (Korea Development Bank)'s foreign Borrowings, later extended to commercial
               banks
SExR (1964):   Adopting Single Exchange Rate System with a Change to Realistic 255 Won per US dollar from Previously 130 Won
RintR (1965): Realistic Readjustment of Interest Rate with Upper Limit adjusted to annual 40% from 20%
ChB (1967):   Chartering Korea Exchange Bank, Korea Trust Bank, Korea Housing Bank, local banks, branch offices of foreign
               banks
ChNB (1972–74): National Investment Fund, National Savings Association, Export–Import Bank (1969), investment finance
               companies, mutual savings and finance companies
Aug 3 (1972): Presidential Emergency Decree with unorganized money-market loans being rescheduled to be repayable over
               8 years with 3 years grace pds at an interest rate of 1.35% per month
GoPub (1972): Public Corporation Inducement Law to designate eligible corporations and force them to go public
IntLib (1991): Interest Rate Liberalization (1991) with full implementation accomplished at 3 steps until 1995
FExR (1997):   Adopting Flexible Exchange Rate System

Figure 7.7 Intervention and innovation in financial market.

in the analysis, which presents a new theoretical territory where government intervention through public policy becomes justified.

Since institutions inadequately protect property rights, intervention through public policy makes up for institutional incompleteness and makes an effective impact on the investment decisions of the private sector. A theoretical possibility is presented, that a change of norm from property rule to liability rule has a significant positive effect on investment decisions.

In this chapter, the case of the HCIPP in Korea is presented as an empirical example of effective industrial policy. The establishment of institutions as an outgrowth of the evolutionary process enabled the explanation of industrial policy as an effective process of public policy, which is compatible with the theoretical structure of economic analysis. That is, this research offers a new institutional dimension in development economics in which the institution creates conditions calling for the innovativeness of governance in the public sector.

The case of financial market policy is presented to disclose how institutions evolve to achieve the advancement process, which harmonizes with economic development in the operation of the market mechanism. In the early stage in the 1960s, when market institutions were not developed, the policies were more interruptive and more proactive (innovative). However, in the later stage, when market institutions achieved development, the policies became less interruptive and less proactive (less innovative).

Acknowledgement

This research was supported by Soongsil University Research Fund of 2011.

Notes

1 Kim (1988: ch. 2, p. 220).
2 Kim (1988: 236, table 6.2.10).
3 Oh (1996, vol. 3: ch. 12).
4 Kim (1988: ch. 5).
5 The Office of Statistics, Government of Korea: http://nso.go.kr (accessed December 2007).
6 D.S. Kim's (2004) computation of total factor productivity for individual industrial subsectors for each year reveals that the contribution of TFP growth in the growth of H-C industries more or less outnumbered those in light industries from 1975 to 1980.
7 This is the impression from the reading of Cole and Park (1983), ch.3.
8 Ibid.

Bibliography

Bloomfield, A.I. and J.P. Jensen (1951) *Banking Reform in South Korea*, New York: Federal Reserve.
Chang, H.J. (2009) 'Industrial Policy: Can We Go Beyond an Unproductive Confrontation?' Annual Bank Conference on Development Economics, Seoul, Korea, 2009.
Choi, Y.B. (1999) 'Conventions and Economic Change: A Contribution Toward a Theory of Political Economy,' *Constitutional Political Economy*, 10, 245–64.
Cole, David C. and Yung Chul Park (1983) *Financial Development in Korea, 1945–1978*, Camridge, MA: Harvard University Press.
Demsetz, Harold (1967) 'Toward a Theory of Property Rights,' *American Economic Review*, 57, 2, 347–59.
Hayek, F.A. (1982) *Law, Legislation and Liberty*, London: Routledge & Kegan Paul.
Heckscher, Eli F. (1931) *Mercantilism*, ed. E.F. Soederlund, rev. edn. 1955, London: Allen & Unwin.
Kim, Dong Suk (2004) *Sanoupbumunbyeol Sungjangyoinbunseok Mit Kookjebikyo* [Sources of Growth Accounting Measurement by Industrial Subgroups and International Comparisons], Seoul: Korea Development Institute.

Kim, Kwang-Mo (1988) *Hankookwui Sanupbaljeongwa Choonghwahakkongup jeongchaek* [Industrial Development in Korea and Heavy-Chemical Industrial Policy], Jikoomunhwasa.

Kirzner, Israel M. (1973) *Competition and Entrepreneurship*, Chicago: University of Chicago Press.

List, Friedrich (1827) *The National System of Political Economy*, repr. 1977, Fairfield, NJ: Augustus M. Kelley Publishers.

Oh, Won-Chul (1996) *Hankookhyung kyeongje kunsul* [Korean Model of Constructing Economy], vol. 1–7.

Ostrom, Elinor (1990) *Governing the Commons: The Evolution of Institutions for Collective Action*, Cambridge: Cambridge University Press.

Rhee, Sung Sup (2007) 'Institution as a Linchpin to Connect Individualism and Holism' (in Korean), *JaedoWa Kyungjae*, 1, 1, 5–16.

Rhee, Sung Sup (2008) *Cases and Analyses of the Heavy-Chemical Industrial Promotion Policy (1973–79) in Korea*, Report in Korea Knowledge Sharing Program, KDI School of Public Policy and Management and Ministry of Strategy and Finance.

Rhee, Sung Sup (2009a) 'Fundamental Coase Theorem and Institutional World of Non-Zero Transaction Cost,' 2009 Annual Meeting of Asian Law and Economics Association, June 20–21, 2009, Seoul, Korea.

Rhee, Sung Sup (2009b) 'Institutions and Entrepreneurship,' 2009 Conference of Korea Institution and Economics Association, August 17–20, 2009, Seoul, Korea.

Schumpeter, Joseph A. (1934) *The Theory of Economic Development*, New Brunswick, NJ: 2006, Transaction Publishers.

Simon, Herbert A. (1955) 'A Behavioral Model of Rational Choice,' *Quarterly Journal of Economics*, 69, 1, 99–118.

Smith, Adam (1776) *The Wealth of Nations*, New York: Modern Library, 1937.

Stiglitz, J. and S. Yusuf (2001) *Rethinking the East Asian Miracle*, Washington, DC: World Bank.

Thurow, Lester (1993) *Head to Head: The Coming Economic Battle among Japan, Europe and America*, New York: Warner Books.

Tullock, Gordon (1965) *The Politics of Bureaucracy*, Washington, DC: Public Affairs Press.

Yoo, J. *et al.* (1995) *Industrialization and the State: The Korean Heavy and Chemical Industry Drive*, Cambridge, MA: Harvard Institute for International Development.

8   The myth about Korea's rapid growth

Jungho Yoo

1 Introduction

Few observers in the early 1960s expected the Korean economy to grow and industrialize as rapidly as it did, for neither was the country well endowed with natural resources nor were its science and technology highly advanced. In the following two decades Korea transformed from one of the poorest countries in the world, with an agrarian and stagnant economy, into a country of rapidly rising per-capita income with an industrializing and dynamic economy. This and similarly rapid growth in Hong Kong, Singapore, and Taiwan are often referred to as the 'East Asian Miracle.'

There are diverse opinions regarding what to make of the phenomenon and why it happened. Some take issue with using the word *miracle* on the grounds that the rapid growth can be accounted for by increases in inputs of productive resources and that little is left unexplained.[1] This chapter proposes to use the word, although the phenomenon may not be beyond human understanding, in the sense that the pace of growth was unprecedentedly rapid in world economic history.[2] A more interesting issue is why and how it was possible. This is of practical interest for policy-makers in many developing countries aspiring to achieve rapid growth and also of theoretical interest to economists. But, there still is no consensus on why or how it happened, especially regarding the role of government. Widely held among economists as well as among laypersons is the view that the miracle was made possible by the government's replacing the market in resource allocation.

This view seems to acquire additional credibility in the Korean context, partly because the beginning of dramatic economic growth coincided with an equally dramatic political event. President Park Chung-Hee took power through a military coup in 1961, promising 'to save the people from under the poverty line.' As much as he was dedicated to the goal of 'rich nation, strong military,' he was merciless to his opponents. For the goal of economic development, he could sacrifice almost anything. Individuals' freedom and property rights were on a short leash and could always be restrained or snatched away. The commercial banks were nationalized shortly after he took power. There is little doubt that he regarded all financial and non-financial firms as agents or pawns in the grand plan he had in mind for the economy. The economy was only nominally a market economy. The government did not hesitate to intervene in the market; therefore, it was a government-controlled economy.

As is well known, rapid growth and industrialization followed, far in excess of the goals of the government's plans. This raises a question concerning whether the government's control of or heavy intervention in the market economy accelerates growth. Many take the Korean experience to be the evidence for a strong 'yes' in answer to the question.[3] However, in Korea's experience, as in any other countries, the association or coincidence of a policy with a certain economic performance does not prove the causality between the two. The relation has to be examined, which is what this chapter does.

This chapter considers, first, how the rapid expansion of exports began in the early 1960s; second, the export promotion policy since the mid-1960s; and third, the Heavy and Chemical Industry drive in the 1970s, the archetypal example of government economic management. Based on these considerations, this chapter concludes that it is an unwarranted myth that the rapid growth miracle was made possible by the government's intervention in the market or control of the economy.[4] This is not to say that the Korean government made no contribution to rapid economic growth. Provision of a stable macroeconomic environment, conservative management of fiscal policy, reform of tax administration, and so on, must have contributed to rapid growth in important ways. Besides, there must have been institutional roles the government played, such as the protection of freedom and private property, which were admittedly imperfect but were indispensable for the country's phenomenal growth. This chapter merely asserts that, whatever the government may have done right, it was not its control or micromanagement of the economy. Lastly, this chapter considers the influence of world market size on the pace of industrialization.

2 How rapid export expansion began in the early 1960s

Korea's exports began to expand suddenly and rapidly in the early 1960s, and rapid expansion continued in the following decade, without which the country's rapid growth and industrialization may not have been possible. Early studies of the growth experience tend to attribute export expansion to the change in development policy from import substitution in the 1950s to export promotion in the 1960s, while mentioning as underlying factors the abundance of hardworking workers and a favorable world economic environment.[5]

There appear to be some grounds for the claim that export expansion could happen because of the government policy of export promotion, for there were a number of export promotion measures in place at the time. However, as Yoo (2008) shows, the rapid export expansion followed three devaluations between February 1960 and February 1961 that raised the official exchange rate from 50 won to 130 won to the dollar, nearly wiping out the overvaluation of won. The effect of export promotion measures, though numerous, were quantitatively rather small, accounting for 1–2 percent of the exporters' earnings per dollar.[6]

The decisive factor was the devaluations, but they do not appear to have been part of the government's conscious policy decisions for export promotion. Of the three devaluations, the first one in February 1960 changed the exchange rate from 50 to 65 won to the dollar, and it was the result of the tug of war over the official exchange rate that was going on between the Korean and US governments.[7] The second devaluation in January 1961 raised the rate to 100 won to the dollar, and it took place on the occasion of resuming the aid and economic cooperation between Korea and the United States, which had been disrupted by the Student Revolution in April 1960. The last one, in February 1961, which raised the exchange rate from 100 to 130 won to the dollar under the new Chang Myon government, was a conscious decision to correct currency overvaluation, part of the policy reform for unified exchange rates. The general policy stance, however, was still industrialization under import substitution.

The three devaluations were followed by an explosive expansion of manufactures exports, enabling total exports to increase 40–60 percent in real terms per year during the remainder of the 1960s, and the development policy changed from import substitution to export promotion. It was not, as is popularly believed, that the change in development policy from import substitution to export promotion brought about the beginning of export expansion. The First Five-Year Economic Development Plan, which was adopted by the new military government in 1961, was still putting a policy priority on import substitution and was considering exports as merely a remedy for the foreign exchange shortage. However, a complete turnaround in the policy can be observed in the revised version of the Five-Year Development Plan, written in 1964 well after rapid export expansion had already begun, which now explicitly stated that the promotion of the export industry, not just an increase in exports, was the policy goal. In June of the same year, the government adopted the first Comprehensive Export Promotion Program, which intended to provide export promotion with a comprehensive and consistent policy framework. The well-known monthly Expanded Meeting for Export Promotion, presided over by President Park, began in 1965.

It was only natural that the government switched the policy from import substitution to export promotion as a result of the rapid export expansion led by manufactures exports. It was a tailor-made answer to a number of difficult problems the government faced, including a severe shortage of foreign exchange, creation of jobs for unskilled workers, and the need to make visible progress in economic growth and keep the promise of saving the people from poverty. Moreover, progress would gain the Park government, which came to power through military coup, legitimacy in the eyes of the people. It is not surprising at all that the government grabbed the opportunity. The government launched an all-out effort for export promotion, beginning in the mid-1960s.

The beginning of rapid export expansion in the early 1960s is an interesting episode from this chapter's point of view. The government made the policy switch from import substitution to export promotion after the rapid expansion of manufactures exports had already begun. In this experience the government did not identify the need for a new policy or policy change but reacted to a new

development. This is one of the reasons why the claim that government intervention in the market made the economic miracle possible is not very convincing.

3 Export promotion in the 1960s

It should be admitted that it is no small feat for a government to recognize the
need for a policy change and actually make the change, even after the need is
revealed; not all governments are willing or capable of making such a change.
The Korean government did just that with export promotion in the second half of
the 1960s, after rapid export expansion began. This change will be considered in
this section.

For the purposes of this discussion, it seems necessary to review briefly the
policy measures the government adopted after rapid export expansion began. In
addition to such measures as reduced income taxes, exemption from tariffs on
imported inputs for export production, and other minor measures that had been
in place, the government greatly expanded credit incentives by increasing the
number of types and volumes of preferential loans for exports, often with interest rates lower than the inflation rate. Also, new incentives were introduced in
the mid-1960s, such as wastage allowance schemes, reduced public utility and
transportation rates, accelerated depreciation for tax purposes of the assets that
were used in export production, and so on. In a word, the government mobilized
all conceivable policy tools to support the policy goals. As for the exchange rate
policy, the government took another major devaluation of about 100 percent in
1964.

The important question for this chapter is whether export promotion measures
were the cause of export expansion. To find out, it is necessary to consider the
1950s as well, for the export promotion measures were not adopted in a vacuum.
In the 1950s the government pursued highly protectionist trade policies for
import substitution industrialization and did not abandon them when it launched
export promotion. So, in the 1960s the government in fact was simultaneously
pursuing two policies that worked at cross purposes. From the producers' point
of view, export promotion made export sales more attractive than domestic sales,
and protection made domestic sales more attractive than export sales. Therefore,
it would be simply wrong to explain away rapid export expansion as the consequence of the export promotion policy without considering the effect of the
protectionist policy. Thus questions arise: which one of the two policies had
stronger effects and what was the net effect?

This question was quantitatively investigated by an empirical study, whose
authors came to the conclusion that the effects of the two policies on Korean
producers nearly offset each other. In other words, the incentives the producers
faced in the late 1960s were virtually neutral between exports and domestic
sales.[8] The accuracy of the study may be debated, but there is no question that
the two policies were working at cross purposes. The export promotion might
not have been necessary had there been no protectionist policy. Also, attention
needs be paid to the unintended effect. Export promotion and protection jointly

had the effect of raising the prices of traded goods vis-à-vis non-traded services. This amounts in effect to a depreciation of domestic currency, making the manufacturing sector more attractive vis-à-vis the service sector. Indeed, in the process of export expansion, many more investments were made in the manufacturing sector than in the other sectors, and workers were lured away from the rest of the economy.

What the government did with trade policy in the 1960s can be summarized as follows. The government in effect blocked the economy's road to the world market by putting up a roadblock with its protectionist policy and then removed the roadblock with its export promotion policy. It is very hard to imagine that this was the effect the policy-makers intended. Viewed in this light, rapid export expansion in the 1960s hardly serves as supporting evidence for the claim that the government's policy and wise economic management made the miracle happen.

4 The heavy and chemical industry drive

The HCI drive was the archetypal example of the government's control of the economy, much more than a mere intervention in the market. It officially began with President Park's declaration in January 1973 and ended with the announcement of the Comprehensive Stabilization Program in April 1979, six months before the assassination of the president. It intended to promote the development of a number of selected heavy and chemical industries.[9] The drive was masterminded by the HCI Promotion Council, which was specially set up in the president's office and headed by a senior secretary to the president. The government prepared a detailed program of investment plans at the plant level, complete with timetables and locations. It handpicked entrepreneurs for key projects and coerced them to undertake the projects, as they were often reluctant because of large investment requirements and uncertain prospects. It was during this period that chaebols, family-owned business conglomerates, emerged and acquired increasingly dominant positions in the economy in terms of sales, employment, assets, and so forth. The HCI drive was little different from a war plan in spirit. The private firms, financial or non-financial, were all agents of the government that pursued the sacred goal of nation building.

The government employed all conceivable policy measures, as it had done in the previous decade with its export promotion policy, to promote the development of selected heavy and chemical industries. Through nationalized commercial banks and other financial institutions, the government directed credits to selected industries at preferential interest rates. The government revised the Tax Exemption and Reduction Control Law to provide tax breaks for the policy-favored industries (Figure 8.1), and it protected the domestic markets by severely restricting competing imports from abroad. This naturally led to much faster growth of heavy and chemical industries compared to light manufacturing industries. Of course, the big question is: did the economy's performance improve because of the HCI drive?

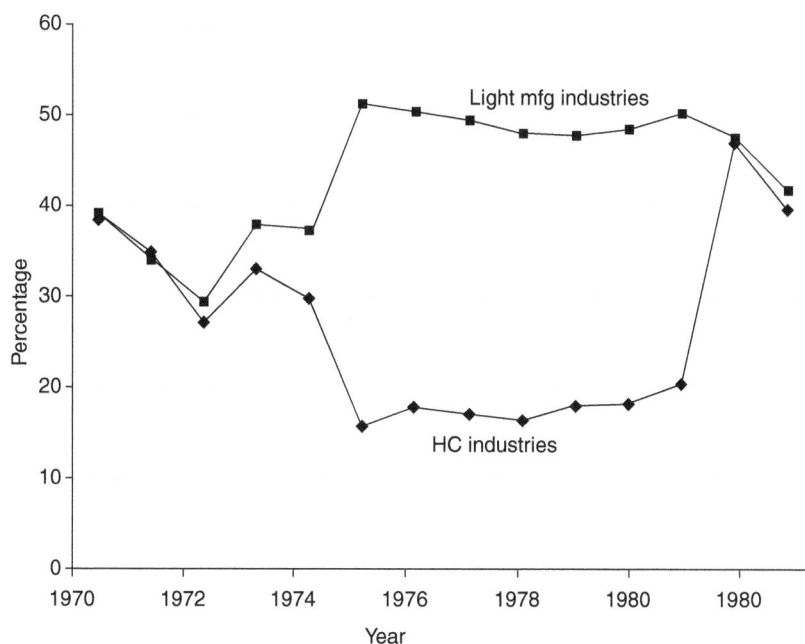

Figure 8.1 Effective corporate tax rate (source: Kwack 1985).

Yoo (1990) investigates this question.[10] First, Yoo attempts to find out whether the HCI policy affected at all the allocation of capital and labor between the policy-favored heavy and chemical industries (HC industries hereafter) and the rest of the manufacturing sector (light industries). Second, it examines whether the resulting allocation was optimal in some sense. It was found that resource allocation within the manufacturing sector was indeed strongly influenced by the HCI policy. Most tellingly, the capital–labor ratio in HC industries rose nearly twice as fast as it did in light industries for the duration of the HCI drive. This was the consequence of lowering the cost of capital for HC industries with easy access to credit at preferential interest rates lower than inflation rates. However, this trend was reversed in the years immediately following the end of the drive: the capital–labor ratio in HC industries nearly stood still while it rose rapidly in light industries because the end of the HCI drive meant that easy access to credits for HC industries dried up, while credits were becoming more readily accessible for light industries. The divergent behaviors of the capital–labor ratio in the two industry groups were the result of the rational response by firms and entrepreneurs to the different capital costs that the HCI policy created in their respective industries.

Was the resulting allocation of capital between the two industry groups optimal? One way of finding out is to compare the productivity of capital in the two industry groups. If it were the same in both, then the allocation was optimal in the sense that one could not increase manufacturing output by reallocating capital from one group to the other. But it was found that capital productivity was higher in light industries than in HC industries by 20–30 percent in the mid-1970s. Even this big difference in productivity may have been an understatement, because the outputs of heavy and chemical industries were overvalued by the trade policy that strengthened their protection. Therefore, it was clear that too much investment was made in HC industries and too little in light industries, and this misallocation of resources must have entailed losses in manufacturing output, at least in the second half of the 1970s, when the effects of the policy were being felt.

It was precisely during this period that the economy's performance deteriorated, and it eventually registered a negative growth in 1980, as exports and investment faltered. The growth rate of exports in real terms precipitously dropped from 36 percent in 1976 to 19 percent and 14 percent in the next two years, and real exports shrank absolutely in 1979. Similarly, investment growth rapidly slowed down for these years, and investment itself shrank in real terms by more than 10 percent in 1980. This decline in investment was not surprising, being highly correlated with exports. These developments in exports and investment led to the economy's downturn. Given this fact and the finding that the HCI drive led to resource misallocation at that time, an intriguing question arises: was the HCI policy responsible for the weakening export performance?

It was. Before proceeding to show this, it would be useful to consider the usual explanation of the economy's negative growth in 1980, which many people seem to find plausible. The explanation blames the second oil shock and the world recession in the late 1970s and thereafter. Since export expansion was the primary impetus for the economy's rapid growth, it is quite plausible that a world recession dealt a major blow to the Korean economy. However, the world recession at the time was not the main cause of Korea's poor export performance, for total world exports changed little during the recession, while Korea's market share in world exports substantially declined. Thus, there is little doubt that the cause of Korea's poor export performance was a decline in its export competitiveness. Why did it decline? Did too much allocation of resources to heavy and chemical industries hurt competitiveness? Yes, because it must have meant not enough resources left for light industries that were producing most of the Korea's exports at that time. This is an important question for this chapter. However, it is not easy to give a definite answer, for the question is essentially counterfactual in nature. Put differently, the question is: what would have happened to Korea's export competitiveness, had there been no HCI drive?

For this purpose, Yoo (1997b) compares Korea's market share with Taiwan's in OECD imports of manufactures. The market share is a good indicator of export competitiveness, since most of Korea's exports were destined for OECD member countries, and manufactures accounted for most of Korea's exports. Taiwan was chosen for comparison, as its economy was similar in many respects to Korea's. It was poor in natural resources, it was at a comparable stage of development, manufactured goods accounted for most of its exports, and the composition of export goods was most similar to Korea's among the developing countries in the mid-1970s. But Taiwan did not have anything like Korea's HCI drive. While it also had its own industrial targeting policy, its policy was much less discriminatory against non-targeted industries, while Korea's HCI drive was highly discriminatory. According to a reliable observer, industrial targeting was often meaningless in the case of Taiwan's policy.[11] Therefore, by observing the market share of Taiwan, one can guess what Korea's market share would have been, had the government pursued not the HCI policy but a much milder version of industrial policy like Taiwan's.

As shown in Figure 8.2, Korea's and Taiwan's market shares were little different in the mid-1970s. Thereafter Korea's market share fell from 1.38 percent in 1978 to 1.29 percent in 1979 and 1.16 percent in 1980 before it bounced back in the following years, while Taiwan's did not undergo such a decline. What were the export goods that led the fall? They were the products of light manufacturing industries, which did not receive policy favors under the HCI drive. This can be seen in Figure 8.3, which shows Taiwan's and Korea's market shares of the HC industry group and the light industry group, with both industry groups identically defined for the two countries. In the case of the HC industry group, the relative position of the two countries' market shares did not change much over the years until the early 1990s, showing no sign that the HCI drive raised the competitiveness of the HC industry group.

In contrast, the market shares diverged in the case of light manufacturing industries. Korea's market share was growing bigger than Taiwan's in the second half of the 1970s but became smaller in exactly those years when Korea's total exports lost ground. No doubt, the competitiveness of Korea's total exports declined because its competitiveness in light industry products declined.

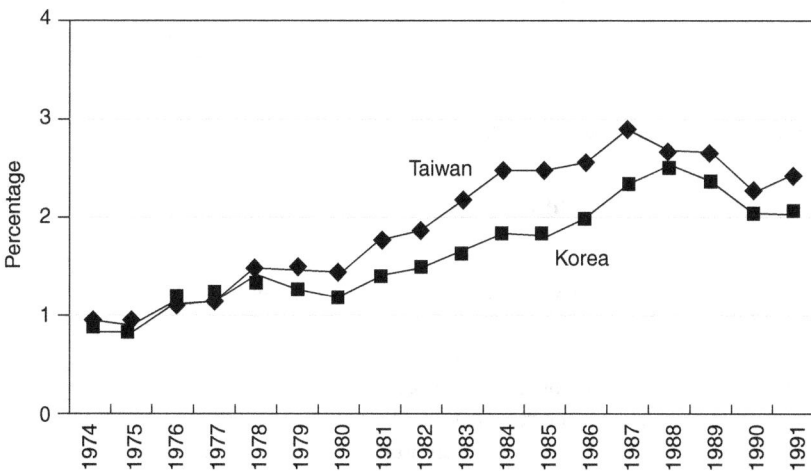

Figure 8.2 Market share in OECD imports in manufactures (%) (source: Yoo 1997b).

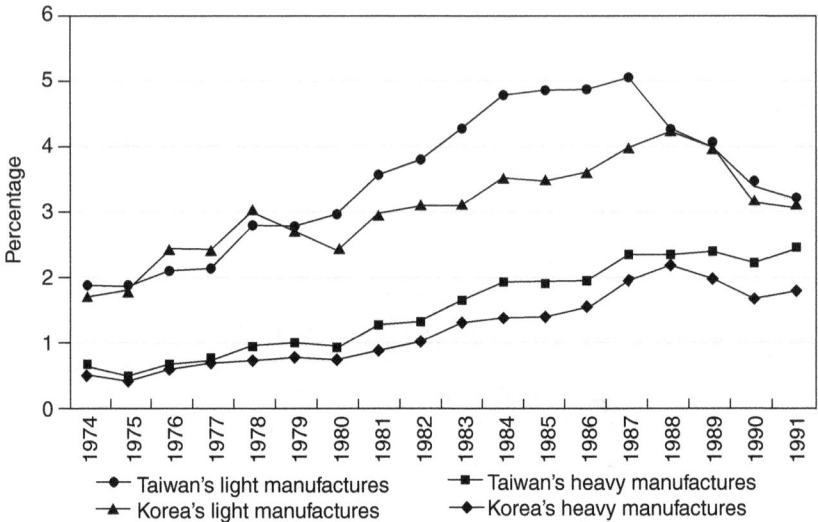

Figure 8.3 Market share in OECD imports of manufactures by industries (source: Yoo 1997b).

Was the decline in light industry's competitiveness caused by the HCI policy? This seems to have been the story. The HCI policy provided the favored industries with tax breaks, trade protection, and directed credits at preferential interest rates. Since no government can create something out of nothing, the costs of providing policy favors had to be borne by someone else within the system. For light manufacturing industries, directed credits for HC industries meant a shortage of credits, tax breaks meant tax-rate hikes (see Figure 8.1), and trade protection meant higher prices of inputs they had to purchase in the domestic markets. For these reasons the light industries' competitiveness was impaired. Had there been no HCI policy, the costs of the policy would not have been borne by the light industries, and it seems reasonable to say that they would have increased the market share as their counterparts in Taiwan did.

5 Influence of the world market size on the pace of industrialization[12]

Then what made Korea's exceptionally rapid growth and industrialization possible? Many observers mention as one of the reasons the high educational attainment of Koreans in the early 1960s, comparable to those countries with three times as high per-capita income. This certainly must have been an important reason. In addition, another reason that has not received much attention so far needs to be mentioned. As shown in Figure 8.4, the volume of total world exports was more than 100 times as large in the early 1960s, when the East Asian economies were beginning to industrialize, as it was in the early 1800s

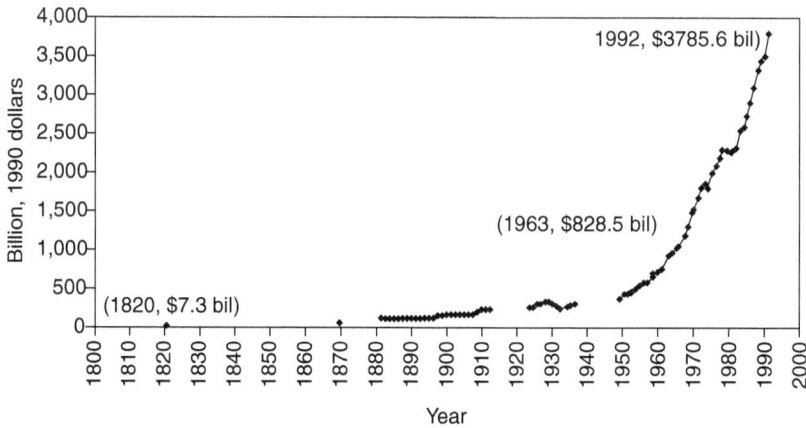

Figure 8.4 Value of world exports (source: Maddison 1995).

when European countries began their industrialization.[13] This is not to reiterate the virtue of outward-oriented policies but to call attention to the influence that the size of the world market exerted on the pace of an economy's industrialization, the importance of which has not been much appreciated.[14] If outward orientation of the policy itself were the main reason for the unprecedented rapid growth of East Asian economies, it should hold that they were more open than their European counterparts were. However, Korea was very much a closed economy in the 1960s and 1970s. It must be the case that Korea's pace of growth and industrialization was very rapid despite the more closed nature of its economy. What enabled the feat, it seems, was the size of the world market that was literally hundreds of times bigger in real terms. But this needs much more discussion than is appropriate for this chapter. It suffices to call attention to Figure 8.5, taken from Yoo (1997a), showing the relation between the beginning date of industrialization and the length of time that different economies took to industrialize. As the figure clearly shows, the later the beginning date of industrialization, the shorter the length. The length of time required for industrialization is negatively correlated with the size of the world market.

6 Conclusion

This chapter reviewed how the rapid expansion of manufactures exports suddenly began in Korea in the early 1960s. It was not brought about by the change in development policy from import substitution industrialization to export promotion. It began as the three devaluations in 1960 and 1961 nearly wiped out the overvaluation of won. After rapid export expansion began, the government made an all-out effort for export promotion in earnest starting in the mid-1960s. Thus, rapid export expansion brought about the policy change, not the other way

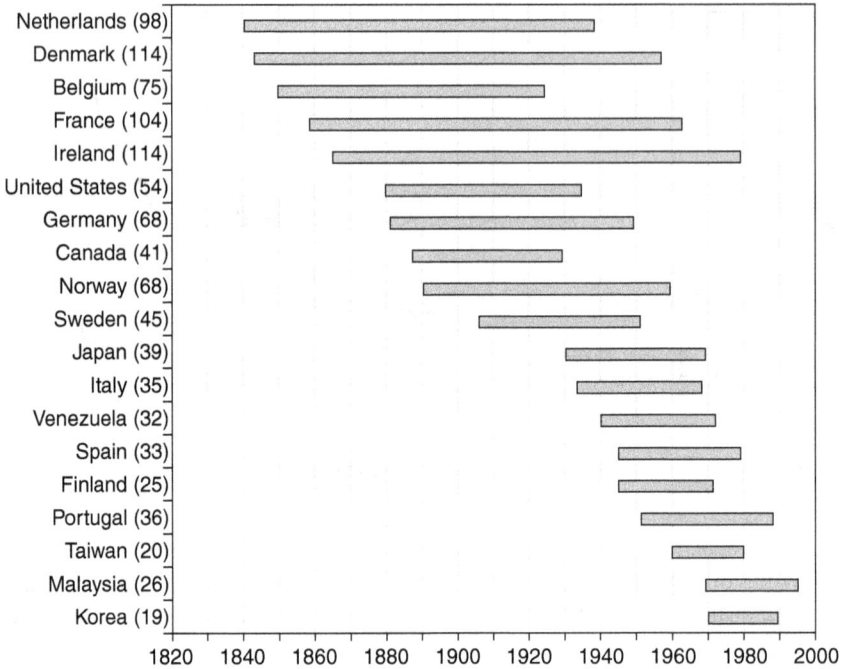

Figure 8.5 Length of time for industrialization (source: Yoo 1997a).

round. It is to the government's credit that it recognized the need for the policy change and actually made the change, for not all governments make a policy change even after the need becomes apparent.

The chapter also reviewed the new policy of export promotion that began in the mid-1960s and the effects of the Heavy and Chemical Industry drive in the 1970s. The main effect of export promotion was that it offset the negative effects of protectionist policies, which were still in place in the 1960s and 1970s, clearing the obstacles from the road to the world market. The HCI drive in the 1970s, which was basically an attempt to promote selected heavy and chemical industries at the expense of light manufacturing industries, very much hurt export performance. Investments, which used to be highly correlated to export performance, plunged in 1979 and 1980, leading to a negative growth of the economy in 1980.

This review shows that the economy was certainly government-led, but its growth was not. The widely held view that the government's interventionist policies made the Korean economic miracle possible is a myth. The rapid growth and industrialization in Korea and other Asian countries cannot be adequately explained without referring to the influence of the world market size. According to Maddison (1995), the estimated volume in 1992 was more than 500 times bigger in real terms than it was in 1820, about the time when European countries began their industrialization. It is inconceivable that China could grow at around 10 percent per year for decades, if the size of the world market remained the same as it was in the 1800s. Only those countries that traded with the rest of the world benefited from the large world market. Korea was no exception. Korea could grow rapidly because the obstacles to benefiting from the international division of labor in the big world market were cleared away: the extreme overvaluation of domestic currency in the 1950s was nearly wiped out by three devaluations in quick succession in the early 1960s; and the export-suppressing effects of protectionist trade policies in the 1960s and 1970s were nearly offset by various export promotion measures.

Notes

1 See, for example, Krugman (1994).
2 According to J. Bhagwati (1999), 'The real miracle that requires explanation is that of the phenomenal rise in private investment rates on a sustained basis to high levels, unparalleled as far as I know in any other region or historical period.'
3 Two well-known examples of such a view are Amsden (1989) and Rodrik (1995).
4 Even the World Bank (1993: 6) says that 'our judgment is that in a few economies, mainly in Northeast Asia, in some instances, government interventions resulted in higher and more equal growth than otherwise would have occurred.'
5 Early studies include Cole and Lyman (1971), Frank *et al.* (1975), Hong and Krueger (1975), Kim and Westphal (1976), Hong (1979), and Krueger (1979), among others.
6 See the estimate of the effect in table 5.8, Frank *et al.* (1975: 70).
7 Korea and the United States had opposite interests regarding the exchange rate, for the rate determined how many dollars the Korean government received for given amounts of won advances to the United Nations Command, which were necessary and were being spent for the United Nations forces to carry out their mission in the Korean peninsula.
8 Westphal and Kim (1982).
9 The selected industries were iron and steel, nonferrous metal, chemical, machinery, shipbuilding, electronics. For a description of the HCI drive, see Lee (1991).
10 See Yoo (1990). Part of this appeared as ch. 4 of Stern *et al.* (1995). Another version, including some extensions, was published as Yoo (1991).
11 Chen (1999: 247) describes the nature of Taiwan's industrial policy:

> Although many policies were aimed at specific industries at the very beginning, many of them were soon extended to other industries that asked for the same privileges.... Therefore, many industrial policies became so general that the private sector could develop the industries they thought profitable without bothering too much about the industrial targets of the Government.

12 This paragraph draws upon Yoo (1997a).
13 Maddison (1995).
14 An exception, Krueger (1991: 470), mentions the larger world market as a factor that makes development in the last half of the twentieth century easier than in the nineteenth century.

Bibliography

Amsden, A.H. (1989) *Asia's Next Giant: South Korea and Late Industrialization*, New York: Oxford University Press.

Bhagwati, J. (1999) 'The "Miracle" That Did Happen: Understanding East Asia in Comparative Perspective,' in E. Thorbecke and H.Y. Wan (eds.), *Taiwan's Development Experience: Lessons on Roles of Government and Market*, Boston: Kluwer.

Chen, P. (1999) 'The Role of Industrial Policy in Taiwan's Development,' in E. Thorbecke and H.Y. Wan (eds.), *Taiwan's Development Experience: Lessons on Roles of Government and Market*, Boston: Kluwer.

Cole, D.C. and Lyman, P.L. (1971) *Korean Development: The Interplay of Politics and Economics*, Cambridge, MA: Harvard University Press.

Frank, C.R., Jr., Kim, K.S., and Westphal, L.E. (1975) *Foreign Trade Regimes and Economic Development: South Korea*, New York: National Bureau of Economic Research.

Hong, W. (1979) *Trade, Distortions and Employment Growth in Korea*, Seoul: Korea Development Institute.

Hong, W. and Krueger, A.O. (eds.) (1975) *Trade and Development in Korea*, Seoul: Korea Development Institute.

Kim, K.S. and Westphal, L.E. (1976) *Korea's Foreign Exchange and Trade Regimes*, Seoul: Korea Development Institute (in Korean).

Krueger, A.O. (1979) *The Developmental Role of the Foreign Sector and Aid*, Cambridge, MA: Council on East Asian Studies, Harvard University.

Krueger, A.O. (1991) 'Benefits and Costs of Late Development,' in P. Higonnet, D.S. Landes, and H. Rosovsky (eds.), *Favorites of Fortune: Technology, Growth, and Economic Development since the Industrial Revolution*, Cambridge, MA: Harvard University Press.

Krugman, P. (1994) 'The Myth of Asia's Miracle,' *Foreign Affairs*, 73(6): 62–78.

Kwack, T. (1985) *Depreciation and Taxation of Income from Capital*, Seoul: Korea Development Institute (in Korean).

Lee, S.C. (1991) 'The Heavy and Chemical Industries Promotion Plan (1973–79),' in L.J. Cho and Y.H. Kim (eds.), *Economic Development in the Republic of Korea, A Policy Perspective*, Honolulu: East-West Center.

Maddison, A. (1995) *Monitoring the World Economy 1820–1992*, Paris: OECD.

Rodrik, D. (1995) 'Getting Interventions Right: How South Korea and Taiwan Grew Rich,' *Economic Policy*, 10(1): 55–107.

Stern, J. *et al.* (1995) *Industrialization and the State: The Korean Heavy and Chemical Industry Drive*, Cambridge, MA: Harvard Institute for International Development.

Westphal, L.E. and Kim, K.S. (1982) 'Korea,' in Bela Balassa and Associates, *Development Strategies in Semi-industrial Economies*, Baltimore: Johns Hopkins University Press.

World Bank (1993) *East Asian Miracle*, Washington, DC: Oxford University Press.

Yoo, J. (1990) 'The Industrial Policy of the 1970s and the Evolution of the Manufacturing Sector in Korea,' KDI Working Paper No. 9017.

Yoo, J. (1991) 'The Effect of Heavy and Chemical Industry Policy of the 1970s on the Capital Efficiency and Export Competitiveness of Korean Manufacturing Industries,' *Korea Development Review*, 13(1): 65–113 (in Korean).

Yoo, J. (1997a) 'The Influence of the World Market Size on the Pace of Industrialization,' *The KDI Journal of Economic Policy*, 19(2): 75–157 (in Korean).

Yoo, J. (1997b) 'Neoclassical versus Revisionist View of Korean Economic Growth,' Development Discussion Paper No. 588, Harvard Institute for International Development.

Yoo, J. (2008) 'How Korea's Rapid Export Expansion Began in the 1960s: The Role of Foreign Exchange Rate,' Working Paper 08-18, KDI School of Public Policy and Management.

9 The new institutional economy and the new traditional economy in Korea

Does the Confucian tradition give it a competitive edge?

J. Barkley Rosser, Jr. and Marina V. Rosser

1 Introduction

The economy of the Republic of Korea (ROK, aka South Korea) has been among the more successful of the rising 'Tiger' economies of East Asia. Caught between the contesting larger powers of China and Japan, Korea has always had a hard time maintaining its independence and been under pressure to keep up economically with these larger countries. It has also at times served as a cultural conduit between the countries, with both Confucianism and Buddhism arguably passing to Japan from China via Korea as an intermediary. While it has played this important international role, at times it has reacted to the external pressures from these neighboring powers by turning inwards and fending off the outside world to be the 'Hermit Kingdom' as it was called in the nineteenth century when the European and American powers (as well as Japan) began seriously to attempt to penetrate it. While useful in the short run defensively, these periods of isolationism weakened the economic dynamism of Korea, making it ultimately more vulnerable to outside interventions, with the Japanese being able to conquer it at the end of this period.

The growth of the South Korean economy from 1960 onwards can be explained largely by its high rate of capital investment. But why and how this high rate of investment proved to be effective in developing industries that have been highly competitive in exporting to the world economy raises deeper questions regarding the sources of this successful effort. Are there institutional or cultural factors that have been and are at work in reinforcing this generally favorable outcome (which is not to say that all has been perfect in the Korean economy, as its vulnerability in the 1997 East Asian financial crisis showed).

Indeed, we wish to explore a new theoretical proposition in order to explore this matter of deeper roots. We propose to combine ideas coming from *new institutional economics* with those associated with the *new traditional economy*. In its formulation due to Oliver Williamson (1975) who drew on the seminal work of Coase (1937), the institutional structure of an economy develops in a way that tends to minimize transactions costs. The new traditional economy idea emphasizes how technologically advanced and modern economies integrated into the world economy may nevertheless have parts of their character crucially dependent on a traditional socio-cultural pattern or structure, often associated with a traditional religion (Rosser and Rosser 1996). It has been argued that both Islam and Confucianism have served as foundations for such new traditional economies (Rosser and Rosser 1998), as well as Hinduism (Rosser and Rosser 2005).

This new proposal argues that these two elements may interact to bring about the essential character of an economy. This can be linked to the argument of Kuran (2009) regarding the *economics of civilizations* in which religion, culture, and law can interact to determine institutions and practices in an economy in distinctive ways, and which can be viewed as a unifying concept here. Transactions cost minimization will operate through the constructs strongly influenced by the cultural and civilizational foundations of a society and economy.

The religious and cultural heritage of Korea is quite complicated, reflecting not only influences from both China and Japan, but also many brought in from much further away, such as from the United States and Europe, with Korea having one of the highest percentages of its population being Christian (about a quarter) of any East Asian nation, only surpassed in that by the Philippines. As in both China and Japan, there is also a tradition of a local native religion, the *Sinkyo* (Osgood 1951), as well as a considerable tradition of Buddhism (in China the local native religion is *Taoism* and in Japan it is *Shintoism*). However, in terms of influencing social behavior, arguably the most important influence in all three nations has been Confucianism, and there have been many careful observers who have argued that at least in the nineteenth century, if not more broadly, that Korea has been the most Confucianist of all of these countries: 'A Korean is more Confucianist than Confucius himself' (Whigham 1904: 185).

This poses a challenge. Traditional Confucianism in many ways did not support economic growth or dynamism. Commercial activity was looked down upon, and an inward-looking perspective was favored. Thus, it is often argued that the height of Confucianist influence in Korea was the nineteenth century, when the highly Confucianist *yangban* elites studied ancient scripts while avoiding business activity and maintaining Korea in its isolationist Hermit Kingdom state. At the same time, the emphasis on family and education and respect for hierarchy have been argued to support economic growth. It can be argued that these competing impulses within Confucianism can be seen within Korea itself, with the more pro-growth aspect being emphasized in South Korea, while the older, more anti-growth version manifests itself in the isolationist *juche* policy found in North Korea, the Democratic People's Republic of Korea (DPRK). Needless to say, it is in the more economically successful ROK economy that we may find a more efficient fusion of new institutionalism and new traditionalism.

This chapter will explore these themes in more detail. We shall review the basic ideas of new institutionalism and the new traditional economy. We shall then consider how Confucianism fits into this discussion. Then we shall apply these arguments to the Korean economy, both in the South and the North, which have contrasted sharply in their respective economic performances, but which also continue to share certain deep similarities arising from their common cultural heritage.

2 New institutional economics

Broadly speaking, the *new institutional economics* can be viewed as an attempt to reconcile the *old institutional economics* with conventional neoclassical economic theory. The split between old institutional economics and neoclassical theory is an old one, arguably dating to the *Methodenstreit* of the late nineteenth century among German-speaking economists, which would be later reproduced within American economics during the first half of the twentieth century, resulting in a victory by neoclassical economics by the 1950s. The earlier debate pitted the German Historical School, led by Gustav von Schmoller (1900–4), against the nascent neoclassical school, led in the German language tradition at the time by Carl Menger (1871), more known now as the founder of the Austrian School whose modern adherents now ironically view themselves as in opposition to the neoclassical approach. However, at that time Menger's role as an advocate of the use of marginal analysis and the idea that rational economizing agents would engage in marginal calculations to optimize was more important than other elements in Menger's analysis such as his emphasis on self-organization (Menger 1892; Rosser 2010).

In contrast to the emphasis on optimizing behavior by rational agents through the use of marginal analysis, the keystone of the neoclassical approach, the German Historical School and the later (old) Institutionalist School in the United States, emphasized the importance of the evolution in history of customs, laws, rules of conduct, organizations, and institutions. This coincided with a deep skepticism about the ability of humans to engage in such precise, rational calculations in general, even if some individuals probably do, although the more formal defense of this view would only come much later with the bounded rationality theory of Herbert Simon (1957). There were a variety of strands within this old institutionalism (Hodgson 2004), but among its leaders in the United States were Thorstein Veblen (1898), John R. Commons (1931), and Karl Polanyi (1944). However, they would come to lose their position of dominance in American economics by the end of the 1950s due to the rising emphasis on using mathematics in economics, which was championed by such leading neoclassicals as Paul Samuelson (1947), while the old institutionalists tended to eschew this as unrealistic.

In more or less creating the new institutionalism, Oliver Williamson was influenced by both of his main teachers, the advocate of bounded rationality, Herbert Simon, and the arch-neoclassical theorist of general equilibrium, Kenneth Arrow. Arguably he set out to combine their approaches, to argue that boundedly rational people nevertheless sought to optimize in creating institutions within the economy. In this he drew upon the long-neglected paper by Ronald Coase (1937) in which he argued that firm sizes arose from rational managers seeking to minimize transactions costs when they decide whether to carry out an activity within the firm or to outsource it to another firm. While some have complained that the concept of transactions costs is poorly defined and too broad, this idea has become the main centerpiece of this approach, which has become widely influential. While there are debates over just what constitute 'institutions' and whether an organization is one or if institutions are more deeply defined (North 2005), a variety of economists have come to argue along new institutionalist lines (Platteau 2000; Aoki 2001; Greif 2006). It should be noted that many of these figures are concerned with questions of economic history and the evolution of institutions, with their otherwise apparently self-organizing aspect seen as reflecting pressures to minimize transactions costs as technological and other changes in the economic environment alter them.

3 The new traditional economy

The idea of the *new traditional economy* was initially introduced by Rosser and Rosser (1996). They developed it as an extension of the division of economic systems due to the old institutionalist, Karl Polanyi (1944) into the three categories of decision-making approaches: *tradition, market,* and *command.* In the first, generally identified with earlier, more 'primitive' economies, decisions were based on what was done in the past, on custom, with this symbolized by labor market decisions, with people doing what their parents did, as in European feudalism or the Hindu caste system.

In the market system decisions are carried out mostly on the basis of market forces, the law of supply and demand. In the command economy, decisions are made on the basis of orders by some authority, usually the state as in the command socialist economy of the DPRK. Polanyi actually saw these forms as having their origins within the more primitive economies, with the truly traditional economy being mostly about *household sharing*, with *reciprocal exchanges* being the foundation of market economies, and the early model of command being the *redistributive* systems sometimes associated with the Big Man systems. This would lead to a controversy within economic anthropology (Rosser and Rosser 1995) between *substantivists* who followed Polanyi's view or variations on it and the *formalists* (LeClair and Schneider 1974) who argued that all economies could analyzed as market economies only using standard neoclassical tools.

In their formulation of the new traditional concept, the element of *familistic groupism* as an important part of an economy was emphasized. Polanyi emphasized the matter of *embeddedness*: what is the dominant institutional structure in an economy within which decisions are embedded? Are markets embedded within some traditional system of past patterns or are social patterns embedded within market forces (or either within a state-run command system)? In a new traditional economy, market forces become at least somewhat embedded within some traditional structure, most likely based on a traditional religion, but also usually emphasizing familistic groupism, which is encouraged by most great world religions. However, in contrast with the old traditional economy of Polanyi, the new traditional economy also uses modern technologies and is integrated into the broader world economy.

Rosser and Rosser (1996, 1998) have argued that there are new traditional elements within the Japanese economy that draw upon its Confucianist heritage. Taiwan under Chiang Kai-Shek openly proclaimed a Confucian orientation, and advocacy of a Confucian perspective has reappeared in mainland China as well. Kahn (1979) was the first to argue that a version of Confucianism could be consistent with economic growth, particularly its emphasis on education. More generally Confucianism has emphasized harmony and hierarchy, with supposedly mutual relations within the hierarchy. So, while those below should obey those above (ultimately the emperor in traditionally Confucianist China), those above were to work for the interests of those below. These relations were to be reproduced in the family, with the husband and father in charge. Within an East Asian economy dominated by family firms, this familistic groupism can be seen as consistent with a Confucianist version of the new traditional economy.

4 The economics of civilizations as a synthesis

We are arguing that the emergence of a new traditional economy may well also involve new institutional processes in that the emergent forms and organizations may also involve moves to minimize transactions costs. This can be seen in general in the concept of the familistic groupist firm. A large literature suggests that high levels of trust are conducive to economic growth (Fukuyama 1995; Zak and Knack 2001). There is also considerable evidence that in many East Asian nations trust is more likely to be associated with close social relations (Buchan and Croson 2004; Carpenter *et al.* 2004). Such characteristics can be argued to go beyond such matters of religion or culture and to involve the broader concept of *civilizations*.

Kuran (2009) argues for the usefulness of the idea of the *economics of civilizations*. This was first put forward by Samuel Huntington (1993, 1996), with an emphasis upon ineluctable conflict between civilizations, such as Islam and Western Christianity. However, Kuran emphasizes that civilizations are flexible and evolve over time. There is no need for such eternal oppositions between them.

The more important aspect of this is that a civilization involves a cluster of many different aspects of a society, an idea also emphasized by Pryor (2008) in his broadened perspective on what constitutes an economic system. At a minimum, a civilization will involve religion, culture, and law, as well as other elements. Kuran provides an example in the third paragraph of his paper.

> Civilization captures more than 'culture,' which comes to mind as a benign alternative. We may speak of the political culture of India, Calcutta's commercial culture, and the musical culture of South Asia. The concept of Indian civilization encompasses all of these, along with the mechanisms that account for their interactions. Serving as a broader unit of analysis, it weaves together social traits and patterns studied by diverse disciplines, including ones that 'cultural studies' specialists typically consider outside their intellectual domain.

In arguing for the flexibility of civilizations, Kuran goes on later in the paper to note the example of Egypt, where Western-style commercial practices began to be introduced in the 1850s, but were very slow to be adopted. In comparison with a place like New Zealand, when traffic lights were introduced, they were initially ignored, but now they are obeyed, at least much of the time. He sees this flexibility of civilizations as key to their development and argues specifically that this has been key to the economic success of certain East Asian economies, notably Japan and South Korea.

In any case, it is easy to argue that given the long historical continuity and identity that Korea has exhibited, there is a distinct 'Korean civilization' that has existed for a long time, despite sharing certain important characteristics with the neighboring Chinese and Japanese civilizations such as strong influences of Confucianism and Buddhism. While Korean civilization has been flexible, it has also exhibited long patterns of path dependence and continuity, as argued regarding its alphabet by Choi (2008). That its current system may involve elements of new traditionalism combining with an economizing new institutionalism is thus possible to be argued.

5 The South Korean economy as a successful neo-Confucian economy

Even as there are and have been critics of its economic success (e.g., Eder: 1996), Noland and Weeks (2009: 117) declare that 'Korea is arguably the premier development success story of the last half century'; strong praise indeed. It has gone from deep poverty at the end of the Korean War to at least the lower end of upper income status in the world economy as a member of the OECD, including surviving the disruptions arising from the 1997 Asian financial crisis (Rosser and Rosser 2004). It has gone from a strongly state-directed economy in the 1970s to one much more market-oriented, with ongoing moves toward privatization and marketization (Mitchell 2009). It has also far outstripped its Communist neighbor to the north, which was ahead of it in real per-capita income well into the 1960s but now faces severe economic problems (Lee 2009). The question is the degree to which this success can be attributed to the persistence of the Confucian tradition in the ROK, and whether or not this tradition is strong enough to qualify the nation as a 'new traditional economy' or not.

The first part of this is to answer how strong the Confucian influence is in South Korea. Although neo-Confucianism (originally a tenth-century Chinese form combining elements of Taoism and Buddhism) had entered Korea earlier, it was with the ascension of the Choson dynasty in 1392 that it clearly became the ruling ideology in Korea over Buddhism, which had arrived earlier. This dynasty would remain in power until 1910, when the Japanese took over, and neo-Confucianism would retain its official position throughout (Cumings 1997; Kleiner 2001; Chung 2006). Indeed, in the succeeding centuries, with Korea arguably one of the world's technological leaders in the 1400s, the Koreans independently developed neo-Confucian doctrines out of debates between contending schools of thought (Deuchler 1992; Chung 1995). This would continue even into the 1700s, culminating in the work of Tasan (pen name of Chong Yak-Yong (1762–1836), late Choson dynasty codifier of Korean neo-Confucianism) who reportedly subtly incorporated Christian influences coming in from China. He stressed the 'three bonds': son to father, subject to king, wife to husband, and the 'five moral relationships': affection between father and son, proper order of old and young, righteousness between king and subject, proper separation of functions between husband and wife, and faithfulness among friends, all of these based on the benevolent harmony of the Confucian concept of *jen* (Deuchler 1992). In the 1800s, this would both ossify as Korea became more insular and backward, even as its *Yangban* elite emphasized its adherence to neo-Confucian doctrine, including its anti-mercantile strand, more and more. As Reischauer and Fairbanks (1960: 426) put it: 'Korea during this period seemed at times even more Confucian and traditionally Chinese than China itself.'

Of course, the economic backwardness brought on by both this insularity and anti-mercantile attitude left Korea open to foreign conquest, and Japan took advantage of this in 1910. While this older Confucian system was overthrown and the Japanese brought in many outside influences, it must be kept in mind that Japan itself was a strongly Confucian society still at this time, albeit one that was absorbing Western influences. This means that Confucianism was not suppressed at a deeper level. After the defeat of the Japanese in World War II and the division of Korea into North and South, Confucianism was fully removed as an official doctrine in both parts of the country, which moved into their competition as examples of capitalism and socialism (Kim 1992; Hwang 1993). However, many observers continue to see strong Confucian influences in both of these successor states (Cumings 1997).

In the ROK modernization has been strongly associated with moving away from the hierarchy and insularity of Confucianism, symbolized by the increase to nearly a quarter of the population that is Christian, with a strong influence of the South's protector in the Korean War, the United States. Its economy would follow more the pattern of that of Japan, both with strong, indicative planning (Kuznets 1990) and with its large industrial conglomerates, the *chaebol*, which resemble the pre-1945 *zaibatsu* of Japan that the United States broke up. What then are the Confucian elements that have persisted?

The main ones are the emphasis on the importance of education and on the central role of the family. In both the ROK and the DPRK there is an enormous emphasis on education, with both of them near the top in the world in terms of the percentage of the population that goes on to college. Unsurprisingly, many see this as a central underpinning of the success of the ROK, even as the constraints of the system in the DPRK have held back its people's potential.

Nevertheless, even as the Confucian heritage ultimately lies behind the emphasis on education, the conflict between it and Western influences is intense within the education sector in South Korea (Chang 2009). Thus, critics see Korean education as too rigid, suppressing independent thought and creativity, with the admiration in society for education emphasizing a 'shallow credentialism' rather than substance. However, even as the problems in Korean education are attributed to the Confucian heritage, it is the Confucian heritage itself that lies behind the push for educational reform.

It is in the area of the continuing importance of the family that many see the role of Confucianism asserting itself most strongly. However, even here there are conflicts over interpretation (Chang 1997). Those in South Korean society who overtly support neo-Confucianism tend to be very politically and socially conservative. They oppose the emergence in the ROK of nuclear families of the US sort as many people have migrated from rural areas to cities, especially the mega-city of Seoul. This breaks up the more traditional extended family that they prefer. However, even within these nuclear families, traditional views of relations between men and women persist more strongly than in most other societies, and the idea of filial obedience retains its hold, again, Confucian influence surviving even as its more open advocates are repudiated.

This importance of the family and hierarchy shows up in the economy in the structure and functioning of the industrial chaebol. The overwhelming majority of these are family-owned firms, and all grew out of family firms (Cumings 1997). The CEO of a chaebol is both a father of his 'family' and the king of his company, combining two of the three bonds of traditional neo-Confucianism. This extends to their attitudes to workers, who are supposed to be docile and obedient, although they are not always so (Koo 2001). As Cumings (1997: 327) puts it: 'So these large kingdoms, [are] said to be run by men of unimpeachable morality and integrity in good Confucian fashion, expecting loyalty and distributing beneficence, even more than [in] the old court system.'

Needless to say, the chaebol have become controversial, and some of them have been broken up in the wake of the upheavals following the 1997 Asian financial crisis, which hit the ROK hard (Chang 2003). Nevertheless, they remain the dominant organizations within the Korean economy, their structure representing an internalization of activity along Japanese lines. More than any other element of the South Korean economy, they represent the confluence of the new institutionalist aspect of the economy and its new traditionalist element, a minimization of transactions costs within a hierarchically organized entity that runs itself along traditional Confucian lines within a technologically advanced economy integrated into the world economy.

Nevertheless, we must admit that the ROK cannot be fully labeled a new traditional economy, despite having these significant elements. As defined by Rosser and Rosser, such systems involve some advocacy of their own approach, as in the Islamic economy of Iran. In South Korea we see most of the society running from this heritage, viewing it as backward and oppressive, even as central elements of the society continue to fundamentally reflect its ongoing influence. In this regard, it could be argued that the ROK is a new traditional economy in spite of itself.

6 The North versus the South redux

At this point let us reiterate the contrasting way that the two Koreas reflect their common Confucian heritage. Certainly they are sharply contrasting in their relative economic performances, with the North in such bad shape that some observers have forecast its complete collapse (Eberstadt 1999). Also, while there is widespread opposition in the ROK to any sort of official Confucianism, this opposition is even stronger in the North, with communism seen to have fully supplanted Confucianism.

Even so, the DPRK exhibits several Confucianist aspects. We have already mentioned that it shares the obsession with education that one finds in the ROK. Also, while there is less official emphasis on families, the emphasis on filial piety and obedience to the leader has exhibited itself in the politics of the society at its top. Kim Jong Il succeeded his father, with all expected to obey the son as they were the father. As Cumings (1997: 413) puts it, 'It is Neo-Confucianism in a communist bottle.'

Indeed, in at least two respects, the DPRK is more Confucianist than the ROK. This is in both its anti-mercantile attitude and also in its insular imitation of the nineteenth-century 'Hermit Kingdom' with its *juche* policy of self-sufficiency. These two together go a long way to explain the poor economic performance of the North relative to the South. We draw again on Cumings (ibid.) to express how this seems to careful observers.

> The resonance with Korea's past means that the DPRK often impresses foreign visitors precisely in its cultural conservatism: a Japanese visitor old enough to remember prewar Japan remarked on the similarities he found in the 'antiquarian atmosphere' of North Korea ... The antiquarian aspect of this regime thus extends to an elite that has the same sense of birthright and entitlement as the old yangban (and for a minority that travels abroad, a life of world-class privilege). There is a yawning chasm between the elite prerogative and the difficult daily lives of nearly everyone else.

We close this discussion by noting that while it may be that the chaebol of the South reflect a new institutionalist outcome that has reduced transactions costs so that the ROK has become 'the premier development success story of the last half century,' the nature of the political economic system in the DPRK has suppressed any development of institutions or organizations that would reduce costs or increase efficiency as it has been managed on completely different grounds for completely different goals.

7 Conclusions

We have examined the hypothesis that the economy of South Korea (ROK) represents a fusion of the new institutional economy that organizes itself to minimize transactions costs within its organizations with the new traditional economy that embeds itself within a traditional social or religious structure while operating in a technologically advanced modern economy, with this fusion representing the economics of the Korean civilization. We find this not to be fully the case as the modern ROK substantially resists its Confucian heritage in many ways. However, the large chaebol firms have driven the export sector of the ROK economy very successfully over the last half century, while also reflecting values of familistic groupism and hierarchy, while drawing on a highly skilled labor force produced by an educational system inspired by the Confucian heritage of Korean society. South Korea at least partially fulfills this idea.

In contrast, the economy of North Korea fails to fulfill the new institutionalist aspect of this possible fusion with its inefficient and unproductive economic structures and organizations. Nevertheless, while its government is even more opposed to any sort of official Confucianism than that in the South, the DPRK is in some ways even more Confucianist, also admiring education, but also following the traditions of an earlier Korea in its refusal to open to the outside world, a neo-Hermit Kingdom in its anti-mercantile and poverty-stricken isolation.

Acknowledgment

We acknowledge valuable advice from Woosik Moon and Hee Jwa Sung, neither of whom should be held responsible for any errors of fact or interpretation remaining in this chapter.

Bibliography

Aoki, M. (2001) *Towards a Comparative Institutional Analysis*, Cambridge, MA: MIT Press.

Buchan, N. and Croson, R. (2004) 'The boundaries of trust: own and others' actions in the US and China,' *Journal of Economic Behavior and Organization*, 56:467–84.

Carpenter, J.P., Daniere, A.G., and Takahashi, L.M. (2004) 'Cooperation, trust, and social capital in southeast Asian urban slums,' *Journal of Economic Behavior and Organization*, 56:533–51.

Chang, K.-S. (1997) 'The neo-Confucian right and family politics in South Korea: the nuclear family as an ideological construct,' *Economy and Society*, 26:22–40.

Chang, S.-J. (2003) *Financial Crisis and Transformation of Korean Business Groups: The Rise and Fall of Chaebols*, Cambridge: Cambridge University Press.

Chang, S.J. (2009) 'A cultural and philosophical perspective on Korea's education reform: a critical way to maintain Korea's economic momentum,' *KEI Academic Paper Series*, 2:157–77.

Choi, Y.B. (2008) 'Path dependence and the Korean alphabet,' *Journal of Economic Behavior and Organization*, 66:185–201.

Chung, E.Y.J. (1995) *The Korean Neo-Confucianism of Yi T'oege and Yi Yulgok: A Reappraisal of the 'Four-Seven Thesis' and Its Practical Implications for Self-Cultivation*, Albany: State University of New York Press.

Chung, Y.-I. (2006) *Korea under Siege, 1876–1945: Capital Formation and Economic Transformation*, Oxford: Oxford University Press.

Coase, R.H. (1937) 'The nature of the firm,' *Economica*, 4:386–405.

Commons, J.R. (1931) *The Legal Foundations of Capitalism*, Madison: University of Wisconsin Press.

Cumings, B. (1997) *Korea's Place in the Sun: A Modern History*, New York: W.W. Norton.

Deuchler, M. (1992) *The Confucian Transformation of Korea: A Study of Society and Ideology*, Cambridge, MA: Harvard University Press.

Eberstadt, N. (1999) *The End of North Korea*, Washington: AEI Press.

Eder, N. (1996) *Poisoned Prosperity: Development, Modernization, and the Environment in South Korea*, Armonk: M.E. Sharpe.

Fukuyama, F. (1995) *Trust: The Social Virtues and the Creation of Prosperity*, New York: Free Press.

Greif, A. (2006) *Institutions and the Path to the Modern Economy: Lessons from Medieval Trade*, New York: Cambridge University Press.

Hodgson, G.M. (2004) *The Evolution of Institutional Economics: Agency, Structure and Darwinism in American Institutionalism*, London: Routledge.

Huntington, S.P. (1993) 'The clash of civilizations?' *Foreign Affairs*, 72:22–49.

Huntington, S.P. (1996) *The Clash of Civilizations and the Remaking of the World Order*, New York: Simon and Schuster.

Hwang, E.-G. (1993) *The Korean Economies: A Comparison of North and South*, Oxford: Clarendon Press.

Kahn, H. (1979) *World Development: 1979 and Beyond*, Boulder: Westview Press.

Kim, B.-L.P. (1992) *Two Koreas in Development: A Comparative Study of Principles and Strategies of Capitalist and Communist Third World Development*, New Brunswick: Transaction.

Kleiner, J. (2001) *Korea: A Century of Change*, Singapore: World Scientific Press.

Koo, H. (2001) *Korean Workers: The Culture and Politics of Class Formation*, Ithaca: Cornell University Press.

Kuran, T. (2009) 'Explaining the economic trajectories of civilizations: the systemic approach,' *Journal of Economic Behavior and Organization*, 71:593–605.

Kuznets, P.W. (1990) 'Indicative planning in Korea,' *Journal of Comparative Economics*, 14:657–76.

LeClair, E.E. and Schneider, H.K. (eds.) (1974) *Economic Anthropology: Readings in Theory and Analysis across Cultures*, New York: Macmillan.

Lee, S.H. (2009) 'North Korea and international financial organizations: political and economic barriers to cooperation,' *Korea's Economy*, 25:76–88.

Menger, C. (1871 (1981)) *Principles of Economics*, trans. James Dingwell and Bert F. Hoselitz, New York: New York University Press.

Menger, C. (1892) 'On the origin of money,' *Economic Journal*, 2:239–55.

Mitchell, T. (2009) 'Economic policy reforms in the Lee Myung-bak administration,' *Korea's Economy*, 25:33–44.

Noland, M. and Weeks, E. (2009) 'Korean institutional reform in comparative perspective,' *KEI Academic Paper Series*, 2:117–42.

North, D.C. (2005) *Understanding the Process of Economic Change*, Princeton: Princeton University Press.

Osgood, C. (1951) *The Koreans and Their Culture*, New York: Ronald Press.

Platteau, J.-P. (2000) *Institutions, Social Norms, and Economic Development*, Amsterdam: Harwood.

Polanyi, K. (1944) *The Great Transformation*, Boston: Beacon Press.

Pryor, F.L. (2008) 'System as a causal force,' *Journal of Economic Behavior and Organization*, 67:545–59.

Reischauer, E.O. and Fairbanks, J. (1960) *East Asia: The Great Tradition*, Boston: Houghton Mifflin.

Rosser, J.B., Jr. (2010) 'How complex are the Austrians?' in R. Koppl (ed.) *What Is Austrian about Austrian Economics? Volume 14 of Advances in Austrian Economics*, Bingley: JAI Press, pp. 165–79.

Rosser, J.B., Jr. and Rosser, M.V. (1995) 'A comparison of comparative economic anthropologies,' *History of Economics Review*, 23:96–107.

Rosser, J.B., Jr. and Rosser, M.V. (1996 [2004]) *Comparative Economics in a Transforming World Economy*, Chicago: Irwin (2nd edn, 2004, Cambridge, MA: MIT Press).

Rosser, J.B., Jr. and Rosser, M.V. (1998) 'Islamic and neo-Confucian perspectives on the new traditional economy,' *Eastern Economic Journal*, 24:217–32.

Rosser, J.B., Jr. and Rosser, M.V. (2005) 'The transition between the old and new traditional economies in India,' *Comparative Economic Studies*, 47:561–78.

Samuelson, P.A. (1947) *The Foundations of Economic Analysis*, Cambridge, MA: Harvard University Press.

Schmoller, G. von (1900–4). *Grundriss der allgemeinen Volkswirtschaftslehre, Vols I and II*, Berlin: Duncker & Humblot.

Simon, H.A. (1957) *Models of Man*, New York: Wiley.

Veblen, T. (1898) 'Why is economics not an evolutionary science?' *Quarterly Journal of Economics*, 12:373–97.

Whigham, H.J. (1904). *Manchuria and Korea*, London: Isbister.

Williamson, O. (1975) *Markets and Hierarchies: Analysis and Antitrust Implications – A Study in the Economics of Internal Organizations*, New York: Free Press.

Zak, P. and Knack, S. (2001) 'Trust and growth,' *Economic Journal*, 111:295–321.

10 The effect of fiscal drag on tax revenue and tax burden

Sung-Kyu Lee

1 Introduction

As far as income tax is concerned, most OECD countries seem to have had a similar experience in recent years. That is, statutory rate cuts combined with base broadening and/or fiscal drag have left income tax burdens *not reduced* as a proportion of GDP. In addition, the combination of fiscal drag, base broadening, and statutory rate cuts has meant that income tax revenues as a proportion of GDP or total tax revenues has changed *little* over the past 25 years across OECD countries.

For instance, Ireland is a typical example of a country in which in recent years the progressive income tax system has allowed Irish government revenues to swell due to both nominal and real fiscal drag without either increases in tax rates or decreases in the thresholds. This is because Ireland has experienced considerable economic growth, and this growth has resulted in high wage inflation.

Fiscal drag describes the phenomenon whereby more people move into higher tax brackets because tax allowances and tax thresholds are not adjusted in line with inflation or earnings growth.[1] Particularly, for the case of earnings growth, since incomes tend to rise more quickly than prices, if tax allowances and thresholds are only up-rated with prices, then over time *more people will pay taxes and more of them at higher rates*.

Fiscal drag is not a trivial issue, since fiscal drag is a sly way of extracting more taxes from earners while avoiding headline increases in tax rates. Over time, people pay at higher average and marginal tax rates and they don't really know why. And with these higher marginal rates come reduced work incentives, resulting in damaging effects on the economy.

Normally, with unchanged tax policies, the tax burden is expected to increase, reflecting the effects of *real fiscal drag*. Fiscal drag is a feature of the tax system which means that the total tax burden has a tendency to rise each year unless the government takes action to stop it. In addition, where taxes are indexed, only price inflation is adjusted, but the growth in earnings is not adjusted. Given that earnings tend to grow faster than prices, the result is that the government automatically collects more tax revenues each year without having to raise taxes.

In general, fiscal drag is a phenomenon that appears in income tax. In addition, fiscal drag also occurs in other taxes where allowances fail to keep pace with underlying growth in the tax base. For instance, the fiscal drag phenomenon can be seen, even on a smaller scale, for taxes such as capital gain tax and stamp duty on properties, where the tax base tends to grow more quickly than the rise in thresholds.

We will attempt to explain the significance of fiscal drag in both tax revenue and tax burden in an illustrative way, and then to propose some policy implications to eliminate fiscal drag. Public finance scholars often propose that government should reform the tax system in a *low tax rate and broad tax base* way. Instead of following this fundamental principle, government seeks a different scheme: *narrow tax band and broad number of taxpayers*. The most widely advocated remedy for fiscal drag is the indexation of tax thresholds. However, this research will suggest that the institution making fiscal policy should be transparent in order to avoid fiscal drag.

This chapter is organized as follows. Section 2 describes the conceptual definition of four different fiscal drags, which section 1 classifies. In Section 3, we examine the relationship between fiscal drag and tax revenue and, in turn, in Section 4, we analyze the effect of fiscal drag on the tax burden based on the OECD (2007) results. Section 5 deals with several implications derived from fiscal drag and some policy adjustments to offset it. Finally, Section 6 presents concluding remarks and further research.

2 Fiscal drag: conceptual framework

In this section, we discuss briefly the mechanics and driving factors of fiscal drag in a conceptual framework. Studies looking at the effects of fiscal drag have mainly focused on the role of inflation.[2] The mechanisms are, however, the same regardless of whether rising earnings levels are due to inflation or real earnings growth. But, tax increases as a result of inflation are likely to be of greater concern as they may occur in the context of largely unchanged real earnings so that real after-tax incomes may decline when tax burdens go up.

Inflation reduces the real value of tax-band limits. In a progressive income tax, this pushes taxpayers with unchanged real incomes further up the tax schedule into higher marginal rates (hence the term *bracket creep*). However, as greater proportions of their taxable income are taxed at higher rates, tax burdens change even for those who do not move into the next tax band. In addition, inflation erodes the real value of tax-free allowances, flat-rate tax deductions, tax credits, and cash benefits. As some of these are targeted toward low-income taxpayers, fiscal drag can make tax systems *less progressive*.

Empirical results show, however, that this does not necessarily mean that they become less redistributive.[3] The reason is that, even with reduced progressivity, income taxes still reduce inequality, as tax burdens are higher for the rich. In fact, because fiscal drag increases overall income tax revenues, the equalizing effect of income taxes is likely to be strengthened, despite declining progressivity.

2.1 Traditional fiscal drag and fiscal dividend

The definition of *fiscal drag* was first developed by the Council of Economic Advisers (1962) in the United States. They state that

> automatic stabilizers work in a fashion that may inhibit the long-run expansion of demand. As the economy moves along the potential output path with reasonably stable prices, the Federal tax system generates an increase in revenues of about 6% a year. Unless this revenue growth is offset by reductions in taxes or by increases in expenditures, it acts as a 'fiscal drag' by siphoning off income.[4]

Moreover, according to Heller (1966),

> In a growth context, the great revenue-raising power of our Federal tax system produces a built-in average increase of $7 to $8 billion a year in Federal revenue. Unless it is offset by such 'fiscal dividends' as tax cuts or expansion of Federal programs, this automatic rise in revenues will become a 'fiscal drag' siphoning too much of the economic substance out of the private economy and thereby choking expansion.[5]

Musgrave and Musgrave (1989) stated that 'given a passive policy which holds tax rates and expenditure programs unchanged, a built-in increase in revenues leads to a rising surplus at a full-employment level of income, thereby exerting a drag on the economy.' The slowdown of the economy in the late 1950s and early 1960s was attributed to this development. Thus, a *passive* or *do-nothing policy*, which leaves tax rates and expenditure levels unchanged, is in effect *a policy of restriction* as the economy grows. This implies that discretionary action is needed to offset it. Musgrave also argued that fiscal drag can be offset through *fiscal dividend*.[6]

Income tax burdens are expected to increase automatically as a result of a progressive rate structure, coupled with an increasing growth in nominal income. Inflation tends to accelerate the tempo of such growth. This function of the individual income tax system is often regarded as a stabilizing effect which compensates counter-cyclically for the fluctuations in national income over changing business conditions. This is referred to as the *built-in flexibility* of taxation.

However, this flexibility does not always have a beneficial effect on the economy. In the long-run process of economic growth, it tends to depress the level of aggregate demand, especially during recoveries, and to slow down the potential path of economic growth. Thus, it is generally acknowledged that the depressing effect of progressive income taxes is not desirable from the standpoint of long-term policy objectives.

Even if the distortion of inflation on income taxes can fully be offset, tax revenues grow faster than real incomes, and thus effective tax rates increase constantly. In the United States, the phenomenon has been called *fiscal drag*, drawing attention to the fact that it is one of the shortcomings in the mechanism of built-in tax stabilizers in a growing economy. There are two policy measures that can cure fiscal drag: (1) tax reductions and (2) increases in government expenditures. These remedies together are frequently called *fiscal dividend*, in contrast to the concept of fiscal drag.[7]

The most conspicuous characteristic of postwar tax policy in Japan was the successive rounds of annual tax reductions that occurred until the late 1970s, focusing primarily on individual income tax. This policy seems closely related to fiscal dividend. The Japanese government adopted 'tax reductions,' rather than increases in government expenditures, as the means of making fiscal dividend effective, mainly because it considered the tendency toward increasing tax burdens as undesirable. As a result, this policy option has prevented the level of government expenditures from expanding rapidly in the past years, and has contributed to the construction of a comparatively small government.

On the other hand, the Japanese government did not adopt any measures of inflationary correction in the income tax system in the 1980s. As a result, there are two points worth noting related to fiscal drag. First, real tax burdens rose in Japan because of bracket creep as nominal income increased. Thus, fiscal drag occurred, demanding a higher proportion of the taxpayers' rising money income as taxes. Second, the government automatically received increasing tax revenues as a result of inflation. Thus the impact of inflation on the Japanese tax system was obvious because individual income tax revenues *rose* relatively rapidly, while revenues from indirect taxes *fell* throughout the whole tax system in Japan. This represents *a switch from indirect to direct taxation*, and thus this could be regarded as an unintended byproduct of inflation in the absence of proper adjustments in Japan.[8]

2.2 Fiscal drag: nominal and real

Fiscal drag refers to the process whereby tax thresholds are either not adjusted for inflation or fail to keep pace with earnings growth and thus, in either case, an automatic rise in tax revenues occurs. On the other hand, fiscal drag means the effect of inflation on tax revenues. If tax allowances are not kept in line with inflation, individuals pay relatively higher amounts of tax, thus dragging down post-tax incomes. Consequently, the demand for goods and services falls.[9]

In order to understand the concept, we can take an example of nominal fiscal drag as follows. Suppose a person earns $20,000 per year and is liable to pay 20 percent tax on earnings above a threshold of $5,000 per year. Then they pay $(20,000 - 5,000) \times 0.20 = \$3,000$ in tax, or 15 percent of their income. Now suppose that due to inflation, their wages go up by 5 percent, but the government only increases the tax threshold by 2 percent. Now they must pay $(21,000 - 5,100) \times 0.20 = \$3,180$, or 15.14 percent of their income. The proportion of income as tax has increased and this process is referred to as *nominal fiscal drag*. Thus, nominal fiscal drag refers to the increase in tax revenue caused when the threshold of a tax is not increased in line with inflation.

Nominal fiscal drag is conceptually the same as *bracket creep*. Bracket creep is the process by which inflation pushes wages and salaries into higher tax brackets. A progressive tax system is usually not adjusted for inflation. As wages and salaries rise in nominal terms under the influence of inflation, they become more highly taxed, even though in real terms the value of wages and salaries has not increased at all. The net effect is that in real terms taxes rise unless the tax rates or brackets are adjusted to compensate.

On the other hand, *real fiscal drag* takes place when tax thresholds are increased in line with rising prices (inflation) to avoid nominal fiscal drag, but where a growing economy means that earnings rise faster than inflation, thus increasing taxes as a proportion of earnings.[10]

2.3 Modern fiscal drag

Finally, thresholds are as important as rates in income tax. In recent years, increasing attention has been devoted to how many people are paying at higher tax rates in addition to the overall number of income taxpayers. Much of the rise in the *number of taxpayers* and in the *number of higher-rate taxpayers* can be explained by the process of *fiscal drag*. Income tax and national insurance thresholds are increased every year in line with inflation unless the government explicitly decides to adopt measures for adjustments. But incomes tend to rise more quickly than prices, so over time an increasing amount of people's incomes crosses the threshold and moves into higher tax brackets. Fiscal drag is not restricted to income tax and national insurance: it applies to any tax or benefit with thresholds that increase less quickly than the 'tax base' over time. Thus, the government explicitly overrides statutory up-rating arrangements and means-tested benefits cover ever fewer people, while inheritance taxes, for example, capture even more.

The rise in the number of taxpayers and in the number of high-rate taxpayers is not solely due to above-inflation income growth. Fiscal drag can be accelerated if thresholds are increased by less than inflation is. For instance, this can happen if personal allowance is frozen or the basic rate limit is frozen. Conversely, fiscal drag can be slowed if thresholds are increased by more than inflation is. Moreover, the increased number of people in a tax band will increase inequality in pretax incomes. For example, high-income people will have faster income growth than average, while low-income people will have lower-than-average income growth. This means that the number of higher-rate taxpayers will increase even more quickly, but the total number of taxpayers more slowly, than average real income growth.

Clearly, *increases in the number of taxpayers and in the number of high-rate taxpayers increase government revenues*, both in real terms and as a proportion of GDP. To an extent, therefore, *fiscal drag can do the same job as raising tax rates*. Thus, for example, in the United Kingdom, normal fiscal drag is already built into the treasury's medium-term revenue forecasts. Taken together, Table 10.1 classifies fiscal drag based on the above arguments.

Table 10.1 Classification of fiscal drag

Type	Cause	Solution
Traditional fiscal drag	Economic growth	Fiscal dividend
Nominal fiscal drag	Inflation	Price indexation
Real fiscal drag	Earnings growth	Earnings indexation
Modern fiscal drag	Not adjusted to thresholds	Fiscal transparency

3 Fiscal drag and tax revenue

In this section, we first examine the relationship between fiscal drag and tax revenue. Tax revenues as a share of GDP tend to increase over time. In effect, tax revenues as a share of GDP have increased during the past two decades across OECD countries. There are various reasons why the ratio of taxes to national income can change, the most important of which are economic growth and discretionary tax change.

We will attempt to discuss the effect of economic growth on fiscal drag. A given tax system will tend to produce tax revenues that are higher as a share of GDP during periods when the economy is running above trend output and lower when the economy is operating below trend. This is due to, for example, changes in levels of employment and profits affecting income tax and corporation tax receipts. In addition to this *cyclical* effect, there is over time a tendency for taxes to increase as a share of GDP as the economy grows. This phenomenon is known as *fiscal drag* and is partly a product of the progressivity of the tax system. Income tax allowances are normally raised in line with retail price inflation, while earnings tend to grow in real terms. As a result, more income is taxed at each rate of income taxation. The government will also tend to receive more revenue in social security taxes. Therefore, the government must take into account in its fiscal projection that in the absence of offsetting measures, the ratio of taxes to GDP will rise by, for example, 0.23 percentage points a year when the economy is growing at close to trend rate.

Second, we examine discretionary budget and tax measures. The proportion of national income taken in taxation is affected by discretionary changes in taxation. These can be implemented in several ways: changes in tax rates, changing the tax base, and introducing new taxes.

The increase in tax revenues over time is usually influenced by the following four factors:

1 *Discretionary budget and tax measures*: explicit net tax increases announced by the government's Budget Report.
2 *Real fiscal drag*: the government's decision not to raise thresholds and allowances in line with growth in the underlying tax base: for example, through not increasing income tax thresholds in line with growth in incomes.
3 *Economic cycle*: tax revenue is higher when national income is thought to be stronger.

4   *Other economic factors*, such as the composition of national income and the
     health of financial sector.

In particular, an important factor that contributes to boost tax receipts is the phenomenon known as *fiscal drag*. In general, the government conventionally
assumes that income tax allowances and thresholds rise in line with prices rather
than earnings. However, as earnings tend to grow in real terms over time, this
definition of *unchanged policy* will see revenues increase as a share of national
income or GDP over time as people migrate into higher tax brackets. Acquiesc-
ing to this fiscal drag is, in effect, a *policy choice* of government. This implies
that, if unchecked, fiscal drag will raise tax revenues. In fact, fiscal drag has gone
largely unchecked, which helps explain why the number of people paying
income tax has risen and why the number paying it at the higher rate has risen.

For instance, Table 10.2 shows the impact of discretionary policy measures
(i.e., budget/tax measures) over the period 1997–2008 in the United Kingdom.
In addition, it shows the decomposition into the cumulated impact of fiscal drag,
the economic cycle, and other economic factors on revenues of 2007/8 in the
United Kingdom.

The effect of budget and tax measures on the government revenues in 2007/8
in the United Kingdom was 2 percent of the national income. On the contrary,
fiscal drag increased tax revenues in a cumulative way by 2.2 percent of GDP in
the United Kingdom. That is, by 2007/8, fiscal drag had contributed 2.2 percent
of the national income for 11 years. In addition, the economic cycle was estimated to have contributed 0.2 percent a year and other economic factors decreased
revenues by 2.3 percent of GDP a year.[11] Figure 10.1 illustrates this.

4 Fiscal drag and tax burden

In this section, we explain the effect of fiscal drag on the tax burden based on the
OECD (2007) results. Changes in the tax burden do not result only from policy
action; in a changing economic environment, they can also occur if policies are
not adjusted. In particular, since tax rates depend on income levels, higher or

Table 10.2 Cumulated contributions to change in tax revenues from 1997 to 2008 in the
           United Kingdom

Main factors	*Impact on revenues in 2007/8 budget (% of GDP)*
Budget/tax measures	2.0
Fiscal drag	**2.2**
Economic cycle	0.2
Other factors	−2.3

Source: IFS, *The Green Budget 2008* (2008).

Notes
1 The figures are cumulated number for 11 years from 1996/7 to 2006/7.
2 Fiscal drag is estimated using the UK Treasury's estimate of 0.2% a year.

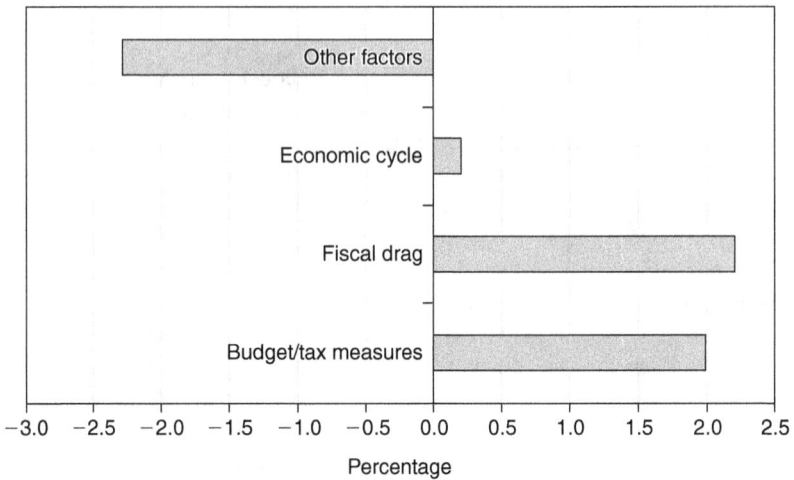

Figure 10.1 Impact on UK tax revenues in 2007/8 (unit: % of GDP) (source: IFS, *The Green Budget 2008*, 2008).

lower earnings will alter the share of gross earnings that taxpayers are liable to pay in taxes. In a *progressive* tax system, rising earning levels result in higher tax burdens. This mechanism is often referred to as *fiscal drag*.

Fiscal drag tends to impact on both tax burden and tax revenue. Here, we will focus on the tax burden aspect. If the earnings of many taxpayers move in the same direction due to either inflation or real earnings growth, then the effect on average tax burdens and total tax revenues can be substantial, and thus this must be taken explicitly into account when addressing tax policy. Therefore, we can raise one important question, whether policy must be changed or adjusted so as to offset fiscal drag, and, furthermore, to what extent each government should rely on the fiscal drag effect as a means of increasing tax revenues.

Inflation and real earnings growth increase the tax burden, which is often measured by the 'tax wedge.' The tax wedge denotes the difference between labor cost to the employer and after-tax pay by the employee.

OECD (2007) uses the tax wedge to measure the tax-burden indicator.[12] The tax wedge denotes the difference between labor cost to the employer and after-tax pay received by the employee.[13] The tax wedge is expressed in a percent of a measure of labor cost to the employer.

Figure 10.2 shows the tax wedge between 2000 and 2006 for both a single worker earning an average wage and the fiscal drag effect. First, tax wedges for a single worker earning an average wage remained unchanged on average across OECD countries. But a number of countries, such as Japan, Iceland, and Finland, observed substantial changes in the tax burden between the years 2000 and 2006. Second, we can observe *significant fiscal drag effects* in some countries such as Mexico, Ireland, Greece, and Hungary. In spite of these effects, the tax wedge in

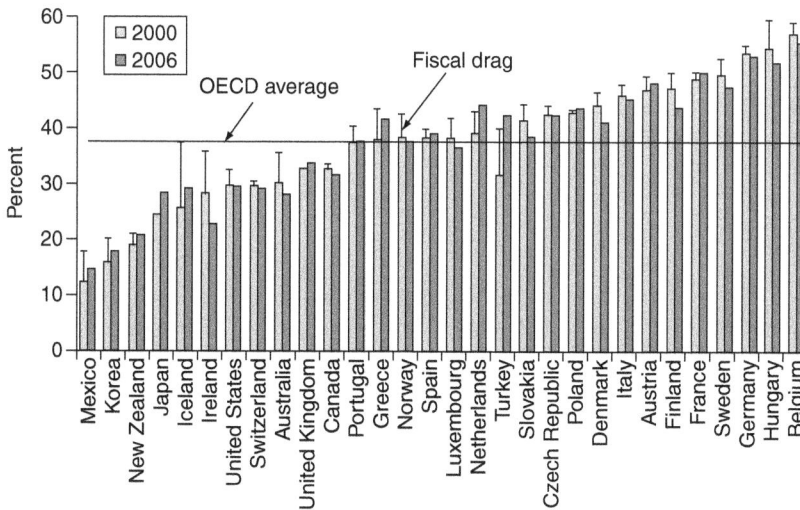

Figure 10.2 Tax wedge in 2000 and 2006 and fiscal drag effect in the case of average wage for single worker (source: OECD, *Taxing Wages 2006–2007*, 2007).

2006 was not substantial. This implies that these countries appear to have offset policy measures that tended to lower tax burdens for average-wage earners. In the absence of either automatic or discretionary policy adjustments, inflation and real earnings growth would have increased tax wedges by 2.6 percentage points on average (see Table 10.3).

In Figure 10.2, the *fiscal drag effect* accounts for both inflation and real earnings growth. It is the change in tax burdens that would have been observed between 2000 and 2006 in the absence of any discrete policy measures or automatic adjustments, such as 'indexing for inflation.' The fiscal drag effect in the Figure 10.2 was added to the tax wedge in 2000. This implies that the *sum* of the fiscal drag effect and the tax wedge in 2000 represents the tax wedge that would have resulted in the unadjusted tax system from the year 2000 for someone earning an average 2006 wage.

Table 10.3 shows the tax-wedge change between 2000 and 2006 in the case of an average wage. In most countries that saw rising tax burdens, increases in tax burdens tended to fall short of the fiscal drag effect. This implies that fiscal drag was partly offset by automatic or discretionary tax policy adjustments. In Korea, the fiscal drag effect exceeded the actual change in the tax wedge. That is, the actual change of the tax wedge was increased by 1.8 percentage points in 2006, but the fiscal drag effect was 4.2 percentage points. But three countries are exceptions: New Zealand, Japan, and Turkey. In New Zealand, the tax-wedge increase of 1.7 percentage points was entirely due to positive fiscal drag. In Japan, tax wedges went up by 4 percentage points in the absence of fiscal drag. In Turkey, in the absence of counterbalancing measures, inflation was running at

Table 10.3 Tax-wedge *change* between 2000 and 2006 for average wage of single worker (unit: %)

Country	Actual change	Fiscal drag
Australia	−2.2	+5.0
Austria	+0.9	+2.1
Belgium	−1.6	+2.1
Canada	−1.3	+0.7
Czech Republic	−0.1	+1.6
Denmark	−3.1	+2.3
Finland	−3.7	+2.4
France	+0.6	+0.6
Germany	−0.8	+1.1
Greece	+3.4	**+5.4**
Hungary	−2.7	+4.9
Iceland	+3.4	**+11.6**
Ireland	−5.9	**+7.1**
Italy	−0.9	+1.5
Japan	+4.0	−0.0
Korea	**+1.8**	**+4.2**
Luxembourg	−2.0	+3.4
Mexico	+2.4	**+5.4**
Netherlands	+4.7	+3.5
New Zealand	+1.7	+1.7
Norway	−1.1	+4.1
Poland	+0.6	+0.5
Portugal	+0.1	+3.2
Slovakia	−3.2	+2.9
Spain	+0.5	+1.5
Sweden	−2.4	+2.6
Switzerland	−0.6	+0.7
Turkey	+2.3	−8.3
United Kingdom	+1.5	+0.4
United States	−0.5	+2.5
OECD average	−0.1	+2.6

Source: OECD, *Taxing Wages 2006–2007* (2007).

more than 200 percent over the six-year period and this resulted in a negative fiscal drag of 8.3 percentage points.

Table 10.3 and Figure 10.3 show that inflation and real earnings growth would have increased tax wedges by 2.6 percentage points on average in OECD countries between 2000 and 2006. In particular, in Greece, Iceland, Ireland, and Mexico, the fiscal drag effect amounted for more than 5 percentage points.

Most importantly, the size of potential fiscal drag effects is, to a large extent, determined by the magnitude of changes in *wage levels* rather than inflation. Table 10.4 demonstrates that, during the 2000–6 period, average wages increased by more than 40 percent in nine countries: the Czech Republic, Greece, Hungary, Iceland, Korea, Mexico, Portugal, Slovakia, and Turkey. This implies that in the absence of automatic or discretionary counterbalancing policy measures,

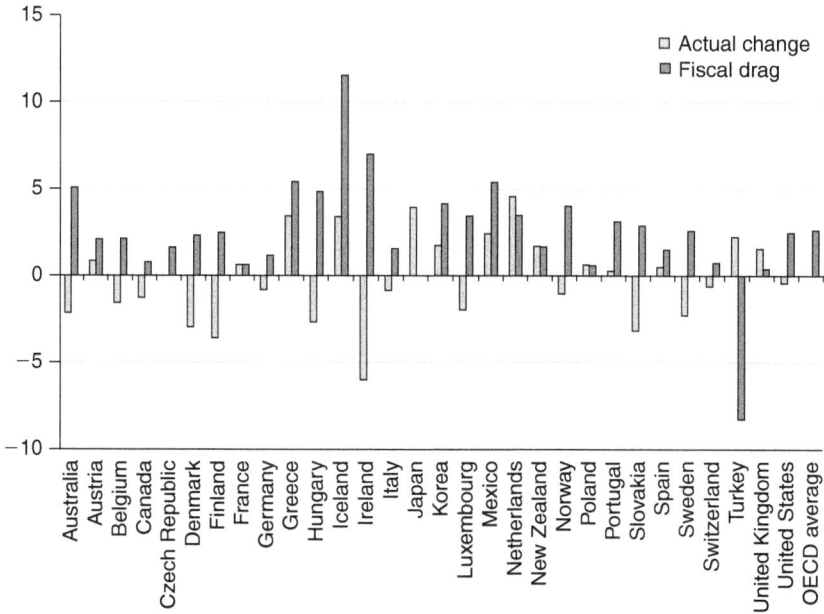

Figure 10.3 Tax-wedge change between 2000 and 2006 for average wage of single worker.

fiscal drag effects would have been *sizable* in these countries. Moreover, in five of these countries, *inflation* was the main driving factor of higher nominal wages: Iceland, Mexico, Portugal, Slovakia, and Turkey. But, in the remaining four countries, real wage growth exceeded inflation: the Czech Republic, Greece, Hungary, and Korea.

Table 10.5 and Figure 10.4 show the link between earnings increases and fiscal drag across OECD countries. In addition, Figure 10.5 illustrates a strong link between the fiscal drag effect and tax progressivity across OECD countries, where the indicator is the elasticity of the total tax burden for a single worker in the base period, or the year 2000.

Now, we turn to examining the fiscal drag effect in Korea from the OECD (2007) results. Figure 10.6 shows how fiscal drag affected tax burdens at lower, average, and higher earnings levels for single individuals in the case of Korea. That is, this figure shows tax-burden differences between 2000 and 2006 for single individuals earning between 30 percent and 220 percent of the average wage. The horizontal axis represents earnings levels between 30 percent and 220 percent of the average wage. The outer area represents the fiscal drag effect due to real earnings growth, and the interior area is due to inflation. In the absence of either automatic or discretionary policy adjustments, *fiscal drag effects would have caused tax wedges to rise significantly in Korea.* This phenomenon is the same for almost all OECD countries. Tax increases resulting from fiscal drag are

Table 10.4 Inflation and real earnings growth in OECD from 2000 to 2006 (%)

Country	Change in average wage	Inflation	Real average wage growth
Australia	32.7	16.1	14.3
Austria	21.1	10.1	10.0
Belgium	17.8	13.2	4.0
Canada	13.5	10.5	2.7
Czech Republic	43.0	10.9	28.9
Denmark	17.4	11.5	5.3
Finland	24.7	7.6	15.8
France	17.7	9.9	7.1
Germany	12.6	9.0	3.3
Greece	47.9	19.6	23.6
Hungary	76.5	31.0	34.7
Iceland	48.9	29.2	15.3
Ireland	37.8	19.3	15.5
Italy	16.5	17.0	−0.4
Japan	0.2	−5.1	5.6
Korea	58.1	20.7	30.9
Luxembourg	21.2	14.5	5.9
Mexico	51.2	37.5	9.9
Netherlands	23.6	14.7	7.8
New Zealand	21.9	11.0	9.8
Norway	33.3	10.8	20.3
Poland	18.9	14.3	4.1
Portugal	40.4	19.2	17.8
Slovak Republic	56.3	34.8	16.0
Spain	22.9	21.7	1.0
Sweden	24.4	9.3	13.7
Switzerland	12.0	5.8	5.8
Turkey	204.1	245.0	−11.8
United Kingdom	30.6	13.0	15.6
United States	18.7	14.6	3.7

Source: OECD, *Taxing Wages 2006–2007* (2007).

often pronounced at lower earnings levels. The main factor driving this pattern is tax relief or reductions targeted to low-income taxpayers. The reason for this phenomenon is that once earnings increase above a certain limit, these tax concessions may no longer be available for them.

5 Some policy implications

In this section, we examine several implications derived from fiscal drag and some policy adjustments to offset it.

Table 10.5 Earning growth, tax progressivity, and fiscal drag

Country	Change in average wage	Progressivity indicator: tax wedge elasticity	Fiscal drag (%)
Australia	0.372354	1.772865	+16.5
Austria	0.234039	1.196391	+4.4
Belgium	0.190557	1.288541	+3.6
Canada	0.105103	1.19802	+2.1
Czech Republic	0.428834	1.153765	+3.8
Denmark	0.174654	1.488082	+5.2
Finland	0.251354	1.355321	+5.1
France	0.169783	1.13108	+1.2
Germany	0.124315	1.114389	+2.0
Greece	0.537132	1.480457	+14.0
Hungary	0.832406	1.247093	+9.0
Iceland	0.624635	2.357229	+44.5
Ireland	0.3613	2.09096	+24.8
Italy	0.169685	1.251551	+3.2
Japan	−0.0075	1.458417	−0.1
Korea	0.586858	1.874463	+25.5
Luxembourg	0.215916	1.618628	+8.8
Mexico	0.527326	2.614819	+42.7
Netherlands	0.229744	1.389584	+8.8
New Zealand	0.230908	1.746364	+8.8
Norway	0.33306	1.513201	+10.7
Poland	0.269286	1.062485	+1.1
Portugal	0.404283	1.397931	+8.4
Slovakia	0.560441	1.240724	+6.9
Spain	0.232389	1.199677	+3.9
Sweden	0.231568	1.331814	+5.2
Switzerland	0.096291	1.430106	+2.2
Turkey	–	0.601527	−20.6
United Kingdom	0.274085	1.293796	+1.1
United States	0.188587	1.636188	+8.2

Source: OECD, *Taxing Wages 2006–2007* (2007).

5.1 Policy adjustment and fiscal drag

To avoid inflation-induced tax increases, many OECD countries operate 'automatic inflation adjustments' that are known as *indexing*. The scope of these measures varies across countries, however, and they generally fall short of adjusting all tax-relevant amounts, thresholds, and limits.[14] Only three OECD countries, Denmark, Norway and Sweden, report that income tax schedules are regularly adjusted to changes in real earnings.

Counterbalancing measures can be used to offset fiscal drag. Table 10.6 shows such measures adopted in OECD countries. In Korea, we see there are no measures to offset fiscal drag due to either inflation or earnings growth.

Thus, in order to keep revenues and their composition broadly unchanged as shares of GDP over the longer term, the government needs a comprehensive

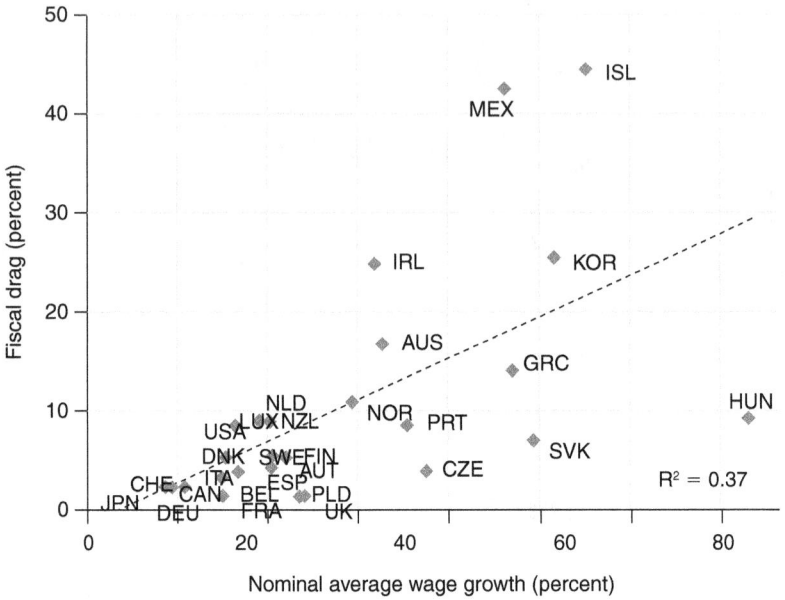

Figure 10.4 Earnings growth and fiscal drag (source: OECD, *Taxing Wages 2006–2007*, 2007).

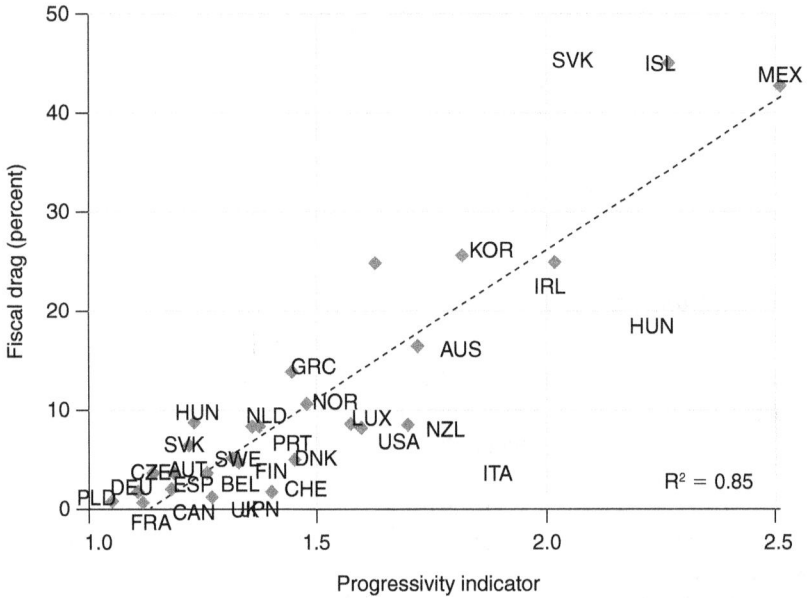

Figure 10.5 Tax progressivity and fiscal drag (source: OECD, *Taxing Wages 2006–2007*, 2007).

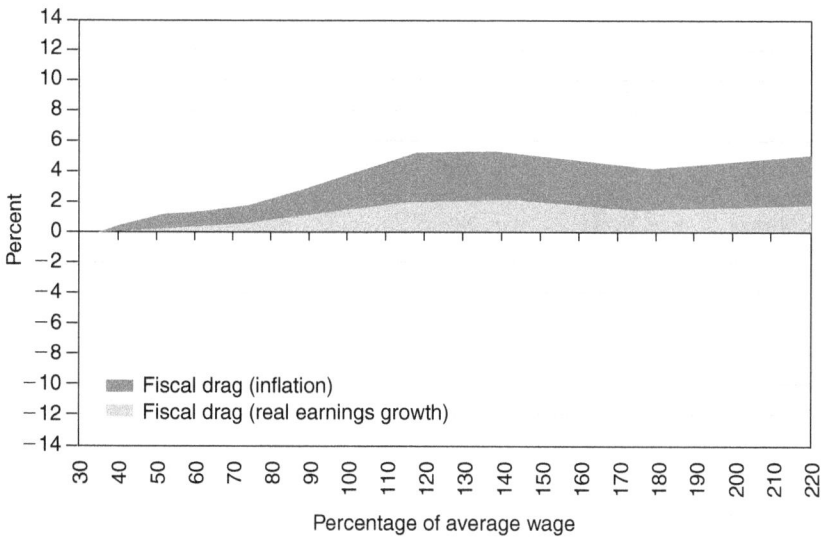

Figure 10.6 Tax wedge difference between 2000 and 2006 for single individuals in Korea's case (source: OECD, *Taxing Wages 2006–2007*, 2007).

form of *real indexation*: this means tax allowances and thresholds must rise in line with growth in the relevant tax base, which is often faster than prices.

5.2 Fiscal drag as a policy choice

The government tends to *exploit* fiscal drag, over the short to medium term, with the increase in marginal, as well as average, income tax rates for many people. Exploiting fiscal drag is the most sensible way for the government to raise extra revenues. But the government will not make this explicit. Therefore, this would, in effect, be a *policy choice* of the government, rather than an economically neutral assumption.[15]

5.3 Institutional tax reform for fiscal drag

On average across OECD countries, tax wedges at most earnings levels declined somewhat during the 2000–6 period. While most OECD countries have implemented tax-cutting measures, such as lowering tax rates or making tax concessions more generous, these measures have not always led to significant decreases in the tax burden.[16]

Where the effect of measures aimed at reducing tax burdens was limited, the main reason was a *lack of regular adjustments* of tax policy parameters to higher earnings levels. In many OECD countries, average full-time earnings have increased considerably over the 2000–6 period. With progressive tax systems in

Table 10.6 Automatic and discretionary adjustments to prevent fiscal drag in OECD countries

Country	Income tax: adjustments for inflation	Income tax: adjustments for real earnings growth	Family benefits	Social contributions
Australia	No	No	Yes	n.a.
Austria	No	No	No	Yes
Belgium	Yes	No	Yes	No
Canada	Yes	No	Yes	Partly
Czech Republic	–	No	Yes	n.a.
Denmark	Yes	*Yes*	Yes	Yes
Finland	Yes	–	–	n.a.
France	Yes	No	–	Yes
Germany	No	No	No	Partly
Greece	No	No	n.a.	Yes
Hungary	Yes	No	Yes	Yes
Iceland	Yes	–	Yes	Yes
Ireland	No	No	Yes	Yes
Italy	No	No	No	Yes
Japan	No	No	No	–
Korea	No	No	No	n.a.
Luxembourg	No	No	Yes	Yes
Mexico	Partly	No	n.a.	Yes
Netherlands	Yes	No	Yes	Yes
New Zealand	No	No	No	n.a.
Norway	Yes	*Yes*	No	Yes
Poland	No	No	Yes	Yes
Portugal	Yes	No	Yes	n.a.
Slovakia	Yes	No	Yes	Yes
Spain	Yes	No	n.a.	Yes
Sweden	Yes	*Yes*	No	Yes
Switzerland	Yes	–	Yes	–
Turkey	Yes	–	n.a.	Yes
United Kingdom	Yes	No	Yes	Yes
United States	Yes	No	Yes	Yes

Source: OECD, *Taxing Wages 2006–2007* (2007).

place, higher earnings usually translate into higher tax burdens: this phenomenon is known as *fiscal drag*. Unless tax systems are *adjusted* to compensate for these effects, the evolution of earnings levels can have substantial effects on the tax burdens faced by employees.

Without counterbalancing policy measures, the combination of inflation and real earnings growth would have led to significant tax-wedge increases in almost all OECD countries. The fiscal drag effect is especially strong where tax systems are particularly progressive or where earnings growth has been above average, which was common in Greece, Iceland, Korea, and Mexico.

Most OECD countries employ some form of *adjustments*, such as *indexing* tax band limits for inflation, in order to prevent large tax-burden changes as a result of inflation or real earnings growth. But, these adjustments are incomplete or infrequent in most countries. As a result, the impact of tax reform that aims at lowering tax burdens in a given year can, to a large extent, offset fiscal drag effects accumulated over extended periods. In a small number of countries that saw tax burdens grow over the 2000–6 period, the fiscal drag effect has, in fact, been the main driver of these developments.[17]

5.4 Price and earnings indexation to eliminate fiscal drag

The government must make policy decisions so as to offset the fiscal drag effect. To illustrate, we take as an example the UK case and thus we can gain some insights from the UK example.[18] In 2003–4, the higher-rate taxpayers numbered 3.3 million in the United Kingdom. Figure 10.7 shows projections of the number of people in each income tax band in 2009–10 under three alternative assumptions for tax thresholds: price indexation, earnings indexation, and freezing. Price indexation represents all thresholds increasing in line with inflation, while earnings indexation means thresholds increasing in line with average earnings growth. Freezing refers to remaining the same in cash terms. First, if income tax thresholds were increased in line with earnings ('earnings indexation scenario') over six years from 2003/4 to 2009/10, then the number of higher-rate taxpayers would remain virtually *unchanged* over that period. Second, if income tax thresholds were increased in line with prices ('price indexation scenario'), then some 300,000 extra people would start paying income tax and more than one million would move into the higher-rate band compared to those in 2003/4. Finally, if thresholds were frozen ('frozen scenario'), there would be 2.6 million more higher-rate taxpayers compared to those in 2003/4.[19]

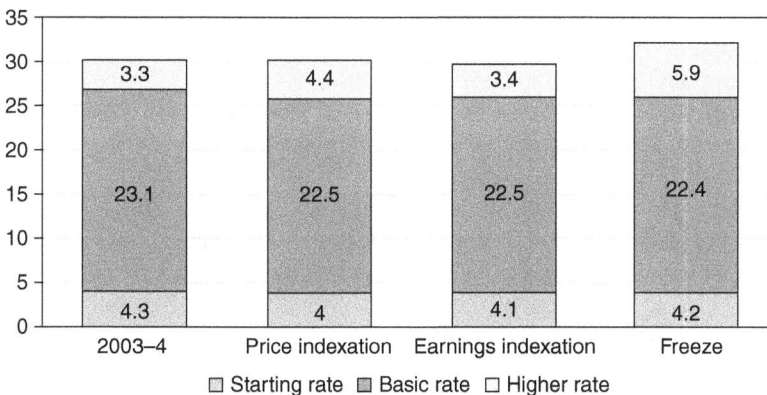

Figure 10.7 UK number of taxpayers expected in 2009–10 as of 2005–6 (unit: millions) (source: IFS, *The Green Budget 2004*, 2004).

5.5 Political dimension and tax transparency

Although nominal fiscal drag can easily be countered by a system of *index-linked tax brackets*, this may be politically undesirable. Many voters do not perceive the effects of fiscal drag, so the government may prefer to adjust tax brackets manually once every few years – in effect restoring the real tax rates to their approximate preinflation levels, but in a way that either gives the government the appearance of cutting taxes, or makes the government seem as if they are giving the taxpayer an additional benefit. Not surprisingly, such changes are usually made right before a general election is to be held.

5.6 Fiscal forecasting and fiscal drag

The government should incorporate a structural increase in revenues arising from fiscal drag in forecasting tax revenues. There is a case for presenting public finance forecasts in such a way that *unchanged* policies imply that, other things being equal, tax allowances and thresholds are adjusted to keep the tax burden constant. Specifically, in some countries, this reflects the government's conventional forecasting assumption that tax allowances and thresholds must rise in line with prices. As earnings typically rise more quickly, this implies a continuous rise in the share of the national income taken in income tax as more people find larger proportions of their income being taxed at higher rates. For instance, the UK Treasury estimates that *fiscal drag increases current receipts by 0.2 percent of the national income, or GDP, a year*. Thus, the government uses a comprehensive form of 'real taxation' when projecting some tax revenues beyond its short-term forecasting horizon.[20]

6 Conclusion

The number of higher-rate taxpayers tends to increase over time because tax thresholds are habitually indexed by price inflation from year to year, whereas earnings normally grow by more than price inflation – a process known as *fiscal drag*. In order to compensate for fiscal drag, it is necessary to raise the higher-rate threshold of income tax. Otherwise, fiscal drag would increase the number of higher-rate taxpayers.

The tax burden (or increase in tax revenue) can change as result of discretionary policy measures, fiscal drag (the fact that 'unchanged' policies are defined in government forecasts in such a way that they lead to a rise in the tax burden over time), the economic cycle, or other economic factors (such as changes in the size and composition of the national income and movements in asset and commodity prices, etc.). The government can choose to offset changes in the tax burden resulting from fiscal drag or economic factors with discretionary measures. Hence, over the medium term, all changes in revenues as a share of national income are, in effect, a *policy choice* of the government.

Over the medium term, any change in government revenues is discretionary since changes due to fiscal drag or economic factors could always be *reversed* through policy decisions of the government. For example, in order to prevent government revenues from increasing as a share of national income over time as a result of fiscal drag, the government could choose to *index tax thresholds or cut tax rates*.

At present, the personal income tax thresholds in Korea are not indexed to both inflation and earnings growth. As a result, as incomes and standards of living rise over time, a larger share of individual incomes is paid in taxes even though real pretax purchasing power may not have changed because of fiscal drag, implying that higher nominal incomes result in higher average tax rates.

Is it fair? It may not be fair for low-income groups. Failing to account for fiscal drag by not indexing the thresholds, and especially the lower-income thresholds, will affect low-income groups more in relative terms than those with higher incomes.[21] Is it efficient? It is not efficient. In general, taxes are said to invoke a degree of dead-weight cost. Increasing, the average tax share when people's real financial position has not changed will exacerbate this inefficiency. Then what is a fairer alternative? One possibility is an indexation system. The income thresholds at which marginal income tax rates change must be *indexed* fully by real earnings growth rather than inflation in order to offset the effect of fiscal drag.

Finally, with these examinations, it might be of interest to perform future research in two directions. First, it will be very interesting to estimate the *existence* of both nominal and real fiscal drag for different kinds of taxes and different countries by using a time series analysis. For this purpose, we can estimate the following panel equation for different tax categories:

$$\ln\left(\frac{T_{it}}{GDP_{it}}\right) = \ln\alpha + \beta_i \cdot \ln\left(\frac{GDP_{it}}{P_{it}}\right) + \upsilon_i \cdot \ln P_{it} + \mu_{it} \tag{10.1}$$

where T_{it}/GDP_{it} denotes tax revenue as a proportion of GDP for country i and year t, P_{it} is price level, GDP_{it}/P_{it} is real economic growth, and μ_{it} is random disturbance. This specification tells us that tax revenues will be affected by real economic growth and inflation. From this estimation, we expect that there will be a difference between tax categories.

Second, it would be more interesting to calculate the size of fiscal drag as a share of GDP. For instance, the contribution of fiscal drag in a revenue category to revenue receipts as a proportion to GDP is calculated on the basis of the elasticity of revenue receipts and growth rate (g_t) in trend GDP, which is assumed to be the base for all revenue receipts. Elasticity of revenue receipts (ε_r) with respect to the tax base is calculated after netting out the impact of legislative changes from the revenue receipts. The contribution of fiscal drag to changes in structural revenue receipts is computed as

$$FD = \frac{(\varepsilon_R - 1) \cdot g_t \cdot R_{t-1}}{NGDP_t} \tag{10.2}$$

Where ε_R denotes the elasticity of revenue category R with respect to the tax base, g_t is the growth rate in nominal trend GDP, R_{t-1} is the revenue category of the past trend year, and *NGDP*$_t$ is the trend nominal GDP. Thus, fiscal drag for a specific category arises when the elasticity of the revenue deviates from one. Kremer *et al.* (2006) applied this method for six European countries and suggested that the fiscal drag associated with a positive income change can even be *negative*. For instance, this applies to excise taxes: as they are volume based, price increases may leave tax revenues unaffected or lead to revenue decreases while the corresponding nominal tax base would rise. Consequently, the ratio of excise taxes to the nominal trend base would decrease. The basic idea of the broader definition is to capture any change in the revenue ratio that arises automatically: that is, without changes in legislation, there will be trend growth differentials between the tax base and GDP.

Notes

1 Literally, the word *drag* has two different meanings. On the one hand, if something is a *drag* on the development or progress of something, it slows it down or makes it more difficult. On the other hand, to *drag* something or someone *into* an event or situation means to involve them in it when it is not necessary or not desirable.
2 For instance, see Heinemann (2001).
3 See Immervoll (2005).
4 See Council of Economic Advisers (1962), pp. 72–3.
5 Refer to Heller (1966) and Blinder and Solow (1974).
6 See Musgrave (1989).
7 See Ishi (1993: 133).
8 See ibid.: 134–8.
9 This definition comes from the *Wikipedia*.
10 See *Wikipedia*.
11 Refer to *The Green Budget 2008*.
12 See OECD, *Taxing Wages 2006–2007* (2007).
13 It includes social security contributions paid by employees and payroll taxes paid by employers, and income taxes minus any family cash benefits. Thus, it is a comprehensive measure.
14 In addition, adjustments can operate with significant time lags and may be suppressed if inflation remains below a certain threshold.
15 See IFS, *The Green Budget 2007* (2007).
16 See OECD, *Taxing Wages 2006–2007* (2007).
17 See ibid.
18 See IFS, *The Green Budget 2004* (2004).
19 See ibid.
20 See IFS, *The Green Budget 2007* and *The Green Budget 2008*.
21 Buddelmeyer *et al.* (2004).

Bibliography

Adam, S. and H. Reed, 2004. 'Options for Raising Revenue,' *Green Budget 2004*, Institute for Fiscal Studies, January.
Alesina, A. and R. Perotti, 1995. 'Fiscal Expansion and Adjustments in OECD Countries,' *Economic Policy*, Vol. 21, pp. 205–48.
Alt, J., I. Preston, and L. Sibieta, 2007. 'The Political Economy of Tax Policy,' Mirrlees Review Conference, April 2007.

Blinder, Alan S. and Robert M. Solow, 1974. 'Analytical Foundations of Fiscal Policy,' in *The Economics of Public Finance*, Washington, DC: The Brookings Institution, pp. 3–115.

Buddelmeyer, H., P. Dawkins, J. Freebairn, and G. Kalb, 2004. *Bracket Creep, Effective Marginal Tax Rates and Alternative Tax Packages*, The Melbourne Institute.

Chote, R., C. Emmerson, C. Frayne, and G. Tetlow, 2007. 'The Public Finances under Mr. Brown,' *The IFS Green Budget 2007*, Institute for Fiscal Studies, January.

Chote, R., C. Emmerson and G. Tetlow, 2008. 'The Public Finances under Labour,' *The IFS Green Budget 2008*, Institute for Fiscal Studies, January.

Clark, Tom and Howard Reed, 2001. *Election Briefing 2001*, IFS Election Briefing Note No. 7, May 2001.

Council of Economic Advisers, 1962. A*nnual Report of the Council of Economic Advisers*, pp. 72–73.

Creedy, J. and N. Gemmell, 2007. 'Tax Revenues and Fiscal Drag: An Introduction,' *Australian Economic Review*, Vol. 40, No. 3, pp. 323–38.

Denham, Mike, 2008. *The Great British TaxPayer Rip-Off*, UK Taxpayers' Alliance, May.

Emmerson, C., C. Frayne, and G. Tetlow, 2005. 'The Tax Burden under Labour,' *The IFS Green Budget 2005*, Institute for Fiscal Studies, January.

Heinemann, F., 2001. 'After the Death of Inflation: Will Fiscal Drag Survive?' *Fiscal Studies*, Vol. 22, No. 4, pp. 527–46.

Heller, Walter W., 1966. *New Dimensions of Political Economy*, Cambridge, MA: Harvard University Press.

Immervoll, H., 2005. 'Falling Up the Stairs: The Effects of "Bracket Creep" on Household Incomes,' *Review of Income and Wealth*, Vol. 51, No. 1, pp. 37–62.

Institute for Fiscal Studies, 2001. 'An Audit of the Public Finances,' *The IFS Green Budget 2001*, January.

Institute for Fiscal Studies, 2004. *The IFS Green Budget 2004*.

Ishi, Hiromitsu, 1990. 'Taxation and Public Debt in a Growing Economy: The Japanese Experience,' *Hitotsubashi Journal of Economics*, Vol. 31, pp. 1–22.

Ishi, Hiromitsu, 1993. *The Japanese Tax System*, 2nd edn, Clarendon Press.

Kremer, J., C.R. Braz, T. Brosens, G. Langenus, S. Momigliano and M. Spolander, 2006. 'A Disaggregated Framework for the Analysis of Structural Developments in Public Finances,' *ECB Working Paper Series*, No. 579, European Central Bank, January.

Kremer, J., C.R. Braz, T. Brosens, G. Langenus, S. Momigliano and M. Spolander, 2006. 'A Disaggregated Framework for the Analysis of Structural Developments in Public Finances,' Deutsche Bundesbank, *Discussion Papers*.

Musgrave, Richard A. and Peggy B. Musgrave, 1989. *Public Finance in Theory and Practice*, 5th edn., McGraw-Hill Book Company.

Nowotny, E., 1980. 'Inflation and Taxation: Reviewing the Macroeconomic Issues,' *Journal of Economic Literature*, Vol. 18, September, pp. 1025–49.

OECD, 2007. *Taxing Wages 2006/2007*, pp. 23–55.

Packer, Stephen B., 1965. 'Economic Significance of Fiscal Drag,' *Financial Analysts Journal*, November–December, pp. 127–33.

Tanzi, V., 1977. 'Inflation, Lags in Collection and the Real Value of Tax Revenue,' *IMF Staff Papers*, Vol. 24, pp. 154–67.

Tanzi, V., 1980. *Inflation and the Personal Income Tax: An International Perspective*, Cambridge: Cambridge University Press.

UK Conservative Party, 2004. *Income Tax and National Insurance Thresholds: A New Direction*, November.

US Council of Economic Advisers, 1969. *Economic Report of the President*.

11 Alternative visions of incomplete property rights

Md. Dulal Miah and Yasushi Suzuki

1 Introduction

Property rights is the basic building block of an economy that dictates the allocation of scarce resources in society, which in turn affects the economic outcome. Countries providing greater security to private property can grow faster than countries designed with inappropriate structures of private property (Knack and Keefer 1995). North and Thomas have sketched a historical account of the rise of the Western world and attribute the rise to an efficient economic organization that requires an individual's

> exclusive rights to use as he sees fit his land, labor capital and other possessions ... the right to transfer his resources to another, and that property rights are so defined that no one else is either benefited or harmed by his use of his property.
>
> (North and Thomas 1973: 91)

The system is efficient because secure property rights provide individuals with the incentive to innovate and produce, and conversely inhibit those activities that are unproductive so that the system brings a private rate of return close to the social rate of return.

Private and social returns coincide if rights to property are completely specified *ex-ante*, or in other words, all externalities are internalized. Externalities are intended or unintended consequences of an action for which the actor cannot be made liable for adverse effects of his actions on others, or for which he is not paid for positive effects. Internalizing all externalities is not feasible if the cost of transacting (search and information cost, measurement cost, negotiation cost, contract cost, cost of policing and enforcing, etc.) between interacting parties is high. However, transaction cost can be reduced if the person that affects most greatly the value of an asset becomes the residual owner (Barzel 1997; Milgrom and Roberts 1992). Residuarity is an arrangement of rights in which residual control rights and residual return rights are tied together to facilitate the evolution of an appropriate form of property rights. For instance, a taxi driver who is also the owner of the taxi he drives would be more careful to maintain the taxi than the driver of a rented taxi. In this sense, the notion of well defined property rights can be rephrased as well defined rights over residual control. Once such an arrangement of ownership is achieved, the problem of transaction cost is resolved not by completely eliminating it but reducing it to such an extent that Pareto optimality is attained. If this postulation is held, we can conclude that property rights arrangements in which residual control and return rights are held by the same entity are economically more beneficial than if they are separately arranged.

The case of China's township and village enterprises (TVEs) does not conform to this standard prescription of property rights. Weitzman and Xu (1994) term TVEs as 'vaguely defined cooperatives' because rights to them are poorly defined. However, they are performing spectacularly. Jefferson and Singh point out these facts and rightly so:

> China's economy has been dominated by publicly owned firms, both state- and collective-owned. Although these factories display many of the negative characteristics that economists ascribe to public ownership, they accounted for most of the extraordinary growth of Chinese industry during the critical early years of transition.
>
> (Jefferson and Singh 1999: 6)

Not only are growing amazingly but they are also outperforming private enterprises. Svejnar (1990) shows that in many circumstances, private firms could not achieve productivity gains as large as those of collectives. This evidence is further supported by Dong and Putterman (1997), who have shown that firms owned by TVEs were at least as productive as those owned by private entities. This anomaly has lead many scholars to argue that the case of TVEs is indeed a paradox in terms of the traditional property rights paradigm. For instance, Weitzman and Xu (1994) argue that the successful existence of TVEs seems to represent 'a paradox or challenge for traditional property rights theory.' By the same token, Svejnar (1990: 247) points out that 'productive efficiency is not related to ownership.' Surprisingly, this is a threat to the standard theory of property rights.

While these conclusions deserve attention, we should interpret them cautiously because private ownership (privately owned firms) in China is constrained to enjoy its full potential by the growing uncertainty embedded in the country's legal and political system. In contrast, TVEs have been able to cope with these uncertainties due mainly to their involvement with the state at various levels – local, provincial, and central. This chapter aims to contribute to this hypothesis by analyzing legal institutional structures under which private and TVEs are operating. We argue that vaguely defined property rights in the TVEs work as a 'slack' to safeguard against uncertainty faced by private ownership. In so doing, we discuss the fundamental uncertainty involved with Chinese political and legal systems that is hindering the growth of privately owned firms. The chapter is structured as follows: Section 2 elaborates the concept of incomplete property rights; Section 3 describes the general features of property rights in TVEs; Section 4 focuses on the legal and political institutions under which TVEs operate; Section 5 argues that current institutional settings for protecting property rights function as a 'slack' or buffer against uncertainty for TVEs while at the same time they impede the proper functioning of privately owned firms; Section 6 finally concludes.

2 Nature and causes of incomplete property rights

Property rights bestow on owners certain attributes in relation to an asset. Essential attributes comprise the right to consume or benefit from the use of an asset; the right to exclude others from uncompensated use of property; the right to sell, dispose of, or transfer the asset; and also the right to derive income from the asset. When all these attributes related to an asset are perfectly specified, property rights are complete. Or in other words, if property rights are defined as a *complete bundle* of rights, the term *complete bundle* implies that the bundle encompasses all the possible uses of the resource over which property is defined and that each use embedded in the bundle is completely specified. Complete specification requires an *ex-ante* collection of information regarding all harmful and beneficial effects caused by a particular assignment of rights over property. It, however, relates to a number of future contingencies. According to Shavell (2004: 9), 'A completely specified act includes in its description the place, time, and the contingency under which it is committed – for example digging at a designated location, on Thursday at 4:00 p.m. if it is not raining (the contingency).'

In reality, the contingencies are many. For example, how a particular use in the future relating to a specific property affects other parties is unknown because it requires a great deal of information a priori. Only some beneficial and harmful effects are easily known for most uses of the property, and the remainder can be known only by incurring great cost (Demsetz 1966). This is because uncertainty increases in terms of whose rights will be affected and by how much. So a point will be reached beyond which the cost of determining effects a priori outweighs the expected benefits. The greater the uncertainty of the effect, the lower is the probability that prior compensation is paid to those harmed or prior fees are charged to those benefited. Moreover, great uncertainty imposes a great cost of sorting out and measuring legitimate claims that undermine efficient resource use. In this regard, the cost of acquiring information is expected to be lowered once property has been put to a particular use so that assessment of effects may become easy enough that payment of compensation is economical. From this vantage point, the functionalist model of property rights attributes incompleteness of rights to the existence of high transaction costs (see Barzel 1997; Coase 1960; Milgrom and Roberts 1992).

The model has overlooked some important dimensions of incomplete property rights. For instance, it views uncertainty simply as an information problem, which is an element that increases transaction costs. In so doing, contributions of other determinants to incomplete property rights are not properly emphasized. Some dimensions of uncertainty, which North (1999) calls 'non-ergodic' aspects, cannot be overcome simply by collecting information. With this sort of uncertainty, we must grope around and we have much less assurance that we are going to solve the problems. As a result, our decision process becomes complex and volatile. Since the consequences of an action extend into the future, accurate forecasting is essential for making objectively rational choices. But in the real world, most choices are made under conditions of uncertainty. Keynes (1937) has emphasized, and rightly so, that all economically meaningful behavior derives from agents' efforts to protect themselves from uncertainty.

The second and most important aspect skipped by the model is 'bounded rationality.' The model assumes that humans' computational capability is unlimited. As a consequence, income-maximizing strategy can be figured out with available information. This is a very strict assumption, however. Simon (1993: 156) points out 'they [human beings) would be unable to make the computations required for optimal choice even if they had perfect knowledge.' In practice, economic actors are *intendedly* rational but *limitedly* so, partly because of information problems but mainly because of the complexity of computing the best strategies (Simon 1996). Putting it differently, even if zero transaction cost facilitates the accumulation of all relevant information *ex-ante*, it is still possible to inaccurately model property rights because the human brain possesses limited capacity to process and analyze information. Since assets have multiple attributes, many of them may not be specified perfectly. As such, the very notion of ownership may remain vague.

Williamson (1985) rationalizes the contracting problem, admitting two important aspects of human behavior: bounded rationality and opportunism. He asserts that, assuming the human brain possesses unlimited calculative power, problems arising from opportunism can be tackled by writing a comprehensive contract *ex-ante*, and thereby *ex-post* opportunism can be averted by taking into account every contingency from which opportunism may likely result. Similarly, if human beings are nonopportunistic, contracting problems arising *ex-post* due to bounded rationality can be overcome since parties have agreed to cooperate (being non-opportunistic) and disclose all the relevant information generated once the events occur. From this view, Williamson concludes that contracts remain incomplete if we admit both bounded rationality and opportunism, two natural traits of human beings.

We have constructed a matrix (Table 11.1), deriving the basic idea from Williamson to stress the importance of bounded rationality for incomplete property rights. Assuming that human beings possess unbounded rationality, what is relevant for a complete definition of property rights is sheer transaction cost. At this stage, if transaction cost is insignificant, we can reach a situation where property rights are perfectly delineated (quadrant I). However, this is a utopian world, attainment of which is impossible.

Let us assume that human beings are unboundedly rational but there exists high transaction cost (quadrant IV). Possessing supernatural powers to analyze information does not guarantee precise specification of property rights so that income is maximized, due to the fact that high transaction cost impedes collecting necessary information. Likewise, the availability of all relevant information

Table 11.1 Matrix showing nature of incomplete property rights

		Bounded rationality	
		Absent	Admitted
Transaction cost	Low	I. Property rights are perfectly delineated	II. No guarantee that the low transaction cost will lead to state of property rights where income is maximized
	High	IV. It is unlikely that unlimited computing capability leads to a state of property rights where income is maximized	III. Property rights are incomplete

facilitated by zero transaction cost unlikely leads to perfectly delineated property rights if we assume that human beings possess limited capacity to accurately interpret and analyze collected information (quadrant II). By the same token, admitting both transaction cost and human bounded rationality means that rights are inevitably incomplete (quadrant III). This implies that transaction cost is a necessary condition but not sufficient on its own to explain incomplete property rights. There are other factors, of which bounded rationality is one among them.

Bounded rationality often encourages agents to become docile, which contributes to the power of individual survival in evolutionary competition. Simon (1993: 156) defines docility as 'the tendency to depend on suggestions, recommendations, persuasion, and information obtained through social channels as a major basis for choice.' According to Simon, such behavior is not unrealistic due to the fact that it contributes to an individual's own fitness. This is because the information on which suggestions and recommendations are based is superior to individually collected information, which tempts individuals to exhibit a large degree of docility. From this view, Simon (1993) concludes that on average, docility contributes to an individual's fitness and hence drives out non-docility in evolutionary competition. However, it is not guaranteed that docility always contributes to individuals' power of survival in competition. Rather, society can tax them by sometimes influencing them to take altruistic actions that decrease individual fitness. Even if this is true, so long as the gain obtained from contributing through altruistic behavior outweighs the cost of altruism, docility continues. At this stage, society will gain from altruism in competing with other societies.

This postulation has a profound implication for explaining incomplete property rights, particularly the issue of the efficiency of the imperfect delineation of property rights. Instead of trying to reach a state of perfectly delineated property rights, actors can sometimes work with vaguely defined property rights without hampering efficiency so long as docile actors contribute to the group. The case of Chinese TVEs is a case in point. Even though rights in regard to them are not clearly specified, their performance is not inferior to that of privately owned enterprises.

3 Ownership characteristics of TVEs

The predecessors of the Chinese Township and Village Enterprises (TVEs) were the Chinese Commune and Brigade Enterprises (CBEs) that consisted of rural sideline production and agriculture cooperatives. In 1958, by the directives of the Political Bureau of the Central Committee of China's People's Congress (CPC), 740,000 agricultural cooperatives all over the country were merged into 26,000 people's communes (Hantang 2000). However, CBEs were a big failure; they suffered from insufficient capital, poor management, and lack of any market skills, which pushed many CBEs to shut down (Bouckaert 2007). Moreover, the social norms and practices for viewing CBEs were also adverse to their survival. For instance, they were regarded as the 'tail of capitalism' and their operation during the first period of the Cultural Revolution (1966–75) was strictly constrained. This attitude changed slightly in the later period when the political leadership emphasized the need for modernization over ideological class struggle. CBEs were then given a major task in the campaign for the mechanization of agriculture. In 1984, communes and brigades were abolished and the CBEs were renamed TVEs through widening their scope. In addition to the enterprises formerly run by the township and village, the concept of TVEs now included cooperative enterprises jointly run by some commune members, other forms of cooperative industries, and individually owned enterprises (Hantang 2000).

What is the property rights arrangement in the TVEs? Who owns use rights, control rights, and residual rights? One of the major features of TVEs is the ambiguity of their property rights. They are neither state-owned enterprises (SOEs) nor privately owned entities. It seems that TVEs are similar to SOEs, but the former differ significantly from the latter in a number of important characteristics. For example, the sources of capital in TVEs are private savings, loans from rural cooperatives, Agriculture Banks of China, and also surpluses in township and village government revenues (Pollard 2003). These sources are almost exclusively local in nature. TVEs possess a greater degree of autonomy than SOEs and face greater budget constraints than do SOEs.

For typical TVEs there is no owner in the spirit of standard property rights theory. In general, collectively owned TVEs are owned by the local residents. All the community members are nominal owners, and they become the owners by dint of residing in the community. Thus, a member's leaving the community means the revocation of ownership. In the similar fashion, an outside individual automatically gains ownership by marriage to a community member. Even though use rights or ownership of TVEs rests on local residents, TVEs are controlled, managed, and supported by the local governments or by hired managers.

> Many Chinese economists report that TVEs are usually controlled by local governments and typically there is no separation between the communal

government and the TVEs. These reports describe a situation where many TVEs do not have genuine autonomy in business transactions; the communal government has major influence in the determination of managerial personnel and employment.

(Weitzman and Xu 1994: 132)

In the early stage of TVEs, they were directly controlled and managed by local governments in the sense that approval of new projects, raising funds, and managing human resources were under the discretion of local governments. Once this stage is passed, the local government can decide to delegate some authority to professional managers and not remain in direct control of the daily operations of the TVE. Even if the local government delegates full operational responsibility to management, it retains the power to appoint managers (Chang and Wang 1994). This gives managers a sense of belonging to the local government and they feel a responsibility to consult with local government officials prior to making major decisions.

Workers sometimes have voting power to select or appoint managers. However, this power is nominal (Chang and Wang 1994). This is due to the fact that the local government is the ultimate initiator of voting. If the local government is satisfied with a manager, the necessity for voting is eliminated. Moreover, workers' employment in the TVEs is also controlled by the local government. Because of this conflict of interest, workers rarely raise their voices against administrative bodies. This implies that workers have almost no power to select or have any say about the appointment of managers. Song (1990) reports that almost 83.3 percent of TVE managers believe that they are appointed by local governments. Another important aspect is the residual return right. The typical community member waits passively to receive or to enjoy the benefits, the major part of which is not in monetary form but in the form of communal social investment. It seems that both parties (local government and citizens) share the residual returns of TVEs. They are entitled to retain a major portion (60 percent or more) of the after-tax profit earned by TVEs and to distribute the remaining among the workers as bonuses and as payment of fees to the local government (Weitzman and Xu 1994).

Despite the fact that residual return and control rights are held by separate entities, which is not the best arrangement according to standard property rights theory, TVEs have been playing a significant role in the growth of the Chinese economy since the economic reform in 1978. They accounted for 47 percent of the total industrial output in the year 2001 and their annual average real growth rate over the period 1988–99 was 19 percent (Fu and Balasubramanyam 2003). In 1978, TVEs accounted for 9.1 percent of China's total industrial output, rising to 36.8 percent in 1992. Moreover, their economic efficiency is very close to that of privately owned enterprises in China (Svejnar 1990). From this view, the case of Chinese TVEs is a paradox in terms of standard property rights theory.

The complete definition of property rights, which the standard model advocates, is an ideal case that requires the existence of perfect legal systems and their strict enforcement. However, countries lacking such characteristics may institute a different system of property rights, conforming to the basic norms and standard practices of the society. In China, there are many uncertainties stemming from the current legal and political systems. Vaguely defined property rights in TVEs are successful in coping with these uncertainties, whereas private firms find it excessively costly to exercise their rights.

4 Uncertainty in the Chinese political and legal systems

Brunetti and Weder (1997) group *uncertainty* into four broad categories: government instability, political violence, policy uncertainty, and enforcement uncertainty. We restrict our analysis to enforcement uncertainty. Enforcement uncertainty focuses on the relation between the private sector and the state. Or in other words, it is the degree of confidence private firms can have that their rights will be protected and contracts will be enforced properly, and that they will not be subject to arbitrary behavior. These measures concentrate on the discretionary behavior of the judiciary as well as the bureaucracy. Private property requires an impartial legal system by which contracts are drawn and enforced. Once rights are assigned, they should be enforced by a third party, which is usually the government. In this sense, a legal system provides the basic building blocks for private property in that it governs the contractual relationship between parties or enforces contractual rights and provides security for a person's property. In this respect, legal systems determine the degree to which private property rights are secure.

The Chinese Communist Party (CCP) founded a new China, the People's Republic (PRC), as a socialist state in 1949 by successfully unifying mainland China. The Kuomintang legal system was abolished, which left the formal legal system in a complete vacuum. This required establishing a new judicial system; but the urgency to fill this legal vacuum was not felt by the authorities in the first three to four years of the PRC. This lack of urgency was partly due to heavy reliance on the pre-1949 communist experience of law, which was basically an extension of military force (Chen 1999). At the end of 1952, the Central Committee of the CCP focused on economic reform for socialist industrialization and socialist transformation of agriculture and other commercial activities. The implementation of this plan gave birth to the 1954 constitution by which the necessary condition for a planned economy and the socialist transformation was set.

The new communist government tried to safeguard and build the country to follow Marxist-Leninist-Maoist instruction both economically and politically until 1978. The socialist ideology of Maoism directly and explicitly renounced the notion of private property and cemented the party as the guardian of public welfare. For instance, China enacted land reform in 1949–51, which deprived the landowners of their land and distributed it among the landless peasants or smallholders. Landowners were politically ruined and they also lost all their rights. Being obsessed with Marxist doctrine – that private ownership of the means of production is the root of all social evils – the government under Mao initiated land reform by forcing Chinese peasants to organize themselves into millions of production units and to pool their land and other significant means of production. Every member of a collective became a part owner of the pool and as such was entitled to a share in the collective's harvests. Under the new system, individual peasants no longer possessed any means of production, and no collective member could do anything about his or her share of the pool. Thus, the interests of the individual were subordinated to those of the collectives.

Collectives were communally owned. Thus, members received more or less the same share of the harvests, regardless of differences in individual contributions. This system helped to generate a tendency to shirk. Consequently, agricultural productivity was low and the resultant food shortages troubled the government to a good extent (Wu 2000). In order to reduce the possibility of a threat that might come from the starving peasants, the government agreed that a small piece of the collective land could be used by each farming household to plant crops of its own choice and that the harvest from that land could be retained by the household. However, this policy threatened the basic tenet of socialism. To offset the possibility that such an ideology would emerge, the government emphasized that the private land could not be more than a small fraction of the collective land and that peasants should not be allowed to farm their private land until they had finished their daily work for the collective. Such a system of abrogating rights over the means of production caused China to suffer a great deal from the chaos and endless class struggle that followed (Bin 2007).

Mao's death in 1976 presented China with a chance to break with its past. The Chinese elite, led by Deng, seized that chance and terminated the Cultural Revolution immediately. After about a year, he launched economic reform, and the 1978 reform brought a change in the Chinese legal tradition as well. Indeed, 1978 was a pivotal epoch in Chinese history and a turning point for development in the legal system because a legal system was required as a necessary tool for social modernization. Moreover, party leaders also repeatedly emphasized that law would provide a social order conducive to economic development (Chen 1999). While Mao's China was virtually without law, Deng's China witnessed massive and rapid enactment of laws and regulations, especially laws and administrative rules related to economic and commercial relations. For instance, legal relationships such as contracts, property, and foreign business relations have been brought gradually within the ambit of a range of formal and increasingly detailed legislative and regulatory enactments. The General Principles of Civil Law (GPCL) enacted in 1986 codified broad principles of property rights, albeit subject to the provision that they do not conflict with state policies and public and social interests. The GPCL reflected CCP policies that had at once begun to limit the intrusion of the state into social and economic relationships while still asserting the basic provisions of state control. Despite these improvements, enforcement remains a serious problem, and as a result, the PRC law regime tends to be ineffectual in lending predictability to economic activity (Potter 1997).

However, in the post-Mao period of economic reform, the state remained a key player in property relations – state property rights remained dominant, albeit purportedly in the service of social interest. The 1982 constitution extended the protection to property, but only to the extent that it is 'lawful property,' the definition of which remains exclusively at the discretion of the state. Article 10 of the constitution stated that land in rural and suburban areas, except those which have already been defined as under state ownership, belongs to the collectives, while the state owns the land in cities. This implies that at this stage of modernization, the law prohibits private land ownership. Moreover, the constitutional requirement that the exercise of citizens' rights, including the right to own property, does not conflict with the state or social interest effectively grants the state a monopoly of power in interpreting that interest and in determining the extent to which private property rights that might possibly conflict with it will be recognized and enforced. Article 11 of the 1982 constitution acknowledges only the property rights of individual enterprises, defined as self-employed businesses. This conspicuous silence on the property rights of privately operated firms stems from an ideological consideration – the specter of exploitation raised by such firms. Contrary to the Western legal tradition, the communist constitution was believed to be a tool for party rule and intended more as a statement of policy goals (James 2007).

The first round of the constitutional review took place in 1988. The amendments stipulated that the state permits the private economy to exist and grow within the limits prescribed by law as a 'complement' to the public economy. In 1988, Article 11 was amended to include a clause that permits private firms and promises to protect their 'lawful rights and interests.' The new paragraph stated that the state permits the private economy to exist and develop within the limits prescribed by law. The private economy is a supplement to the socialist public ownership economy. However, the amended article allows the state to exercise guidance, supervision, and control over the private sector of the economy. The amendment also carefully subordinates the private sector as a supplement to the socialist public economy (Huang 2003). This means that private firms are allowed to grow but only to the point of not attenuating the socialist character of the economy and only to the extent that they complement the SOEs.

Meanwhile, there was no formal legislation to govern private enterprises. Shortly after the amendment of the constitution, national legislation governing private enterprises was enacted in June 1988. The State Council promulgated three sets of regulations: the Provisional Regulations of the PRC Concerning Private Enterprises, and two other shorter statutes relating to taxation of private enterprises and their investors. Soon after, some other supplementary regulations were enacted, and by early 1989, private enterprises were subject to the most extensive legislation for governing them since the founding of the PRC in 1949 (Conner 1991). The regulations themselves placed few limitations on the scope of business activities for private enterprises, but they were subject to restrictions contained in other legislation. Private enterprises could not engage in military or financial industries, or do business in commodities prohibited by the state, which included cultural objects and antiques, jewelry, rare minerals, stamps, firearms and ammunition, military industrial products, cars, and civilian explosives. The regulations therefore enumerated the rights of private enterprises and their investments, particularly their property and management rights.

In 1993, the PRC constitution was amended for the second time to facilitate the transformation of planned economy to socialistic market economy. The genesis of the 1993 constitutional amendments emphasized that China was still only in the initial stage of building 'Socialism with Chinese characteristics.' Nevertheless, through the third amendment of the constitution in 1999, the role of the private sector was upgraded to make it an essential part of the socialist market economy. Even though the amendment introduced the primary stage of capitalism, it did not include a provision concerning the sanctity of private property rights. Instead, the language provided that self-employed, private, and other non-public sectors constituted an important component of the socialist market economy, whose lawful rights and interest would be protected by the state. While this was touted as a major step forward in the China's reform process, the reference to state protection of lawful rights and interests signaled that the private sector would remain subject to state control at a significant level.

A further amendment to the constitution of China was written in 2004 to enshrine private property rights. Prior to this amendment, the constitution stated that the state may, in the greater public interest, requisition land for its use in accordance with the law. The fourth amendment of the constitution was executed including a provision for compensation for land expropriated or requisitioned. Before the current amendment took place, the constitution protected the rights of citizens to own and inherit lawfully earned income, savings, houses, and other lawful property. However, the new amendment decreed that Chinese citizens could now have inviolable rights to private property. But the constitution is less a prescriptive document than a constantly changing description. It will unlikely bring the full property rights revolution China's development demands due to the fact that the constitution's ability to constrain the government is very limited, which implies that uncertainty regarding the protection of private property remains.

Another critical point of concern about the enjoyment of private property remains regarding land-use rights. The Land Administrative Law in the PRC was introduced in 1998 and was further revised in 2004. It stated that urban land is owned by the state, and that rural and suburban lands are collectively owned by peasants. So in a nutshell, all land in China is owned either by collectives or by the state, which means that private rights to them are precarious. Since individuals cannot own land, the law allows individuals to lease from the collectives for a term of 30 years. However, the use of the land is limited to those purposes expressly allowed by the lease. If leaseholders desire to alter the land-use rights, they must receive approval from a variety of governmental bodies, including two-thirds of the villagers' congress or representatives (James 2007). This implies that land-use rights for private purposes are insecure and precarious.

This insecurity is further exacerbated by the state expropriation risk. The only limit of the state's expropriation is that such takings must be 'in the public interest,' which is further defined by the state. Chinese courts must rely on the legislature to codify a definition of the public interest. This provides the state with enormous discretion in defining public interest. Moreover, Chinese law does not provide any provision for individuals wishing to check the due process of the takings. If an individual files a suit against local government officials, questioning whether an expropriation is truly in the public interest, the judges hearing the case would be hired and paid by local officials sitting as defendants, who further have the right to demote, promote, or even fire the judges. At this juncture it can be implied that that judicial independence to protect and enforce private property is not duly instituted, even though the Chinese government enacted a new Property Law in 2007.

The obvious drawback is that there is no third party to enforce the rights. If the contracting parties are free to violate the agreement they have entered into without any fear of reprisal, it is natural that very few would enter into contracts. A third party is essential either to ensure the terms of the contract or to ensure justice when the contract is violated. This role is played by the state through an independent judicial system. In the case of China, state and collective entities appear to be contracting parties against individuals, which means that a contracting party itself is the enforcer of rights. Despite the fact that the constitution provides a provision for compensation in the case of takings, the lack of third-party enforcement or an independent judicial system means that compensation is rarely paid. Zhang (2006) quotes Han (2004), stating that on average the compensation farmers received accounted for only about 5 to 10 percent of the total market value. Clearly, a large fraction of the land rent is appropriated by local governments.

Apart from the compensation issue, there are other ambiguities that are also threats against private property. For instance, the law does not stipulate the relationship between collectives and individuals, particularly the farmers of rural land. Therefore, in reality, in the process of land requisition, the local government needs only to deal with the village committee. Sometimes, the committee colludes to extract as much rent as possible from a farmer's land. To a large extent, farmers do not have much voice in the land requisition process. Thus, in the case of China, while the policy of the socialist market economy would permit individual enterprises and private firms to play an important role, ultimate property rights remain subject to the policy priorities of the party/state and are not to receive absolute constitutional sanction.

5 Coping with adversaries

Uncertainty makes taking all valuable attributes of property into account *ex-ante* impractical. However, legal and political uncertainties prevalent in China cannot be avoided simply by incurring high transaction costs because they are embedded within the basic institutions of the country. This means that privately owned firms are operating in a world of great uncertainty caused by the state or local and provincial governments. If this is the case, it is natural that private ownership might not be the first choice for entrepreneurs. This is manifested by the fact that many private entrepreneurs want to develop under the guise of TVEs (Lo and Tian 2002).

This preference is not whimsical but is rather a rational choice due to the fact that the discriminatory legal environment is unlikely to contribute to the successful performance of the collective sector. As a result, the Chinese experience cannot pose a challenge to property rights theory but rather demonstrates the importance of legal protection for private property rights. Under the existing Chinese system of highly concentrated political powers, citizens may find it difficult to obtain key resources that are crucial for the success of TVEs (Chang and Wang 1994). From this perspective, vaguely defined ownership in TVEs may provide some institutional advantages over private firms in solving the agency problem. Moreover, the assignment of property rights to the local government may be an efficient response to Chinese institutional constraints, which we call 'slack,' in response to uncertainty.

Hirschman (1970) introduces 'slack' as a cushion to which firms can resort when they encounter difficulties. Similarly, existence of some sort of slack in an economy is necessary for responding to uncertainty. At the organizational level, slack consists of payments to members of any entity in excess of what is required to maintain it (Cyert and March 1992). It absorbs a significant portion of the variability of the firm's environment, especially threats emanating from external environments propelled by various institutional changes. For example, a precipitating change in demand for the product of a firm might threaten its extinction, which might cause it to fail when operating at equilibrium. Slack that can be called in when a firm is in need plays a crucial role to provide firms with supportive means. In recognizing the importance and pervasiveness of slack, Hirschman argues,

> It assumes not only that slack has somehow come into the world and exists in given moments, but that it is *continuously being generated* as a result of some sort of entropy characteristic of human, surplus-producing societies.... Firms and other organizations are conceived to be permanently and randomly subject to decline and decay, that is, to a gradual loss of rationality, efficiency, and surplus producing energy, no matter how well the institutional framework within which they function is designed.
>
> (1970: 14–15)

The notion of general equilibrium, or Pareto optimality, implies that there should be no slack in organization. Thus, entrepreneurs should not earn abnormal profit in the long run. However, slack at both organization and economic levels exists for responding to uncertain economic conditions. For example, organizations do have more employees than they need, and firms maintain cash more than is immediately necessary. In accordance with this presumption, the degree to which an attainable level of property rights deviates from a perfectly delineated, or Pareto optimal, structure of rights arrangement can be marked as slack that acts as a buffer against uncertainty.

The TVEs in the Chinese countryside are part of a large government institution with broad powers given by the fundamentals of a political system. For this reason, the full support of the local government provides the citizens and other stakeholders in the TVE with a sense of security needed for long-term development. In this sense, ambiguous property rights are a response to high transaction costs and high uncertainties in the marketplace. Moreover, a government bureaucrat or a government agency can properly work around the obstacles and make the transaction possible. Facing such uncertainties in the marketplace, entrepreneurs may want to include the government as an ambiguous owner.

The advantage that an ambiguous structure of property rights can achieve is that involving government as a contractual partner makes it possible for firms to get help from bureaucrats easily. TVEs do not have the same fear of confiscation of the fruits of their investment that private enterprises have because TVEs are the creatures of local government, precisely the same body that farmers fear will confiscate or redistribute their land. While private entities may face uncertainty as to the results of long-term investments, TVEs, whatever their other problems are, face no real uncertainty in this respect. As a consequence, an emerging non-state firm finds it highly beneficial to include the local government as part of the firm. This gives rise to vaguely defined property rights, which sometimes outperform private enterprises. If the market is full of uncertainty, or when a firm has trouble with market transactions, the local government can intervene on behalf of TVEs. For a purely private firm, asking for help from the local government may not be so easy, because the firm and the government do not share inside information about the firm (Li 1996).

This provides our basic point of analysis – that when formal institutions are precarious or uncertain, societies may attempt to evolve along alternative existing institutions to protect their economic activities. That is the reason private firms tend to disguise themselves as TVEs. Under current institutional settings, they find it prohibitively costly to write a complete contract. In this context, an ambiguous property rights arrangement, which often involves local officials as shareholders of TVEs, may be a better option because it can help secure protections from the local government and reduce impediments to reform at the local level. In other words, high transaction costs provide an environment where ambiguous property rights can be more efficient under certain conditions than well-defined property rights. From this vantage point it can be concluded that once all uncertainties emanating from legal and political environments are eliminated, it is highly likely that private firms would outperform TVEs.

Now the question is how long this 'slack' can work for the Chinese economy. This is the issue that Chinese policy-makers should consider seriously. We have mentioned, referring to Simon, that so long as the gain for by individuals through contributing to the group exceeds the cost of individual fitness, altruistic behavior continues. However, there is plenty of room for rent seeking in the current arrangement of property rights; there are many externalities involved with TVEs. It is understood that any profit from TVEs benefits both the local government and residents. However, beneficiaries are not being rewarded according to their input into TVEs. This usually generates a tradition of shirking, which needs to be monitored (Alchian and Demsetz 1972). Again, monitoring by local government is costly. Thus, it is a matter of serious concern which system of monitoring – private with residual arrangement or collectives with government monitoring – is cheaper. On the other hand, currently a lion's share of the profit is paid to the local government in the mode of fees and other charges, money which is usually spent for building infrastructure and other such development activities. Indeed, this creates a possible hotbed for corruption. As a result, monitoring should be ensured so that the cost of altruistic behavior outweighs the benefits. Otherwise, vaguely defined property rights would be an obstacle for the nascent Chinese economy.

6 Conclusion

Transaction cost is one of the crucial elements for perfect delineation of property rights. However, it is not wise to assume that transaction cost is the sole reason for property rights to remain incomplete. We have shown that fundamental uncertainty, embedded with various political and legal institutions of a country, also matters. We are in accord with the mainstream view that uncertainty increases transaction cost. But our point of disagreement is that transaction cost cannot completely eliminate uncertainty. Drawing on Keynes, we have argued that uncertainty appears to be a more serious concern than has been emphasized in the standard model. We have further pointed out that zero transaction cost does not always lead to perfect delineation of property rights. Since human beings are boundedly rational, they may find it difficult to figure out the best strategy even if all necessary information is collected *ex-ante*. From this vantage point, we conclude that transaction cost is a necessary condition but not sufficient in its own to explain incomplete property rights. Uncertainty and human-bounded rationality are also fundamental to the problem.

The second aspect we have emphasized in this chapter is that perfect delineation of property rights is not always warranted for income maximization. Rather, there might be alternatives to complete property rights. Property rights arrangement in Chinese TVEs can be considered to be one of them: TVEs are performing spectacularly even though control rights and residual return rights are held by different entities. Such a structure of rights, however, is not an irrational choice. As Simon mentioned, bounded rationality encourages agents to become docile; their altruistic behavior contributes to the group so long as the cost of altruistic behavior is less than the benefits received. The key to the successful continuity of TVEs is to maintain this slack. Since the 'exit' option (leaving the group and working individually) has not always proven to be efficient in China, agents are likely to exercise either the 'voice' option (early warning against unproductive rent seeking) or 'loyalty' (accepting whatever the result is). As a consequence, policy-makers should encourage members to raise their voices in a timely way while leaving the option of remaining loyal.

Bibliography

Alchian, A. and Demsetz, H. (1972) 'Production, Information Costs, and Economic Organization,' *American Economic Review*, 62: 777–95.

Barzel, Y. (1997) *Economic Analysis of Property Rights*, Cambridge: Cambridge University Press.

Bin, L. (2007) *The Changing Chinese Legal System, 1978–Present: Centralization of Power and Rationalization of Legal System*, New York: Routledge.

Bouckaert, B. (2007) 'Bureaupreneurs in China: We did It Our Way – A Comparative Study of the Explanation of the Economic Successes of Town–Village-Enterprises in China,' *European Journal of Law and Economics*, 23: 169–95.

Brunetti, A. and Weder, B. (1997) *Investment and Institutional Uncertainty*, International Finance Corporation, Washington, DC: World Bank.

Chang, C. and Wang, Y. (1994) 'The Nature of the Township-Village Enterprise,' *Journal of Comparative Economics*, 19: 434–52.

Chen, J. (1999) *Chinese Law: Towards an Understanding of Chinese Law, Its Nature and Development*, Cambridge: Kluwer Law International.

Coase, R.J. (1960) 'The Problem of Social Cost,' *Journal of Law and Economics*, 3: 1–44.

Conner, A. (1991) 'To Get Rich Is Precarious: Regulation of Private Enterprise in the People's Republic of China,' *Journal of Chinese Law*, 5: 1–57.

Cyert, R.M. and March, J.G. (1992) *A Behavioral Theory of the Firm*, Malden, MA: Blackwell.

Demsetz, H. (1966) 'Some Aspects of Property Rights,' *Journal of Law and Economics*, 9: 61–79.

Dong, X. and Putterman, L. (1997) 'Productivity and Organization in China's Rural Industries: A Stochastic Frontier Analysis', *Journal of Comparative Economics*, 24: 181–201.

Fu, X. and Balasubramanyam, V. (2003) 'Township and Village Enterprises in China,' *Journal of Development Studies*. 39: 27–46.

Hantang, Q. (2000) 'The Evolution of Chinese Township and Village Enterprises,' in F.J. Richter (ed.) *The Dragon Millennium: Chinese Business in the Coming World Economy*, Westport and London: Quorum Books: 13–34.

Hirschman, A.O. (1970) *Exit, Voice, and Loyalty: Responses to Decline in Firms, Organizations, and States*, Cambridge, MA: Harvard University Press.

Huang, Y. (2003) *Selling China: Foreign Direct Investment during the Reform Era*, Cambridge: Cambridge University Press.

James, B.W. (2007) 'Expanding the Gap: How the Rural Property System Exacerbate China's Urban–Rural Gap,' *Columbia Journal of Asian Law*, 20: 451–91.

Jefferson, G. and Singh, I. (1999) 'Overview,' in G. Jefferson and I. Singh (eds) *Enterprise Reform in China: Ownership, Transition, and Performance*, New York: Oxford University Press, pp. 1–22.

Keynes, J.M. (1937) 'The General Theory of Employment,' *Quarterly Journal of Economics*, 51: 209–23.

Knack, S. and Keefer, P. (1995) 'Institution and Economic Performance: Cross Country Tests Using Alternative Institutional Measures,' *Economics and Politics*, 7: 207–27.

Li, D. (1996) 'A Theory of Ambiguous Property Rights in Transition Economies: The Case of the Chinese Non-State Sector,' *Journal of Comparative Economics*, 23: 1–19.

Lo, V. and Tian, X. (2002) 'Property Rights, Productivity Gains and Economic Growth: The Chinese Experience,' *Post-Communist Economies*, 14: 245–58.

Milgrom, P. and Roberts, J. (1992) *Economics, Organization and Management*, Upper Saddle River, NJ: Prentice Hall.

North, D.C. (1999) 'Dealing with a Non-ergodic World: Institutional Economics, Property Rights, and the Global Environment,' *Duke Environment, Law, and Policy Forum*, 10: 1–12.

North, D.C. and Thomas, P. (1973) *The Rise of the Western World: A New Economic History*, Cambridge: Cambridge University Press.

Pollard, D. (2003) 'Chinese Township and Village Enterprises,' in I. Alon (ed.) *Chinese Economic Transition and International Marketing Strategy*, Westport, CT: Praeger: 280–93.

Potter, P. (1997) 'Law Reform and China's Emerging Market Economy,' in Joint Economic Committee, Congress of the United States (ed.) *China's Economic Future: Challenges to US Policy*, Armonk, NY: M.E. Sharpe: 221–42.

Potter, P. (2001) *The Chinese Legal System: Globalization and Local Legal Culture*, New York: Routledge Curzon.

Shavell, S. (2004) *Foundations of Economic Analysis of Law*, Cambridge, MA: Belknap Press of Harvard University Press.

Simon, H. (1993) 'Altruism and Economics,' *American Economic Review*, 83: 156–61.

Simon, H. (1996) *The Sciences of the Artificial*, Cambridge, MA: MIT Press.

Song, L. (1990) 'Convergence: A Comparison of Township and Local Enterprises,' in W. Byrd and Q. Lin (eds.) *China's Rural Industry: Structure, Development and Reform*, London: Oxford University Press: 392–412.

Svejnar, J. (1990) 'Productive Efficiency and Employment,' in B. William and L. Qinsong (eds.) *China's Rural Enterprises: Structure, Development and Reform*, Oxford: Oxford University Press: 243–54.

Weitzman, M. and Xu, C. (1994) 'Chinese Township-Village Enterprises as Vaguely Defined Cooperatives' *Journal of Comparative Economics*, 18: 121–45.

Williamson, O. (1985) *The Economic Institutions of Capitalism: Firms, Markets, Relational Contracting*, New York: The Free Press.

Wu, D. (2000) 'China's Quite Property Rights Revolution,' *Cato Policy Paper*, 22: 10–13.

Zhang, X. (2006) 'Asymmetric Property Rights in China's Economic Growth,' DSGD Discussion Paper No. 28, International Food Policy Research Institute. Online: www.ifpri.org/sites/default/files/publications/dsgdp28.pdf (accessed 3 November 2008).

12 Economic development and institutions

Sung-Hee Jwa and Yong Yoon

1 Introduction

The British economic historian Angus Maddison, Emeritus Professor of Economic Growth and Development at the University of Groningen, reminds us that economic development is a recent phenomenon in the history of humankind. Although humans have existed for at least 2.5 million years, economic development as we know it today is something that appeared only around the 1850s (see Figure 12.1). But not all nations have been fortunate, for one reason or another, in achieving economic development. Only a couple of dozen of the world's 200-plus nations today have achieved the status of advanced economy, while no less than one-third of the 6.5 billion living on Earth are still locked in the grip of poverty. Moreover, within any country, whether viewed in any single year or through time, the differences between the rich and the poor are usually highly visible. Be that as it may, economic development, now the goal of every single modern nation on Earth, has remained elusive and highly misunderstood as well as misrepresented; clearly, there are many mysteries to be solved.

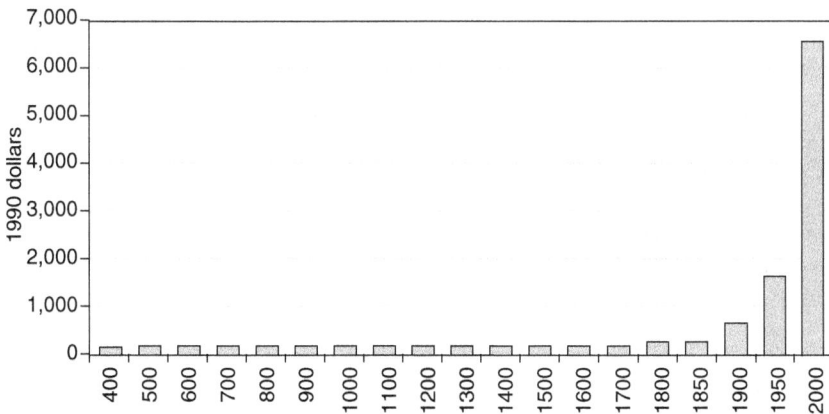

Figure 12.1 Average world GDP per capita, 400–2000 (source: http://econ161.berkeley. edu/TCEH/1998_Draft/World_GDP/Estimating_World_GDP.html).

In this chapter, we begin by highlighting what we believe to be some important but often ignored characteristics of economic development. By doing so, we confirm the notion that institutions do matter, in line with New Institutional Economics (NIE) thinkers, and furthermore, we venture into searching for *what* institutions really matter to economic development. We conclude with some policy recommendations that follow from the discussions found in the body of this chapter.

2   Some myths and realities about economic development

Many current commentaries provide not only a wealth of statistical information on countries' economic performances, but also provide anecdotal and historical accounts of economic change for the better or for the worse in various regions of the world (see works by the World Bank, William Easterly, Jeffrey Sachs, Joseph Stiglitz, Paul Krugman, and many others). In this section, we will make a few observations that we characterize as myths and realities about economic development, which are later invoked in arguments that follow as we enter into the discourse or quest to answer the question, 'What institutions matter to economic development?'

MYTH: Economic development is achievable by all nations
REALITY: At least since the end of World War II, nearly all nations in the world have adopted some kind of development plan. Despite decades of careful planning, however, most have failed to meet their development goals and many have even struggled to get even the basics right. This has led the Peruvian diplomat and former ambassador to the United Nations, Oswaldo De Rivero, to write in his *The Myth of Development* that a large majority of Third World countries are in fact only mistakenly called 'developing' countries. Many of these countries in Africa, Asia, and Latin America, he argues, are not actually in the process of becoming Newly Industrialized Countries (NICs), but are indeed Non-viable National Economies (NNEs) – that is, feeble infant-states born out of self-determination or historical accident, completely void of economic and scientific progress. The bottom line is that economic development, whatever its manifestation might be, is a pretty rare phenomenon.

MYTH: Economic development is the addition of a nation's resources
REALITY: Mainstream economics teaches us about the production function and how goods and services are produced by an efficient combination of economic resources. Development economists have for a long time found this simple formulation somewhat unsatisfactory and can often be found arguing that mere efficient utilization of resources does not necessarily result in economic development. Development is a much more highly complex phenomenon. The eminent development economist Irma Adelman, for example, warns us that one cannot single out a unique factor that will guarantee economic development. More specifically, she argues that trade, education, capital, technology, management, and so on (what she terms 'factor-X') cannot on their own serve as

sufficient conditions for economic growth and development. Furthermore, it could be argued that not just the combination of resources, but rather the emergence of a new order, is what constitutes development. On this notion, Joseph Schumpeter's first footnote in his work *The Theory of Economic Development* reads, 'Add successively as many mail coaches as you please, you will never get a railway thereby.'[1] This cleverly hints to us the realities of something more complex, larger, and beyond just the physical combination of coaches upon which mass transportation is built. What some development economists now seem to agree is that institutions can and do play a very important role in creating this new order and, hence, development. Our task is to suggest *what* it is, then, about institutions that give way to a new order, or emergence?

MYTH: Economic development requires *balanced* growth
REALITY: Modern social democracy strongly advocates equality. Often, inequality is seen in a bad light, working in general against real social or economic progress. Despite the spread of democracy on a global scale in recent decades, economic performance has hardly been impressive.[2] In contrast, the development experiences of some countries, particularly in the latter half of the twentieth century (e.g., the Asian Tigers and more recently China), clearly demonstrate that equality might not be that much of an important concern when it comes to economic growth and development. Contrary to the warnings of Western democratic advocates, history has proven that economic development and prosperity are indeed possible with *unbalanced* growth and, more often than not, development is itself intricately associated with imbalances in the economy.[3] Development is simply a very lopsided affair.

MYTH: Markets are the elixir of economic development
REALITY: Harvard Divinity School's Harvey Cox recently pointed out that it is not difficult to relate how economists view markets to how Christians view God.[4] By this he suggests that mainstream economists tend to place (at times blind) faith in markets as a kind of God and ultimate cure for the problems of less developed regions. Given that markets are usually imperfect, if not altogether absent, in most underdeveloped regions of the world, it would be difficult for nations to rely on markets alone in bringing about economic development. In contrast, the Economics Nobel Laureate Herbert Simon can often be heard stressing the importance of organizations as being even more fundamental to the economy than are markets. That is, it is markets that depend on organizations for their existence and functionality, rather than the other way round. We will argue later that rather than distinguish between markets and organizations, it is better to underscore their common function, particularly with respect to their selection and reward of economic winners, which act as the engines of economic development.

MYTH: Economic policy should avoid the biases of ideology
REALITY: Mainstream economists eager to avoid political connotations in their work have often stressed that economic policy prescription, whether imported

from abroad or produced within the borders of developing countries, should avoid the biases of ideology. Rather, economic policy, it is said, should be tested and accepted mainly through rigorous analysis and empirical testing. In what has now culminated in the neoclassical approach, another Economics Nobel Prize winner, Milton Friedman, argues that economics can be made into a legitimate science rather than a warring set of ideologies.[5] But reality presents a different picture – it is not difficult to find examples of cases when the power of ideology has indeed shaped the course of a nations' achievements (and failures), including its economic development experiences. Rather than avoid ideology, perhaps, nations will be better off accepting its enormous influence and take into account the significance of those institutions responsible for the genesis and diffusion of the prevailing ideologies. We feel strongly about this position and will argue that pro-developmental ideologies in the form of self-help, diligence, and coopera-tion are what must be emphasized if a nation can have any hope of speeding up its development process.

MYTH: Democracy before growth
REALITY: One of the most defining characteristics of modern history, particu-larly with the birth of the modern state in the eighteenth century and the collapse of communism in the late twentieth century, has been the idea of democracy. It remains a puzzle to many observers, however, when history also discovers that this beautiful idea of democracy does not guarantee economic prosperity and development. On the contrary, in a number of regions in the world, non-democratic regimes have shown that significant economic progress is indeed possible without a democracy. So, one is left asking what it is about the institu-tions of democracy (and of non-democratic regimes) that makes development possible or impossible? Incidentally, an interesting argument championing democracy over non-democratic systems is the secure private property rights system. It is argued that a secure property rights system is crucial in maintaining incentives for investment and innovations, and hence economic development. But, as we shall see shortly, the preoccupation of the literature with the institu-tion of property rights, often to the exclusion of other important institutions, has severely limited our understanding of the development process. Essentially, a secure property rights system, although helping to reduce transaction costs, does not guarantee economic growth and development. Rather, as we will elaborate later, secure property rights systems allow for the effective selection and ampli-fication of desirable economic actors and behaviors.

MYTH: Markets versus governments
REALITY: Not unrelated to the myths mentioned above, much of the confusion about economic development also comes from one of the most defining debates of the twentieth century, that of markets versus governments. An interesting story of the struggles between the two titans can be found in Daniel Yergin and Joseph Stanislaw's best-selling book, *The Commanding Heights* (2002). Essen-tially, the authors see modernization in the new era (after World War I) as

spearheaded by globalization, free markets and free trade, immigration, and exchanges of information among nations. Broadly speaking, the authors seem to acknowledge the defeat of the Keynesian influence, especially since the 1980s, which was overtaken by Hayekian ideas that essentially opposed government regulations.[6] Although the debate of markets versus governments has historical significance, it is dangerous to overemphasize its importance. Rather, a broader look at the role and functions of markets (as a decentralized coordination system) and organizations (hierarchical structures in the form of firms and governments) in economic development will reveal more important insights into *why* economic development is possible despite differing opinions as to the merits of markets versus governments.

By way of summary, we would like to emphasize, although somewhat obviously, the fact that economic development is a highly lopsided and uneven affair. Not only does economic development not happen to everyone and in every place, but it does not happen, if it happens at all, equally across people, regions, nations, and even through time. Also obvious, but too often ignored in the analysis (or sometimes over bitterly opposed), is the fact that the bulk of economic resources and benefits have always gravitated toward economically competent actors, regions, and times. Simply put, controversial as it is, economic resources are attracted to better economic performers almost by definition, moving away from less competent and economically lagging counterparts and contemporaries. Of course, this is not to say that development is a permanent state of affairs. Rather, one is sure to find an ever-changing landscape where successful agents eventually fall and are succeeded by other aspiring up-and-comers, and history can be seen repeating itself over and over again.

Before moving on to the next section, we would like to ask the reader to bear in mind that the approach adopted in this chapter is somewhat unique in that we have taken the liberty to more or less borrow freely from New Institutional Economics, evolutionary theory, and complexity economics as we try to better understand the process of economic change and development. Although we are not offering an apology for our fluidity, this multidisciplinary approach, we believe, has various advantages including, among others, (1) the modeling of increasing returns, (2) providing a fuller treatment of dynamism and change, (3) the modeling of non-linear interaction, (4) a better appreciation of self-emergent systems, and (5) providing a view consistent with the second law of thermodynamics. We hope that the justification for experimenting with such a heterodox approach when thinking about economic development will become more evident in the following section as we discuss the recent contributions of the institutional approach to economic thinking about change and development.

3 Economic institutions and economic development

From the 1950s to the early 1970s, mainstream economics, with its adherence to rather strict assumptions – namely, (1) identical, independent agents; (2) utility/ profit maximization; (3) rational choice; (4) complete, symmetric information;

(5) fixed preferences; and (6) unique equilibrium outcomes – did influence economic discussions in a context that largely left out the prevalence and importance of institutions. Essentially trained to think in the mindset of the first law of thermodynamics (e.g., Newtonian physics), much of mainstream economics in the twentieth century tended to downplay differences of whatever kind in favor of building models where assumptions were characterized by a number of equality constraints such as homogeneous goods, identical consumers and firms, and information symmetries, as well as 'democratically consistent' notions such as free entry and exit, perfect information, equal income distribution, and so on. Not only did these models assume away any differences in economic agents, but analyses were essentially static and were inherently unable to properly deal with the process of economic change and development. It is therefore unsurprising to find that for much of the twentieth century, economics remained silent and ineffective when it came to providing real solutions to tackle the problems of developing nations around the world. To this end, mainstream economics has been described as a science of equilibrium; a science of the allocation of scarce resources, which takes place in a timeless and institution-free framework.[7]

In recent years, a number of notable institutionalists have worked consistently on creating a more analytical form of institutional economics. Largely influenced by Coase, Williamson, and North, and also based on ideas developed by Simon, Arrow, Hayek, and others, the result is New Institutional Economics (NIE).[8] Essentially microeconomics in perspective, NIE is now reckoned as a powerful way of looking at the economy through introducing new fundamental concepts such as transaction costs, bounded rationality, satisficing, multiple equilibriums, increasing returns, lock-in, path dependence, and so on, many of which have become commonplace in the modern economist's toolkit.[9]

Following Douglass North, institutions are defined as a set of humanly devised behavioral rules that govern and shape human interactions. One can speak of formal (in the form of laws, rules, regulations and their enforcement) or informal (in the form of expectations of what other people will do, cultural norms, ideology, etc.) institutions. Figure 12.2 summarizes the framework of economic institutions affecting economic agents' behaviors. Starting from the outermost layer is the physical world in which we live – the weather, geography, topography, and so on, to which all physical beings are subject. Informal and formal institutions come next as we narrow down; both are broadly speaking dependent on each other and both are enormous influences on economic agents' behavior. Organizations, private and public, and ultimately the individual actors who function within their relevant organizations and though markets, form the core of the system. Put differently, the behavior of individual economic actors and industry is constrained by their immediate institutions, including the laws of the country they find themselves under, as well as the ideology, the cultural norms, and the overall physical environment that encompasses everything.

A synthesis of the entire literature on how institutions influence human behavior is far beyond this chapter's scope, but suffice it to say here that one common feature of the NIE approach is to emphasize the *economizing* effect of

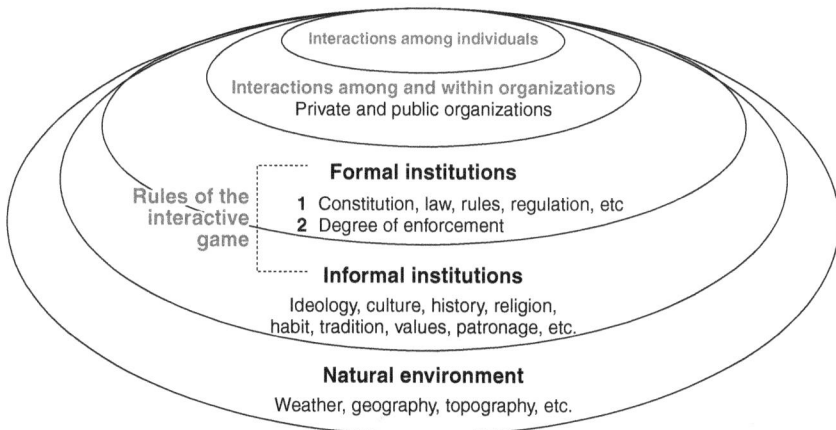

Figure 12.2 Constitution of the complex economy.

institutions. By this, New Institutional economists often mean that institutions are artificial or human-made structures created to help in the handling of transaction costs and market failures (especially free-riding).[10] Furthermore, the importance of institutions suggests that there may be merits and demerits of alternative institutional arrangements.[11]

Be as it may, it is important to appreciate not only the significance of the layers as illustrated in Figure 12.2, but also that there exist vital *interactions* between economic actors (individuals and organizations) across and within the layers. What distinguishes our approach from NIE is our emphasis on non-linear interaction as the essential component to understanding complex systems.[12] And, moreover, the formation, kinds, and patterns of interaction in the economy are largely shaped by the environment, physical as well as cultural, and more directly by the institutions under which economic agents (individuals and organizations) work, which ultimately influence the nature and process of economic change. But what kinds of interaction are associated with economic development? Answering this should allow one to be more specific about the kinds of institutions that policy should support, such as those institutions that encourage the kinds of interactions that promote and sustain economic development. In the spirit of the great institutional development economist Clarence E. Ayres, we are asking, somewhat boldly, 'Can we discover a *megatheory* of economic development?'

One might begin by asking why anyone would wish to interact with anyone else in the first place. A simple answer is to make the claim that we are social animals and as such are destined by genetics to interact with one another. A perhaps more constructive argument would be that we interact with others because we (and our counterparts) derive some sort of positive gain, what we can call *synergy*, from interacting with one another.[13] In short, we interact with one another to derive positive synergy as opposed to negative synergy in the pursuit of economic progress, however it is defined.

Let us make a simple proposition – the key to economic development is 'economic discrimination.' Discrimination is, if you like, the very act of seeing differences differently, which can be contrasted with the act of viewing different things as a common or uniform set.[14] After acknowledging differences, discrimination involves acting on differences to bring about some desired result. Here, with diversity introduced by noticing (and encouraging) differences, discrimination then involves making *judgments*, that is, selecting for favorable treatment those that are preferred over other less preferred alternatives. Essentially, after much deliberation on the development experiences of nations, we find that institutions that embody economic discrimination increase the chances for economic development, while those mitigating economic discrimination eventually experience stagnation and economic depression. In sum, we propose that positive feedback translates into economic development through interaction within institutions that encourage economic discrimination.[15]

Another aspect, not unrelated to the NIE approach we mentioned earlier, is to see the relationship of institutions and market failure. A slightly different interpretation of market failure, rather than defining it in the usual context of externalities, public goods (free-riding), or information asymmetries (moral hazard and asymmetric information), is useful. Market failure, we propose, is caused by ingenuity's not receiving its full reward.[16] In this sense, Marx is placed on his head as it is the workers that can be seen to exploit the capitalist entrepreneur and innovator, rather than the other way round.[17] Such a relationship is not difficult to find, especially in the modern-day context, as more often than not it is business associates who exploit or, if you like, imitate (without full reward) the efforts and success of other business and economic leaders. In other words, the aspect of market failure we find worth emphasizing is the underpayment (and sometimes nonpayment) to economic frontrunners. Ironically, the fact that positive externality generators can never be fully compensated is exactly the source of positive synergies that benefits society. Now, we go one step further to suggest that institutions that embody economic discrimination could resolve market failures as defined above and thus help sustain a good supply of positive synergy generators.

To sum up, within institutions that discriminate economically, each economic actor plays the role of a kind of god 'helping those who help themselves.' A search or discriminatory process is immediately put into action as each economic actor is motivated to look for better partners (increasing the possibility of enjoying positive synergy), which in turn becomes the basis for the emergence of a new and higher order.[18] Economists agree that institutions, history, and, increasingly, cultural considerations do matter, and that the analyses must go beyond the usual fundamentals of resources, technology, and preferences. What we have suggested here is that non-linear interaction encouraged by economic discrimination is a sure way to bring forth positive synergy, which makes development possible.

4 Demystifying economic development

The rejection of bad ideas is as important as the acceptance of good ones. Furthermore, institutional inertia that creates and sustains wrong ideas may make it necessary to reverse or end those policies that generate institutional backlogs – admittedly a very difficult task. In this section, we make some bold statements to see what kinds of notions regarding development consist of good ideas and what institutional reforms might help clean out some of the backlogs that hamper the realization of economic development.

First, we have established that economic discrimination is a good idea for economic development.[19] Armed with the idea of economic discrimination, it is easy to understand the importance of not only markets but also organizations such as firms and the government that operate through a more centralized system utilizing command and control in driving economic development. Specifically, beyond the information-providing and coordinating roles of the market, markets in essence are discrimination mechanisms that help those who help themselves.[20] In a sense, economic actors vote with their dollars in the market. Furthermore, as mentioned previously, a secure property rights system does not guarantee economic development. Rather, it is important as far as it facilitates economic discrimination. Similarly, it is not difficult to see how economic discrimination can generate economic progress under nondemocratic regimes. For example, when referring to the East Asian miracle, one should be careful to avoid circular arguments such as those attributing the 'miracle' to a strong state, credible and benevolent leadership, and so on. The choice of political regimes might matter for society in the long run, but economic progress is possible as long as nations nurture institutions that embody economic discrimination.

The above point in favor of non-market organizations that embody economic discrimination can cause some concern. Specifically, this necessarily links economic development with what might seem like deliberate economic concentration. While frontrunners in the economy serve not only as role models but as sources of new knowledge, of new know-how, and of positive synergies as they interact with others in the economy, it is easy to overlook the benefits and begin worrying that economic concentration associated with economic discrimination must be something terrifying and undesirable. This is perhaps why development has been such a rare phenomenon, particularly in the modern democratic era – it takes some political bravery to go against the popular sentiment of 'equality for all.'

Furthermore, the empirical fact relating modern economic development with the birth and growth of the business firm and corporations becomes clearer when viewed through the economic discrimination lens.[21] Like markets, the business firm is indeed an economically discriminating institution. It comes into existence essentially to internalize those positive externalities we referred to earlier (and those that are not realized in markets) with the aim of generating some kind of profit. That is, because high or formidable transaction costs in identifying synergy make positive externality impossible for markets to exploit, it is often the business firm that can be seen taking risks to internalize these externalities. They can efficiently do so because the business firm has the technical capability of turning externalities that would otherwise go unnoticed into useful and desirable products. By technical capability, we mean the mechanism of 'command and control' by which market transaction costs are avoided – and this can be contrasted with the decentralized decision-making process via the price system.[22] Mainstream economics has often suggested that the government too can act as an important solution to market failures. Given our slight reinterpretation of externalities, firms can be seen as a natural alternative to government intervention in solving the externality problem. Or taking this one step further, beyond market failure and government failure, economic development has benefited from the existence of firms. In the modern era, the economic trinity of firms, governments, and markets, all linked together by their economic discrimination function, has resulted in economic development, albeit in a few privileged countries in the world.

5 Concluding remarks

Another way to pose the question raised in this chapter is 'What institutions are necessary for self-emergence of economic development?' To answer this we have noted that institutions in the standard view have mainly a constraining role, such as constraining the state or other parties from interfering with our property rights. But what we wish to emphasize is that there are many cases of enabling institutions which have a somewhat different role: a firm or government may enable many common people to do positive things they could not do by themselves. And the key to generating positive externalities or synergies, we argue, is economic discrimination. In contrast we need to be aware of myths generated by misunderstandings brought about by an egalitarian ethos.

For example, in Korea, differences and economic concentration have often been scorned in favor of a more equal and uniform society. And more recently such sentiments have also been strengthened by democratic sentiment. We warn that the threat posed to national economic development from this particular brand of egalitarianism, which we term the *Egalitarian Trap*, can act as a serious barrier to economic development. That is, political and economic egalitarianism as exemplified in social democracies tends to work against economic development despite good intentions.[23] As a final note we would like to emphasize that a society's developmental ethos, which can be summed up in the so-called can-do spirit, is much more important to achieving economic development.[24] And it is indeed institutions embodying economic discrimination that nurture this developmental attitude of self-help, diligence, and cooperation.

Notes

1 Schumpeter (1974).
2 In fact, some of the earliest development economic thinkers, notably Paul Rosenstein-Rodan and Ragnar Nurkse, emphasized balanced growth as the only viable way to solve the problem of underdevelopment. Others, including the eminent development economist Albert O. Hirschman, did not believe that the resources needed for a balanced growth strategy would always be available. Rather, he maintained that the resource limitations particularly acute in less developed regions would necessitate prioritizing some areas of industry over others.
3 The early American development economist Clarence Ayres even suggested that by deliberately unbalancing the economy and creating excess capacity in some areas and intensifying shortages in other areas, the pressures resulting would encourage substantial reactions that would speed up the development process.
4 www.theatlantic.com/past/issues/99mar/marketgod.htm.
5 See Friedman (1953).
6 While strongly in favor of this trend, the authors worry that globalization will not last. More specifically, they believe that the current trend will come under threat if inequality in economic growth remains high, and if the Third World is not offered opportunities and incentives to support capitalism. A reason the authors place so much emphasis on narrowing economic gaps is that they believe, following the many interviews they conducted, that there is no *ideological* support for capitalism, and the current system has only the pragmatic fact that it works better than any other (so far).
7 Despite the criticisms here, and to be fair, we must add that mainstream economics has not remained oblivious to the challenges. The neoclassical approach has made enormous strides in recent years, incorporating monopolistic competition, behavior under uncertainly, game theory, asymmetric information, increasing-returns models, endogenous growth models, economics of democracy, and so on.
8 The term *New Institutional Economics* was originated by Williamson (1975). NIE can be contrasted with another modern branch of institutionalism called *European Institutionalism*, essentially organized around the efforts of the European Evolutionary Economic Association.
9 Eggertsson (1990) provides a good survey of the NIE approach. See also Furubotn and Richter (1997) and Drobak and Nye (1997) for more commentaries. Harriss *et al.* (1995) has a summary of recent applications and a number of critical evaluations.
10 For example, different institutions are available that can help improve welfare by, say, reducing the possibility that individuals or groups will make and/or suffer from mistakes. Also, there are various institutions that prevent or limit opportunistic behavior, such as laws, courts, bonding contracts, and so on.
11 Hence, one of the as yet inadequately resolved issues in institutional economics in the context of underdevelopment is why dysfunctional institutions often persist for a long time. Why doesn't the social evolutionary process consistently select 'fitter' institutions over time?
12 The literature on complexity argues that emergence is dependent on the non-linear interaction of economic agents.
13 A more detailed and comprehensive study on synergy can be found by consulting Haken (2004).
14 Discrimination, for example, on two-dimensional geometrical objects means identifying the triangle from the square from the hexagon, and so on. If one wishes not to discriminate, then all two-dimensional objects can be uniformly seen as just two-dimensional shapes or objects and nothing else. There are of course advantages in doing so (just as there are mathematical advantages in looking at shapes either by geometry or by topology), but what we propose is that acknowledging differences is

fundamental to economic discrimination and economic development. To be sure, discrimination brings more variety into the two-dimensional space. Identifying differences, however, is only a part of discrimination, as we shall see.

15 Beinhocker (2006) has suggested that positive feedback arises from increasing returns through non-linear interactions.

16 An analogy might be useful here: 'We as children can never fully repay our parents for their benevolent care and kindness in raising us to become decent human beings.'

17 Karl Marx interprets history as the history of class struggle whereby the entrepreneurs exploit the workers, thereby necessitating the need for a proletarian revolution as the first step toward dismantling the exploitations brought about by capitalism.

18 On the contrary, if interaction generates mainly negative synergy, then the chance of creating a new and better order is largely diminished. Parents seem to know this quite instinctively – they are often concerned about the types of friends their children play with, for example.

19 If the reader needs more convincing, please see other works by the present author.

20 See Jwa (2002b, 2005) for further details.

21 See Micklethwait and Wooldridge (2005) for a fascinating history of the company.

22 See Jwa (2002b, 2008a).

23 The problem sometimes seems to be that adding a political dimension tends to create complications that associate political and economic inequality, despite the fact that political inequality and economic inequality may not be closely associated. See also Jwa (2008b) for the same arguments regarding Korea's economic policy experience.

24 It is said, 'One can take the horse to the river, but one cannot make it drink.'

Bibliography

Beinhocker, Eric D. (2006) *The Origin of Wealth-Evolution, Complexity, and the Radical Remaking of Economics*, Boston, MA: Harvard Business School Press.

Coase, R.H. (1984) 'The New Institutional Economics,' *Journal of Institutional and Theoretical Economics* 140: 229–32.

De Rivero, Oswaldo (2001) *The Myth of Development: Non-viable Economics of the 21st Century*, trans. Claudia Encinas and Janet Herrick Encinas, New York: Zed Books.

Drobak, J.N. and J.V.C. Nye (1997) *The Frontiers of the New Institutional Economics*, San Diego: Harcourt Brace Jovanovich.

Easterly, W. (2002) *The Elusive Quest for Growth: Economists' Adventures and Misadventures in the Tropics*, Cambridge, MA: MIT Press.

Eggertsson, T. (1990) *Economic Behavior and Institutions*, Cambridge: Cambridge University Press.

Friedman, M. (1953) 'The Methodology of Positive Economics,' in *Essays in Positive Economics*, Chicago: University of Chicago Press.

Furubotn, E. and T. Richter (1997) *Institutions and Economic Theory: The Contribution of the New Institutional Economics*, Ann Arbor: University of Michigan Press.

Haken, H. (2004) *Synergetics: Introduction and Advanced Topics*, Berlin: Springer-Verlag.

Harrison, L.E. and S.P. Huntington (2001) *Culture Matters: How Values Shape Human Progress*, New York: Basic Books.

Harriss, J., J. Hunter, and C. Lewis (eds.) (1995) *The New Institutional Economics and Third World Development*, London: Routledge.

Hodgson, G.M. (1998) 'The Approach of Institutional Economics,' *Journal of Economic Literature* 36: 166–92.

Jwa, S.-H. (2002a) *The Evolution of Large Corporations in Korea: A New Institutional Economics Perspective of the Chaebol*, London: Edward Elgar Publishing Ltd.

Jwa, S.-H. (2002b) 'Why Firms and Markets in Economics?' *Seoul Journal of Economics* 15 (2), Summer.

Jwa, S.-H. (2003) 'In Search of "Global Standards": The Fallacy of Korea's Corporate Policy,' *Harvard Asia Quarterly* 7 (2), Spring: 45–52.

Jwa, S.-H. (2005) 'Firms, Markets and Economic Development,' Paper for the AEA/ASSA Annual Meeting in Philadelphia, January.

Jwa, S.-H. (2008a) *Economic Discrimination beyond Evolution* (in Korean), Seoul: Jipyong Publishers Co.

Jwa, S.-H. (2008b) ' "MBnomics": A Review and the Road Ahead,' *International Journal of Korean Affairs* 12 (1), Fall/Winter: 83–100.

Jwa, S.-H. and S.-Y. Hwang (2009) 'A New Interpretation of the Origin of the Subprime Mortgage Crisis: The Failure of Anti-market Government Intervention,' Paper for Beijing Forum 2009 in Beijing, November.

Jwa, S.-H. and Y. Yoon (2004a) 'Political Institutions and Economic Development: A Study in Economic Discrimination and Political Philosophy,' *Seoul Journal of Economics* 17 (3), Fall: 275–307.

Jwa, S.-H. and Y. Yoon (2004b) 'A New Look at Development Economics through Korea's Experience: The Paradox of Economic Development,' Paper presented at the 2004 KDI-KAEA Conference, Seoul.

Knack, S. and P. Keefer (1997a) 'Why Don't Poor Countries Catch-Up? A Cross-National Test of Institutional Explanations,' *Economic Inquiry* 35: 590–602.

Landes, D.S. (1998) *The Wealth and Poverty of Nations: Why Some Are So Rich and Some So Poor*, New York: Norton.

Micklethwait, J. and A. Wooldridge (2005) *The Company: A Short History of a Revolutionary Idea*, London: Modern Library.

North, D.C. (1990) *Institutions, Institutional Change and Economic Performance*, Cambridge: Cambridge University Press.

North, D.C. (1991) 'Institutions,' *Journal of Economic Perspectives* 5 (1): 97–112.

North, D.C. and R.P. Thomas (1973) *The Rise of the Western World: A New Economic History*, Cambridge: Cambridge University Press.

Nurkse, R. (1953) *Problems of Capital Formation in Underdeveloped Countries*, Oxford: Basil Blackwell.

Rodrik, D. (2003) 'Introduction: What Do We Learn From Country Narratives,' in D. Rodrik (ed.) *In Search of Prosperity: Analytic Narratives on Economic*, Princeton: Princeton University Press.

Rosenstein-Rodan, P. (1943) 'Problems of Industrialization in Eastern and South Eastern Europe,' *Economic Journal* 53.

Sachs, J. (2006) *The End of Poverty: Economic Possibilities for Our Time*, New York: Penguin Press.

Schumpeter, J. (1974) *The Theory of Economic Development*, trans. Redvers Opie, Oxford: Oxford University Press.

Simon, H. (1991) 'Organizations and Markets,' *Journal of Economic Perspectives* 5 (2): 25–44.

Williamson, O.E. (1975) *Markets and Hierarchies: Analysis and Antitrust Implications*, New York: Free Press.

Williamson, O.E. (1985) *The Economic Institutions of Capitalism*, New York: Free Press.

Yergin, D. and J. Stanislaw (1998) *The Commanding Heights The Commanding Heights: The Battle for the World Economy*, New York: Simon and Schuster.

Index

Page numbers in *italics* denote tables, those in **bold** denote figures.

For Product Safety Concerns and Information please contact our EU
representative GPSR@taylorandfrancis.com
Taylor & Francis Verlag GmbH, Kaufingerstraße 24, 80331 München, Germany